The IT
Outsourcing
Guide

The IT Outsourcing Guide

Rob Aalders

JOHN WILEY & SONS, LTD
Chichester • New York • Weinheim • Brisbane • Singapore • Toronto

Other Wiley Editorial Offices

John Wiley & Sons, Inc., 605 Third Avenue,
New York, NY 10158-0012, USA

Wiley-VCH Verlag GmbH, Pappelallee 3,
D-69469 Weinheim, Germany

John Wiley & Sons Australia, Ltd, 33 Park Road, Milton,
Queensland 4064, Australia

John Wiley & Sons (Asia) Pte Ltd, 2 Clementi Loop #02-01,
Jin Xing Distripark, Singapore 129809

John Wiley & Sons (Canada) Ltd, 22 Worcester Road,
Rexdale, Ontario M9W 1L1, Canada

British Library Cataloguing in Publication Data

A catalogue record for this book is available from the British Library

ISBN 0-471-49935-8

Typeset in 10/12pt Garamond by Dorwyn Ltd, Rowlands Castle, Hants
Printed and bound in Great Britain by Bookcraft (Bath) Ltd, Midsomer Norton

This book is printed on acid-free paper responsibly manufactured from sustainable forestry, in which
at least two trees are planted for each one used for paper production.

To Margaret Aalders

I am in harbour mists

You live in valley shadows

Mountains, seas, a gulf so vast,

Like the gulf between fliers and divers

Separates us

While this work is done.

Adapted from Lu Yun[1]

Contents

Contents

Foreword

Outsourcing is now a significant and accepted element in the business strategy of most major organisations. Historically, the business drivers of outsourcing have largely been financial cost savings and service improvements, and the benefits can be huge and dramatic.

Now, more than ever, technology solutions are the key to business success as e-commerce becomes an increasingly dominant force. Outsourcing remains a core tool to succeeding in this environment, and the potential benefits remain vast. But the use of outsourcing to support e-business focuses on achieving very different objectives, which now tend to be driven towards attaining:

- absolute reliability
- complete flexibility
- rapid scalability
- radically reduced time to market
- access to industry best practices
- truly global services.

While the outsourcing satisfaction ratings continue to rise, this solution is not problem free. There are numerous pitfalls that the less prepared outsourcer may fall foul of. Outsourcing is more sophisticated and complex than ever, as both the suppliers and the buyers have matured in the market. Furthermore, the technology and business demands coming from the world of e-business are challenging traditional sourcing models. In this market of constant change, organisations often underestimate the time and effort needed to achieve successful outsourcing, or fail to draw upon the appropriate advice from expert sources. As a result of this, in many instances the full benefits from outsourcing are still not realised.

So, are there any magic keys to achieving success with outsourcing?

As one would expect, the answer is not that simple, hence the need for books such as this one. However, the fundamentals underpinning success in outsourcing have remained true for many years, despite the changing technologies and increased expectations from sourcing. And I suspect that they will remain true for a number of years to come, no matter what technology may throw at us. They are simple to define, but extremely difficult to deliver against:

- a clear and unambiguous sourcing strategy that takes account of business needs, in-house capabilities and market conditions;
- selection of an outsourcing partner based on clear criteria for the service, the current and future business drivers, and the relationship sought;
- investment in the management of the relationship, applying the skills and disciplines of excellent service and supplier management.

This outsourcing handbook explores these principles and demonstrates that success in outsourcing comes about by the effective application of good business practice to the management of outsourcing. What you will find here is a no-nonsense introduction to the practicalities of outsourcing, provided by someone with real-life experience of having outsourced his organisation's IT service provision, and then having managed it successfully. Reading this book should help you understand better what might work and what might not, in the context of your own IT environment. Good luck.

David Ballantyne
PA Consulting Group

Preface

I searched the bookshops and libraries for a practical guidebook when I undertook my first outsourcing project. I found nothing. The situation improved over the years as a number of people took pen to paper and wrote about the growing phenomenon. The new authors were, in the main, academics. There was a wealth of advice and guidance on why and why not to outsource, and a growing number of case studies for reference.

However, the bookshelves remained bare of books on the *how* of outsourcing, in sharp contrast to the many texts on how to do marketing, accounting, or even manage information technology. A number of texts professed to provide guidance, but on closer inspection the path from concept to completion was difficult to trace. There was little in the market to guide the novice or inform the veteran. There was even less that tried to take a balanced view of both sides of the outsourcing divide. This was a surprising lapse to a business process built increasingly on the concept of partnership.

This book aims to address that gap and provide those new to outsourcing with a guidebook, and those few veterans with a useful reference that provides a useful source of material that can help in refining and tightening existing arrangements.

The book should also be useful to consultants, independent IT professionals, auditors, lawyers and contractors who are involved in outsourcing agreements. Senior and middle managers should also find it provides a sound reference for them to exercise management governance over an often troubled and risky process.

This book is unique in that it is aimed at meeting the needs, at least in part, of both parties in the outsourcing agreement. Due reference has been made to considerations that the outsource provider should take.

The terms used in this book include "host company", meaning the company that is outsourcing, and "service provider", the company that provides the outsourcing service. Pronouns (you, they etc.) are used whenever it is self-evident which party is being addressed. We have given references to other publications in end notes.

And sadly in this litigious age, I have to issue a disclaimer: The publishers, authors and editors are not responsible for the results of any actions on the basis of information in this work, nor for any errors or omissions. The publishers are not engaged in rendering legal, accounting, information technology or other

Acknowledgements

The case studies and insights from the real world in this book were provided in the main from large international companies that straddle both sides of the outsourcing divide. In every case, they were motivated by a desire to help others achieve a successful outcome in their outsourcing agreements. They have given generously of their time and insight to help others avoid pitfalls. I thank the following for their advice, guidance and generosity: the staff at PA Consulting Group; Graham Bull, Telstra; Vince Graham, National Rail Corporation; Peter Hind, IDG; Howard Morris, Commonwealth Bank; Kym Norley, Booz·Allen & Hamilton; Nick Kovari, formerly of CSC; Tom Hayes and Graeme Stevens, DMR Group Australia; John McNally, VicRoads; Wayne Saunders, Southcorp; Ron Switzer, S2L Consulting Group; Simon Pollard, Gilbert & Tobin Lawyers; Michael Wilkins, Royal & Sun Alliance; Linda Bartlett, British Airways; and David Shoesmith, BASF (UK).

PA Consulting Group calls for special mention. They provided considerable support in the way of case studies and professional guidance. They never sought to influence the content or seek to promote their own position above that of others—the hallmark of a sound professional approach.

PA Consulting Group have undertaken a large number of very successful projects, some of which are referred to in this book. They apply a sound methodology, and the staff I have had the pleasure of dealing with have been unfailingly professional in their approach.

Stacey McGown and Lois Jones supported me during the process, and made time in their busy schedules to ensure that the writing progressed according to plan. Rob McMillan, Paul Dyson and David Ballantyne also provided support and material.

Andy Zaple, formerly of PA, made a major contribution to the early content and provided a significant proportion of the material on cost models for outsourcing. His review of the draft led to a number of improvements to the text, and he has been unfailing in his advice and support.

I am also particularly indebted to: Glenn Sanders, a colleague from Tyndall days, whose skill in removing redundant words and tidying sentence structure has made this book readable; Ron Switzer, who provided a great deal of useful insight and information in the process; Jan Aalders, my brother, who wrote a powerful, well reasoned discussion paper on the subject of outsourcing and, in doing so, honed my thinking; Kathryn Anderson, a writer and poet, whose encouragement and conviction taught me I am a writer; Jane Canfield and Sue Cannon of Canfield Business Designs, who turned my ugly tables and drawings into works of art.

Last but not least my wife Margaret Aalders, who acted as my untiring supporter and personal assistant.

The support and help I received from all these people also provided a vote of confidence and support that helped me through many long hours at my desk. Thank you all for the time and effort you gave to this project. I have tried to represent everyone's views correctly and to place all observations in an appropriate context. Any errors, omissions or misjudgements in this book are mine alone.

1   Introduction

The outsourcing of IT is here to stay. The path to outsourcing is difficult and dangerous. Guidebooks on how to go about outsourcing are rare. Mistakes may jeopardise the business. The costs to switch back to an in-house operation are very high, emotionally, publicly and financially. This book seeks to address the gap by providing a practitioner's handbook, to guide the novice and inform the veteran.

The book provides guidance on how you might undertake or restructure an outsourcing agreement. The approach suggested is top down, and consists of a series of loosely coupled steps that lead from business goals through contract to ongoing management:

- Defining the goals and objectives for the agreement.
- Documenting the current environment.
- Managing the tendering process and selecting the candidate.
- Negotiating the contract.
- Setting performance standards or service level agreements.
- Changing business processes and transitioning staff to their new employer.
- Managing the contract throughout its life.
- Renewing or terminating the contract.

This book includes:

- visual aids
- checklists
- stories from executives who have been through the outsourcing mill.

The book is aimed at executives on both sides of the outsourcing divide: those who belong to the *host company*, i.e. doing the outsourcing, and the *service provider*. It should also be useful to auditors, contractors, lawyers and others involved in setting and managing these agreements.

The book is about *how* to outsource, not about whether to or not to outsource. It does not provide an antagonist or protagonist with a reference for accepting or rejecting outsourcing proposals. Others have written more comprehensively and clearly on this subject, in particular Lacity and Hirschheim.[2] I do believe, however, that outsourcing has much to offer, and I argue the case "for" in Chapter 16.

Nor does this book seek to lay down a rigid methodology for undertaking an outsourcing project. The variations and complexities are too great for a "one size fits all" approach. But there can be little doubt that a structured method will yield better results than one that is unstructured.

The key things to consider in an outsourcing agreement have been summarised by Andy Zaple of PA Consulting Group:

> The success of outsourcing projects depends on planning the outsourced strategy in depth and managing it in practice. Treat outsourcing as a strategic issue rather than a tactical issue. Define what you are trying to achieve, and set out to "buy the outcome" that you seek. Construct service specifications in terms of outcomes rather than supplier inputs. Emphasise quality, flexibility and performance incentives rather than lowest price. Develop positive relationships with your suppliers. Use commercial mechanisms that reward the service provider for meeting your real business objectives. Put as much effort into managing the relationship as into managing the letter of the contract.

I could not agree more. This is not, however, easy to undertake in practice. One sobering consideration is how often best intentions can come to nothing, and hard-won agreement dissolve into bickering and litigation that is harmful to both host company and service provider. Both also need to understand clearly how the motivations of individuals within the negotiating teams can distort the objectives and best intentions of the respective companies.

The host company's negotiating team may consist of staff whose future progress depends on winning a highly cost-effective agreement, while the service provider's team will often consist of sales personnel whose remuneration is dependent on winning the sale. As a result, the outsourcing agreement is often reached in an atmosphere where the host company makes unreasonable demands of an excessively compliant service provider. Neither party benefits as the agreement later dissolves in acrimony and broken dreams.

If both parties commit to a sensible process, as outlined in this book, then the likelihood of a serious mismatch between goals and deliverables will be reduced. Those that use this book as a reference cannot be given a promise that this will eliminate all risk. Most business decisions call on us to make judgements without adequate time or information. However a prudent, soundly structured approach to decision making is a fundamental requirement of good corporate governance.

Structure

The book has been designed to provide you with a sound project reference work. Clearly, the process of reaching agreement will be easier if both parties subscribe to the broad sweep of this book. Indeed, it would be useful to issue all the members of both negotiating teams with a copy so that all are working within a common framework, even if they agree to disagree on the detail.

The text has been structured to support the process, and moves from concept, through implementation to termination or renewal. First, business goals and objectives are considered, and how these are supported by the decision to outsource. The study then moves through the process of discovery, or understanding your own IT, defining your IT management principles, issuing a request for proposal (RFP), and assessing responses and contract negotiation. Transition and ongoing management are considered, and the process is closed with a chapter on renewal and termination.

The book is not ordered in a totally chronological fashion. For instance, evaluation criteria and scoring are discussed in advance of the chapter on issuing the RFP. This approach was taken because it is critical to define what we are going to outsource and what benefit we are seeking from outsourcing before we commence to document what the service provider must be able to do to meet our need.

The appendices contain additional material that should prove useful to any host company or service provider entering into an outsourcing agreement.

Real-life stories

Boxed sections throughout the book highlight real-life stories from people who have been involved in outsourcing. These illustrate some of the issues and challenges, and show how others adapted to them.

Checklists

There is a checklist at the end of each chapter. These quick-reference tools help in quality control and in ensuring that key tasks or components are not overlooked.

Approach

The approach is unashamedly top-down. I subscribe to the simple view that all business activity should be directed towards meeting business goals and believe that "goals provide a guide to action, a basis for problem solving and measuring performance, and also clarify desired outcomes."[3]

The text does not lay down a rigid prescriptive process. No two businesses are exactly alike, and neither are any two outsourcing agreements. No one holds a monopoly on the truth or a single "best" approach. Most managers are intelligent, adaptive beings who may welcome suggestions, ideas and checklists, but can work things out for themselves.

A brief description of the topics covered in each chapter follows. After reading the introduction and these outlines, you should feel this handbook can provide some worthwhile insight into the management challenge of outsourcing, regardless of whether you are a service provider or host company.

Know your motives

This chapter addresses the first and most important question: *why* are you outsourcing? It sets out methods for defining, qualifying and quantifying business goals and objectives for outsourcing. The next chapter shows you how to link these goals and objectives to critical success factors and selection criteria. The checklist helps you ensure the objectives set for outsourcing are sustainable.

Developing critical success factors and selection criteria

This chapter leads you through developing the critical success factors (CSFs) and criteria for selecting your service provider. It shows you how to derive these from the business goals and objectives. Well defined criteria can eliminate much of the difficulty and emotion that surrounds partner selection. Included are short sections on suitable weighing and scoring methods, as well as risk evaluation and management.

Discovering your environment

Establishing the true state of your own environment is critical. Experience shows few companies can easily lay hands on all the IT maintenance and licensing agreements made over the last 10 or 20 years. Many hold poor records on distributed assets. Many others will be surprised at the extent and cost of unofficial or feral IT within the company. The host company must not go to the negotiating table unprepared.

Setting management principles

Setting management principles is probably the most important process in establishing an outsourcing management framework. The principles provide the means for governance of the service provider. They also streamline the processes of management, set your quality goals, and eliminate most of the day-to-day issues in outsourcing.

Preselecting service providers

The preselection process can be undertaken by issuing a request for information (RFI) or by using straight market research. Preselection will:

- help target the right service providers;
- help you tailor the request for proposal (RFP) to ensure you get useful responses to your selection criteria;
- greatly reduce the hack work and drudgery of eliminating substandard providers;
- provide insight into the level and quality of response you can expect when you issue the RFP.

Preparing the request for proposal

This chapter provides some useful tips on preparing the RFP. It suggests an approach and outlines a possible structure. It discusses issues that may arise, and how to avoid them. It also considers some of the common pricing models and their benefits and drawbacks.

Issuing the request for proposal

This section provides some guidance on issuing the RFP, including change control. It covers some of the benefits and drawbacks of formal and restricted RFPs. The aim of this chapter is to ensure that the host company ensures that the right candidates respond, and in the right manner.

Evaluating responses to the request for proposal

This chapter builds on the two previous chapters and moves forward to the business of evaluating responses. The processes cover the initial cull, qualifying responses and then the quantitative and qualitative analysis. It finishes with some recommendations on financial modelling and risk management.

Undertaking due diligence

Due diligence is the process by which the service provider examines in detail the state of the IT environment they are to manage. Up to this point, they will usually have had to rely on descriptions of the environment in the request for proposal. This is the final step before the contract is entered into. This book recommends that the process is done with a joint team, and that it covers all aspects of the future contract, including staffing, organisation, skills, documentation and environment. The two groups must also agree on the gap between existing performance levels and the improvement goals.

Forming the contract

This is the last step in the selection process. How do you get a contract that is fair to both parties, and robust enough to stand the rigours of a multiyear relationship? This book provides some stimulating and novel methods for solving this dilemma.

Managing the transition

Howard Morris, who spearheaded a AUD$5.0 billion outsourcing deal between CBA and EDS, said, "Outsourcing is about change management." And it comes as a surprise to many readers that 80% of the change management effort needs to be directed to business processes *outside* the information technology unit. This chapter covers the tasks and disciplines needed to make the change from an in-house business unit to an outsourced IT unit, including human resources, business processes, change and transition management.

Managing the relationship

How do you manage things now the contract is signed and the function has been passed over to the service provider? What steps can you take to protect yourself against budget blowout, substandard service or poor management practices? How do you avoid disputes, and how do you deal with those you can not avoid? This chapter provides a host of useful suggestions for managing the contract throughout its life.

Renewing or terminating the contract

The time will come when the contract needs to be renewed. Did you consider how this might be done when you drew up the contract? How will you manage yourself out of the dependency if you decide not to renew it? How can you be sure the renewed contract is still consistent with the business goals set years before at contract outset? This chapter considers these questions and many more, and gives some useful approaches to handling them.

Why outsource?

The process of outsourcing is often lengthy and difficult. This final chapter offers some reminders as to why the outsourcing process is worthwhile. There are opposing views and one should not denigrate them. However, this is a book aimed at supporting those who have taken the courageous decision; it is not a dissertation on the pros and cons of outsourcing.

Appendices

Appendix A discusses the importance of future proofing the contract, and provides some guidance on developing a context model. You should study this section: the future may arrive sooner or later, but arrive it certainly will.

Appendix B provides an indicative list of topics that make up an outsourcing contract. This will help define the scope of works that need to be addressed in an outsourcing contract.

Appendices C, D and E offer some forms that are useful for contract negotiation and management. These are the Position Paper, Contract Change Control and Contract Requirement Statement.

Appendix F contains some examples of principles for outsourcing management. If you are new to the concept of principles, this may help you define your outsourcing management framework. This topic is covered in Chapter 5.

Appendix G gives some indicative duration for each stage of the outsourcing project. Each project will differ in size and complexity, and estimates are given solely to guide the novice who may hold unreasonable expectations on how rapidly the process can be completed.

Appendix H suggests a Business Case template. Most large companies, and by inference they are the ones most likely to outsource, have well established templates and procedures governing business cases, or investment decisions. The template is provided for those few that do not.

Appendix I provides a brief description of PA Consulting Group's SMART model for effective outsourcing. PA Consulting Group provided considerable support and advice in the writing of this book.

Conclusion

Michael Wilkins of Royal & Sun Alliance said, "I'd advise new entrants to outsourcing to be rigorous in going about it. I'd also demand that the service provider tell you exactly how *they* intend to go about it, and test the reality of their claims."

This book will help you tie your outsourcing deliverables to earlier defined business goals. It should ensure that the business as a whole enters into the outsourcing agreement, and help minimise risk and maximise benefits. It will also provide an auditable trace to the whys and hows of the outsourcing decision. This can prove important as memories fade, business changes, personnel change and the earlier decision to outsource comes under challenge.

But above all this is an optimistic book. The virtual corporation is here to stay, and outsourcing can improve productivity, competitiveness and effectiveness. I am anxious to ensure that companies that outsource, and those that provide services, reach productive harmony.

It has been said that "outsourcing is a new name for old practices",[4] and that technology staff can seek advice from their colleagues who have, over time, outsourced fleet management, advertising, building maintenance, security and many other areas of the business. This is true. However, few business areas are as sensitive to failure as IT, and few have the potential for greater failure and even business ruin. Managing IT is difficult and dangerous work. Outsourcing it properly is even harder. That is why this book was written.

2 Know your motives

The core of this book opens with a definition of outsourcing adapted from *The Economist Pocket Handbook on Strategy*:[5]

> The handing over of a fundamental corporate process to another organisation; for example the management of a company's information technology (IT) systems, or of its car-fleet management, or of its health insurance scheme.

The definition is followed by the observation:

> There are some that see the present extraordinary rapid growth in outsourcing of all sorts of processes (particularly IT) as a basic abrogation of management's corporate responsibility. Others see it as a shrewd way of turning (high) fixed costs into lower (variable) costs, of improving service and gaining competitive advantage.

Chapter 16 provides some supportive arguments in favour of outsourcing. Outsourcing is not an abrogation of management's corporate responsibility. Managing outsourced IT requires as much management skill and dedication as managing internal IT, if not more. The outsourced unit will be under constant critical scrutiny; costs are harder to hide and mistakes more visible. This text aims to help those outsourcing reduce the challenges to manageable proportions and achieve success.

Outsourcing goals

The essence of the first step in outsourcing was summed up by Michael Wilkins of Royal & Sun Alliance: "Know your motives!" It may surprise those new to outsourcing IT to hear that many companies have not asked themselves why they are outsourcing. The decision to outsource has, in some instances, been based on:

- Intuition—"It felt like the right thing to do."
- Fear—"Our IT was sliding into a black hole."

- Imitation—"We needed to keep pace with the market."
- Frustration—"IT was driving us mad."

Not surprisingly, I do not think these are four good bases on which to make a critical business decision. The approach recommended in this book is to start with goal determination and to move forward through a sequence of logical steps until you reach that last milestone of the contract.

Karpathiou and Tanner[6] questioned why organisations outsourced and were given a number of considered answers:

- To overcome a lack of resources.
- To save costs.
- To focus on core business.
- To gain competitive advantage.

Add to this two more:

- We don't know.
- We are not telling.

The last two reasons may be much more common than research indicates. Psychologists have discovered there is a tendency for people to unconsciously create a justification for actions after the event. This is because most people seek to show there is some consistency between their beliefs and their actions. The term "cognitive dissonance" is used to describe this phenomenon. Those interested in knowing more about this can refer to the work of Leon Festinger (1918–1989).[7]

Alternatively, the reluctance to reveal why a company is outsourcing may be that the truth is unpalatable or inflammatory. The truth may be that the current IT organisation is an unholy mess, or that that the company abrogated responsibility for managing IT. Maurizio Marmotta of Compass Management Consulting said at a recent conference, "Experience tells us that the cause of discontent with outsourcing results from poorly defined requirements. Clients neither understood what they currently had, nor determined what they wanted to achieve".

Identifying the true goals for your company may prove difficult in practice. You may find that the goals are not consistent across the organisation, or that there is a wide difference between stated goals, objectives and company behaviours. This is substantiated by research that indicates there are often notable variances between a company's stated goals as described in their mission statements, annual reports, public relations announcements and statements made by managers. Close inspection will often reveal conflicting and even contradictory stated goals. Robbins and Mukerji[8] observe, "The conflict in stated goals exists because organisations respond to a vast array of constituencies." Identifying the goals and objectives, which link to the outsourcing decision, may prove to be a frustrating process.

To exacerbate matters, the company may have unstated aims that are, again, different from those published. The stated goals in mission statements and public documents are for public consumption. The company may also have unstated objectives that are unpalatable.

For example, Robbins and Mukerji[9] describe how the pilots' strike that grounded Australian airlines for six months in 1990 was fed by the publicly stated intent of adhering to ethical behaviours. The airlines claimed they would not dare break the legal wage-fixing guidelines. However, the real goal of both the airlines and the government was to break the power of the Airline Pilots Federation as a prelude to deregulation in November of that year. You should not be surprised if the organisation's real objectives are quite different from those stated, or that there are contradictions even in the stated goals.

It is also important to probe behind stated goals or objectives. The following bald statements do not tell us a great deal.

- To overcome a shortage of resources.
- To reduce costs.

The sort of questions that should be asked about the first goal include:

- What type of resources, management, programming, technical, help desk?
- How long is the shortage expected to continue?
- What is the cause of the shortage for the company?

If the shortage is caused by below-average remuneration or poor working conditions, then we must ask how outsourcing will change this. If the shortage is industry-wide, then we must ask ourselves how outsourcing will improve supply. Clearly, there are many ways to overcome a shortage of resources. Outsourcing can be a solution, provided that the service provider employs adequate qualified staff and they are available when you need them. Better still, you don't pay for them when you are not using them.

It can be the case that a company needs consistent but intermittent access to rare or specialist skills, such as database administration or system architecture, and these may be best sourced through a service provider. However, the same may not be true of lower-level skills, such as PC support staff or help desk service staff who do not fit comfortably into the higher order consulting profile of the larger service providers.

If a company enters into an outsourcing agreement to overcome a temporary shortage of help desk staff, then they may be taking a sledgehammer to crack a nut. Given the time, cost and contractual ties of outsourcing, this solution could prove to be a slow and expensive alternative to improving remuneration and conditions in hiring staff.

A cost-reduction goal should always be probed further. The internal costs of entering into an outsourcing agreement are large and research indicates cost savings are unlikely to occur in the short term. This is understandable, since the service provider has to add overheads and margin to their staff costs. This typically increases the direct cost per staff member by 20–50%.

Lacity and Hirschheim pointed out that "the preponderance of literature on outsourcing that suggests outsourcing can save 20–50% on IS cost is largely based on expectations. Public sources neglect to report that some outsourcing clients are charged exorbitant excess fees for above baseline measures."[10]

However, there can be no doubt that economies of scale, shared facilities and flexibility have allowed some companies to control IT expense below its continually increasing proportion of enterprise revenues. GartnerGroup estimate that these expenses rose from 2.11% in 1994 to 4.19% in 1999, an estimated 93% increase over the five-year period.[11]

In understanding the goal of cost reduction in IT, we also need to take into account a company's spending on IT outside of the "official" IT budget. The Diebold Group reported that user spending on information systems (IS) outside IT budgets was equivalent to another 64% of the IS departments' spending in manufacturing and 27% in service firms.[12] This IS spend may well sit outside any outsourcing discipline.

The good news on cost savings is that because service providers usually demand greater rigour and adherence to proper practice, this can help reduce costs. Lacity and Hirschheim make the valid observation that "IS costs are directly related to user demands. In most organisations, IS costs [prior to outsourcing] are controlled through general allocation systems which motivate users to excessively demand and consume resources . . . [after outsourcing] users [are] no longer able to call upon their favourite analysts to request frivolous changes, but instead must submit requests through a formal cost control process. This results in the curtailing of excessive user demands and thus reduces overall IS costs."[13]

Outsourcing not only tends to curtail frivolous changes, but also trims the hidden costs of IT in its many guises, including "shadow" IT units hidden within business divisions, uncontrolled "user-developed" applications, and unauthorised purchases of hardware and software assets. These issues are not raised to challenge cost reduction as a legitimate goal for outsourcing. Far from it: there are many benefits to be gained from outsourcing where the service provider has the staff capacity and capability to deliver against the goals and objectives that are beyond the reach of the in-house unit. These issues are raised to illustrate the necessity for the outsourcing team to probe behind stated goals and ensure that the stated goals are legitimate and properly understood.

You must be able to trace your outsourcing process through a logical and tightly coupled sequence that moves from business goals, through objectives, critical success factors, criteria for selecting your service provider, and formation of contract terms and measures that ensure the service provider delivers those things that meet your needs. If this is not done, then the foundation on which the outsourcing agreement is built will be vague and weak.

Before we progress further, it is important to define how the following terms are used in this text:

- goals
- objectives
- critical success factors (CSFs)
- criteria.

These terms have been used interchangeably in management literature. Indeed, Robbins and Mukerji say, "Objectives are goals. We use the terms interchangeably."[14]

I do not use the terms interchangeably; I am grateful to Paul A Strassman for his definitions,[15] and have paraphrased them as follows:

Goals are hopes and aspirations for a distant future, which are not necessarily attainable. Goals are expectations, prospects, possibilities and ambitions. They are lofty ideals. One should not trifle with goals: they are the bonds that bring together all the constituencies in organisations.

Objectives must be explicitly measurable performance commitments. Objectives are reality, schedules, benchmarks, and cost targets. Objectives must be measured to determine how near you are to where you want to be. They should be the products of well considered arguments concerning the balance between ambition and reality.

Critical success factors (CSFs), in our parlance and with apologies to John Rockart,[a] are the few key inputs or characteristics the service provider must have if they are to help us meet our objectives. They should meet the tests of necessity and sufficiency. Each CSF must stand the test of being necessary, and the collection of CSFs must meet the test of being complete, i.e. meeting them alone is sufficient to ensure success.

Criteria are those attributes that we can use to measure the quality and quantity of key inputs or show evidence that the service provider can deliver on the CSFs.

The example in Figure 2.1 is based on goals, objectives, CSFs and criteria for an ambitious athlete. It shows how to break down the goal and, through this process, identify those things that allow us to develop a profile in the RFP against which we can match the profile of service providers.

IT staff familiar with data modelling might like to think as goals being normalised.

This model is illustrated further in Figure 2.2. Note that the goals and objectives will change over time. They need to be revisited periodically, at the very least annually. If this is a concern, let us comfort you. If the objectives don't change over time, then outsourcing is not working because you're not achieving your objectives.

---

[a] John Rockart defined CSFs as "the few key areas where things must go right in order for an organisation to flourish".

Goal

Win a gold medal at the next Olympic Games

Objective (one of several)

Achieve personal best within 0.5 seconds of world record by January

---

CSF (one of several)

First-class coach for 100 metres

Criteria

1. Coach has demonstrated track record in 100 metres
2. Coach is affordable

Figure 2.1—Goals, objectives, CSFs and criteria for an ambitious athlete

The first stage in outsourcing is to define the goals and objectives driving out-sourcing in your organisation, and then to develop the CSFs and criteria necessary to select the best service provider you can afford. This will not be easy. Companies have many reasons (not always compatible or of equal value) for outsourcing. The task you face is to organise these ideas, determine which are most important, and integrate them into a coherent statement of direction to support the initiative.

Identifying goals

The first step in the process is to identify your organisation's goals or objectives that relate to outsourcing your information technology unit. This task is often difficult in practice. Goals may be confused, contradictory or nonexistent. Sprague notes that "less than half the companies surveyed [by Cresap, McCormick and Paget (1983)] specifically consider business practices and plans in their systems plans."[16]

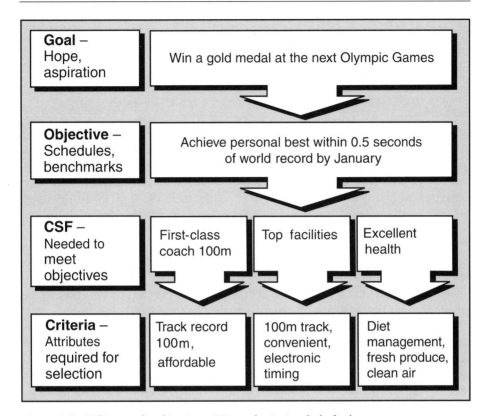

Figure 2.2—Taking goals, objectives, CSFs and criteria a little further

This means that you will probably have difficulty in finding business plans that relate to systems plans, when you seek to determine which, if any, business goals link to the objectives associated with outsourcing.

The goals given as examples below certainly help define why a company might outsource IT.

- Xylog's aim is to remain a virtual corporation focusing on our core competency of interim management of IT. We will outsource all other functions where suppliers offer greater economies of scale or efficiency.
- Pravka will become a global player within the next five years, leveraging other organisations' competencies and skills to achieve its goal.
- Larapinta Ltd will pursue a merger and acquisition strategy seeking to acquire and integrate business and technology and rapidly grow beyond critical mass for our business.

These first two goals certainly imply that goods and services will be provided by external organisations and give some reasons as to why. The third goal does not do so explicitly. However, in researching the third goal, it became apparent that it led to the following objective that could only be met (in this case) by outsourcing:

> We require flexibility in the capacity and capability of our IT unit to the extent we can swell or shrink available numbers by up to 20% within one month and improve the overall skill level from 20% tertiary qualified to 80% tertiary qualified staff within 12 months.

Where do you seek these business goals? Normally they will be contained in company charters, long-term business plans and reports to shareholders. The guardians are often the strategic planning department or the marketing departments. But two cautions. First, goals are often based on rhetoric and sometimes quite devoid of any link to capability and commitment. Second, eyeball people's behaviours in the company and do a reality check on whether the goals are real beliefs or empty phrases.

Generally, you should adopt an approach that assumes there are no goals that point directly to outsourcing. It will usually be necessary for the manager or consultant charged with the outsourcing project to work with the executive and develop or extract the goals and objectives. Some advice is provided later in this chapter on running workshops to derive or develop goals and objectives.

The final caution: a company with many large or semi-autonomous divisions that share a corporate IT function may find it difficult to agree a common set of goals and objectives for outsourcing. Needs may vary widely between the divisions, and goals may stand in direct conflict with one another. If this is the case, then careful consideration will need to be given to hybrid models for outsourcing that can deliver the contrasting needs.

Deriving objectives

It may take some critical analysis to link goals to objectives that support the outsourcing initiative. The objectives "should be the product of well considered arguments concerning the balance between ambition and reality."[17] This process of argument and derivation has the benefits of:

- drawing other executives into the debate and obtaining their views and commitment to any outsourcing objective;
- testing the gap between the ambitions stated in the goals and the business belief and commitment to these goals.

The fortunate may find the company has already broken down goals into stated objectives. Objectives are defined as having "explicit measurable performance commitments", such as the statements below.

- Xylog will outsource the provision of all IT if it can be shown that a service provider can meet our goals of achieving a level of service in desktop and network operations 10% better than we can ourselves, at an equal or lower cost.
- Pravka will outsource IT to a global company in order to leverage their market presence in countries listed in our future development plan. This objective is based on the premise that in doing so we will pay no more than a 5% premium over opening and operating our own global network.
- We will improve the capacity and capability of our IT unit to the extent we can swell or shrink available numbers by up to 20% within one month and improve the overall skill level from 20% tertiary qualified to 80% tertiary qualified staff within 12 months.

The first two business objectives above are quite definite in stating that the objective will be achieved by outsourcing IT.

The manager intending to outsource must still ask *why* outsourcing is the preferred means of achieving the objective. It is important to make sure that the decision to outsource that is explicit in those objectives was not driven by intuition or imitation. Ohmae cautions that you should not "recklessly attempt to come up with a solution on the basis of experience or intuition, without considering the objective factors."[18] Analysis of the factors surrounding the objectives above may very well point to outsourcing as the best solution. However, that analysis needs to be done. You must define a clear and unambiguous statement on why the company is outsourcing, for example:

> Analysis of current IT expenditure on variable costs and quality standards shows that Pentavac IS costs are 17.5% higher than industry average and that our quality, measured in faults per 1000 lines of code and system stability is 14% worse than industry benchmarks. An initial survey of outsourced IT in our industry indicates we can lower the costs and achieve industry benchmark standards of operation within three years compared with in-house operation forecasts.

No doubt most managers charged with outsourcing projects would also be delighted to be given such an unambiguous and well reasoned objective. Sadly, this is rarely so, and few if any managers will be the recipients of such a clear mandate for their project. Indeed, the impression gained from reading Lacity and Hirschheim's study is that most of the firms surveyed outsourced in a knee-jerk reaction to escalating IT costs, and that they made a leap of faith that a service provider would be both better and cheaper than the internal IS department.[19] Peter Hind of IDC said, "IT has too little credibility inside the businesses, the outsiders [service providers] are regarded as Gods who can do no wrong."

It is possible that the dismal picture presented in Lacity and Hirschheim's study of outsourced IT stems in part from poor understanding by some companies of their goals, objectives and drivers for outsourcing. This weakness may in turn have led to poor selection criteria and a misfit between their aspirations and the services delivered by the service provider.

It is difficult to overstress the importance of determining the outsourcing goals and objectives. This step appears to be critical to the success of the venture. The goals and objectives answer the "why" of outsourcing. They must be stated clearly. The senior management group must share them—indeed, they should feel that they wrote them. If the goals are vague and the objectives are not quantified, then the outsourcing agreement that follows is likely to be equally vague and not quantified.

If you have a set of objectives for outsourcing, subject them to the following tests:

- Are the goals achievable, shared and lived?
- Are the objectives explicitly stated, measurable and bound by time?
- Do the objectives lead directly to outsourcing as the best solution?

If the answer to the last question is no, then it is probable that you lack an objective that supports a decision to outsource. Putting it more bluntly, the company does not know why it is outsourcing, and what it expects to achieve from outsourcing, and what measures it will apply to success or over what period.

In reviewing objectives, you should be able to bring them down to a very few. "Focus, focus and focus are the three most important criteria for sifting through [culling] a long list of objectives."[20]

Implications

All objectives carry with them implications. However, these are rarely surfaced and considered at the time the objective is agreed. This is a weakness. It is far better to call out the positive and negative implications of the objective from the start. The task is not arduous. The reward from obtaining some initial agreement on what the negative and positive aspects are likely to be is that it can defuse later criticisms that the decision was not well considered. It is important to obtain agreement from the company executive that they appreciate the implications that lie behind each objective from the start.

One sound method for highlighting the existence of implications and gaining broad acceptance of them is to document the top five or so positive and negative implications associated with each objective and circulate them to your colleagues. Take the following statement: *Our objective in outsourcing our network is to improve network up time to 99.7% and extend the hours of service from 06:00 till 18:00 daily, seven days a week. The current level is 94% between the hours of 07:30 and 17:30 daily.*

For this example, we might state the positive implications to be:

- Staff productivity will increase by 25%.
- Service to customers will not be interrupted by down time to the extent it is today.
- Staff morale will improve and turnover may reduce.

We might state the negative implications to be:

- Existing assets will be disposed of and may fetch little in return.
- We will be tied to the continuing performance of the outsourcer's network.
- The outsourcer will charge for the additional hours of coverage.
- The system will be disrupted as we move to the outsourcer's network.

It is easy to imagine that the implications are self-evident and do not need to be pointed out. Experience suggests that few people outside the IT department give thought to the implications. They often appear as unpleasant surprises and engender unhappy reactions.

Qualifying objectives

It is important to test the robustness of the listed objectives for outsourcing, otherwise you may find that the objectives are based on reckless intuition that outsourcing always results in some specific benefit, typically cost reduction. If the stated objective in your organisation is "We are outsourcing to save costs", then it would be appropriate to ask the following questions:

- What costs—hardware, software, development, maintenance, operations, environmental, recruiting, salary, hidden, management?
- How—through economy of scale, shared facilities, better expense approval?
- At what benchmark—same quality, lower quality, higher service levels?
- How much—10%, 20%?
- When—this year, next year, over 10 years?
- Why is outsourcing the best way to achieve this objective?

If you do not ask these questions at the outset, then you will be asked them when you have to explain the outsourcing decision to staff, customers and the board. Stephen Walsh of Westpac, speaking at a conference on outsourcing, suggested you should "explain the purpose of outsourcing to everyone in the company". In a later discussion, Walsh added, "Organisations need to carefully set expectations as to what information can be shared and when it can be shared, otherwise you lose trust when you say sorry we can't divulge that [commercially sensitive] information yet, or we don't know yet!"

Schedule of objectives

Another failure that appears time and time again is the failure to schedule *when* these objectives are to be achieved. It is critical that a timetable for achievement of objectives is developed and widely circulated, for two reasons. The first is to manage the expectations among staff and management. Regardless of how often the mantra "outsourcing will not be a panacea for all our IT ills" is chanted, most users and managers will expect a panacea. Kym Norley of Booz·Allen & Hamilton spoke of the need to control the expectation among staff that outsourcing means the company could now have the best of everything, immediately. One way of doing this is to prepare a schedule in the form of a bar chart or, preferably, a program evaluation and review technique (PERT) chart that shows timing and dependencies for addressing these goals as part of the contract formation (see Chapter 11).

The second reason is that it is critical to schedule deliverables over the contract so that the overall budgeting and pricing for the outsourcing contract can reflect the approximate quantity and type of skills and related costs that are required at each stage of the outsourcing contract.

Too often the objectives are jumbled together, all expected to start on day one of the contract, and usually end within the first 12 months of a five-year contract. If all objectives are expected to be met within one year, then that is probably a reasonable duration for the contract. However, if the contract duration is expected to be five years and you expect to meet all objectives within 12 months, then you need to question the proposed objectives and contract duration.

The objectives schedule should be supported by reasonable estimations of:

● staff requirements by period, including capability levels and costs;
● infrastructure upgrade costs required to support the changed environment;
● facilities such as office space and equipment required for the number of resources.

These things serve to prepare the company for the contract scope and negotiation phases of the agreement. Andy Zaple of PA said, "Put simply, successful outsourcing is enabled by properly planning why and how you want to do it, and then implementing the plan." The plan must include the schedule of deliverables and the resources required to deliver and operate those processes or outcomes.

Lack of goals and objectives

If the company does not have clear goals and objectives to support the outsourcing project, then there is little option but to develop these goals and objectives with the senior management. This is no small task. The literature on strategic planning is vast and not always consistent in approach or semantics. However there are some clear guidelines. Ohmae suggests, "The first stage in strategic thinking is to pinpoint the critical issue in the situation."[21] That should be fairly easy. The company is about to embark on a risky, expensive, long-term contract without any real idea of why. Ohmae recommends a technique he calls an "issue diagram" (Figure 2.3). The diagram is used to decompose the issue into its component parts and define the actions appropriate to overcoming the issue. (Other strategic planners use similar tools that encourage the analytical process.) For a more complete treatment of the subject, refer to Kenichi Ohmae's book, *The Mind of the Strategist.*

Collins supports Ohmae's view: "Situational analysis is the most appropriate point for most planning exercises . . . The more thorough the exploration of current scenarios the more accurate our forecasts and predictions are likely to be . . . In turn goals set will be more realistic and achievable, and strategies and action plans more appropriate."[22]

The second guideline is that the senior executive must articulate the goals. Again, I borrow from Strassman, who states: "Top executives must articulate shared goals because that is the basis for their legitimacy."[23] Let there be no confusion on this issue. The top executives are employed to lead the business. They must know where they are taking it, and they must be able to communicate that direction to their staff.

An appropriate approach to articulating and defining goals and objectives is to use a workshop. This is often better organised and facilitated by an outsider who is well versed in strategic planning techniques. For this reason, the third suggestion is that the company brings in an external facilitator to workshop goals and objectives. This will help avoid political or personal issues clouding the discussion.

An outsider can bring a level of objectivity and rigour to the process. Outsiders can ask difficult questions about the will, capacity and capability of the business to

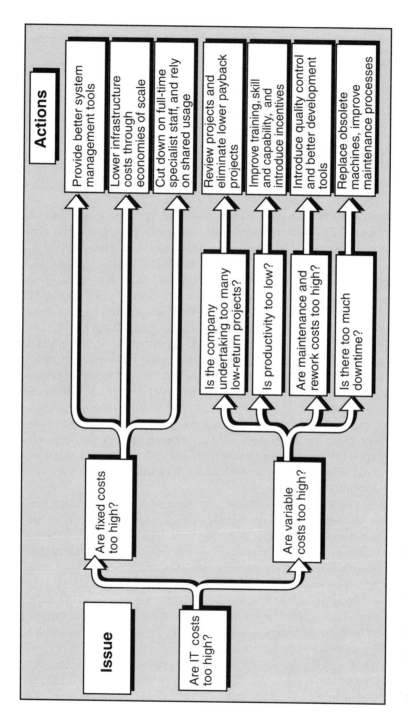

Figure 2.3—Ohmae's issue diagram

achieve stated goals. Techniques such as value added management help ensure that the goals are focused to increasing shareholder value rather than just furthering "feel good" ambitions or ambitions. The outside facilitators will often have access to industry trends and statistics that bring an air of reality to what otherwise may be "blue sky" sessions.

An experienced strategic planner may seem an expensive investment, but a skilled consultant is likely to drive the company to develop more sound goals and objectives than might be achieved in an internal brainstorming session. One drawback is that consultants often find it difficult to manage their desire to create a global strategic plan at great expense. This can be controlled by a tight brief that is specific about the desired outcomes, and limits duration and expense to a cost commensurate with the deliverables.

The scope of the task in this instance is to surface the real reason for outsourcing and ensure the company culture, commitment and resources are available to support those goals and objectives.

The outline of a workshop process would include:

1. Advise the executive that their input is needed to develop goals and objectives related to outsourcing. Include a definition of goal and objective. You may wish to reproduce the definitions in this text and include the goal, objective, CSF and criteria decomposition diagram shown in Figure 2.1
2. Organise research into the current state of the business, previous trends and issues, and establish industry trends and issues. The marketing or planning department should be able to provide some useful material. You may also find it useful to refer to Appendix A for additional recommendations on information gathering.
3. Draw up an issue diagram (Figure 2.3). This does not have to be perfectly correct in its every observation and conclusion. The aim is to illustrate how the business can work from the general (issue) to the particular (action) in a logical manner.
4. Provide the participants with some samples of goals and objectives, including the rationale for selecting them and the potential implications. Figure 2.4 provides a possible format.
5. Hold the workshop to develop the company's goals and objectives related to outsourcing. These can build on the material suggested in the first three steps.
6. Circulate the documented goals and objectives and ask for sign-off that they reflect correctly what was discussed and why the company is outsourcing.

It is important that the stated goals and objectives are circulated and signed off. Plans and objectives drawn up in the ferment of the workshop may not stand critical analysis when executives return to their desks and consider the implications more deeply.

In closing this chapter on goals and objectives, there is one last warning on this subject from Kenichi Ohmae: "The more severe the pressure and the more

Goal: Xylog's aim is to remain a virtual corporation focusing on our core competency of interim management of IT. We will outsource all other functions where suppliers offer greater economies of scale or efficiency.

Rationale: The company believes that maximum flexibility in scale and profit per employee will be reduced if the company eliminates non-revenue-earning infrastructure. The company believes the key to this flexibility lies in outsourcing all processes other than interim management.

Objective: Xylog will outsource the provision of all IT if it can be shown that a service provider can meet our goals of achieving a level of service in desktop and network operations 10% better than we can ourseves, at an equal or lower cost.

Implications (positive):
- This will contribute to business goal #2 of achieving higher than industry average returns on our investments.
- We will not be distracted by the requirements of keeping abreast of, or managing, a non-core activity.
- We can link service performance and rewards in a manner not achievable with our in-house organisation.

Implications (negative):
- We may reduce the flexibility we currently enjoy with personalised desktop environments and hardware choices.
- We may have to share infrastructure and support staff with other customers of the service provider.
- We will have to commit to some level of management of the service provider's performance.

Figure 2.4—Goal template

urgently a broader view is needed, the more dangerously [executives'] mental vision seems to narrow down."[24] This risk can be avoided partially by using an expert consultant who can stand back from the situation, ask probing questions and force broader discussion of the issues than may occur in an internal meeting where the agenda is formed and dominated by internal factions or emergencies.

Finally, know yourself—as a company. Know your company's true values, its style, its culture, its strengths and its weaknesses. Know what your company values and does not value. Don't fool yourself or your intending provider that you are the paragon of virtue described in the mission statement, the service provider likewise. These characteristics will surface in the relationship, so it is worth considering and managing them from the start.

The next chapter moves on to developing CSFs and criteria for selecting the service provider.

Checklist

1. Do you have one or more goals or objectives that lead to outsourcing as an appropriate solution? For example:
    1.1. cost reduction through resource or infrastructure sharing;
    1.2. access to capabilities or skills that are otherwise unaffordable or unobtainable;
    1.3. flexibility to scale your operations up or down at short notice;
    1.4. process improvements that will help control waste and misdirected effort.
2. Have the objectives been quantified adequately?
    2.1. Does each objective have time measures, including duration to achieve milestones or a finite delivery date?
    2.2. Can each objective be measured for success on the basis of increased revenue, reduced cost or other quality?
    2.3. Have the objectives been defined as outputs rather than inputs?
3. Have the resources and infrastructure requirements been estimated for each objective?
4. Are the objectives realistic? Does the company have the money and human resources to achieve these objectives?
5. Has each objective been tested adequately for robustness and longevity? Have the following questions been asked:
    5.1. What benefits are to be delivered?
    5.2. How will the benefits be delivered—through economy of scale, shared facilities, better expense approval?
    5.3. At what benchmark—the same quality, lower quality, higher service levels?
    5.4. How much is the benefit worth—10%, 20%?
    5.5. When will the benefits be realised—this year, next year, over 10 years?
6. Why is outsourcing the best way to achieve this objective?
7. Have the major implications of each objective been defined, and are those implications accepted by the organisation?
8. Are there outsourcing service providers in your geography that have the capacity and capability to deliver the outputs?
9. Have all the senior executive understood and committed to the goals and objectives that will now drive the outsourcing project?
10. Have all the team members of the outsourcing project understood and accepted these goals and objectives?
11. Have the implications been documented and distributed?
12. Have the objectives been signed off?

Outsourcing: a real-life experience

There are many elements that must be right to make the arrangement effective—the contract, the management, the relationship . . . I am going to focus on what is critical to get right at the outset, and how to ensure that all participants in the arduous process of arriving at and transitioning to the outsourcer also understand this.

Having had the opportunity to experience outsourcing from both sides—as a vice-president at DMR Consulting, who led and was responsible for a number of outsourcing deals, to my present position as CIO for Southcorp, where we are currently investigating what opportunity outsourcing might bring our organisation—the most critical element to get right and to continue to focus on throughout the programme is *what are the drivers for outsourcing?*

The business must be engaged in determining the key drivers, as they must relate to the strategies for the business. The drivers focus the development of all other elements of the arrangement—the project team make-up, the style of contract, the types of organisations you invite to respond. They are translated into the criteria by which you measure the success or otherwise of the responses to your RFP.

Typical Drivers

- *Service costing*—represented by annual charges, one-off charges (e.g. transition), consulting rates and variable charges for increases or decreases in service requirement. There is generally an expectation that the outsourcer will be cheaper than insourcing, due to economies of scale.
- *Alignment with business goals*—strategic objectives that must be satisfied or enabled by the outsourcing arrangement. This is where the idea of partnership is becoming more common, although true partnership is difficult to attain without some form of equity arrangement.
- *Achievement of industry best practice*—a major change programme is required to deliver appropriate service to the business.
- *Staff transition*—for many organisations a critical factor is what the outsourcer offers the staff by way of opportunity, entitlements etc.
- *Minimising risk*—scarce resources and limited budgets can create risk profiles for a business, which may limit opportunities in the future.

In engaging the business in the development and sign-off of the drivers for outsourcing, you provide clear focus to the process and, significantly, to the service provider, who need to understand what they must deliver. Importantly, clarity of vision ensures that your business is able to assess objectively whether there is real value in proceeding down the outsourcing path.

If outsourcing does not meet these objectives, then you probably shouldn't proceed with outsourcing. If as an service provider you are not able to meet or understand these objectives, then you probably shouldn't bid.

Wayne Saunders
Chief Information Officer,
Southcorp

Developing critical success factors and criteria

Critical success factors and criteria

We separate these factors from goals and objectives because in some cases, albeit fewer than one would like, companies will have well documented goals and objectives; for them, this chapter will be their starting point.

Critical success factors (CSFs) are the few key inputs or characteristics the service provider must have if they are to help us meet our objectives. They should meet the tests of necessity and sufficiency. Each CSF must stand the test of being necessary, and the collection of CSFs must meet the test of being complete, i.e. meeting them alone is sufficient to ensure success.

Criteria are those attributes that we can use to measure the quality and quantity of key inputs or show evidence that the service provider can deliver on the CSFs.

It has been argued, and with reason, that CSFs and criteria are the same thing: they are both representations of "real" CFSs. While the argument has merit, I still hold to the view that criteria, as used in this text, are measures of evidence CSFs.

For these reasons, the concept of separate CSFs and criteria are promoted in this handbook, and we approach the issue of developing these from the view of the pragmatist rather than the academic.

We start by suggesting that criteria be divided into six grades. These are shown in Table 3.1.

Note the importance of being specific as to the risk if the criterion is not met, and the inclusion of the clarification for the bidder on selection judgement. This is too rarely done and host companies use simplistic grades such as "essential" and "mandatory", without explanation.

This level of clarification is important. The host company must agree what level each criterion is to be set at. The process of defining and agreeing levels will later point to the critical performance issues to be covered in the contract and measured in service level agreements. This clarification must be shared with the bidders so they understand what the host company means by terms such as "critical" or "preferred".

The criteria are used in the RFP to measure the fit of the bidder to the host company's profile of an ideal service provider.

Some may prefer to think of CSFs as subobjectives. This is a legitimate definition. However, by defining CSFs as key inputs or characteristics we differentiate them

Table 3.1—Six levels of criteria

Criteria	Risk if absent	Selection action
6. Essential	Unacceptable	Any RFP not meeting these criteria will be rejected
5. Critical	Very high	Absence will put the company through serious inconvenience and will count heavily against candidates
4. Important	High	Absence will put the company through inconvenience and cost, and will be regarded as a serious shortcoming
3. Preferred	Medium	Absence will create some cost and inconvenience. Absence may be counterbalanced by other criteria
2. Marginal	Marginal	Absence may result in moderate inconvenience or cost. Absence will have a marginal effect on the selection process
1. Low	Low	Absence will not result in any significant inconvenience or cost. The presence of these criteria may sway decisions if all else is equal

from subobjectives by shifting the focus away from business aims and towards the characteristics sought in the service provider.

The previous chapter discussed goals and objectives from the perspective of an ambitious athlete. It used previous track record as one of the criteria that could define the profile of a top coach.

The next step in the progression towards outsourcing is to define the CSFs and criteria used in selecting the bidder that is best able to support the business objectives. For example, here is one of the objectives listed in Chapter 1.

> Pravka will outsource IT to a global company in order to leverage our market presence in countries listed in our future development plan. This objective is based on the premise that in doing so we will pay no more than a 5% premium over opening and operating our own global network at the same standard.

The next stage is to analyse these objectives and isolate the inputs or characteristics we would seek in an appropriate supplier. Those should be broadly based, taking note of the elements mentioned in Kaplan and Norton's book, *The Balanced Scorecard*.[25] The CSFs, like the scorecard, should consider "four balanced perspectives: financial, customers, internal business processes, and learning and growth."

It is not enough to concentrate on the technical resources required to achieve IT project goals. The selection process must consider the service provider's profile from a number of angles, including the commercial and human resource or cultural angle. Host companies should note that the failure of a number of outsourcing projects has been attributed to incompatible cultures rather than underachievement in the technical sphere. We suggest that the CSFs and criteria are grouped into at least three classes: commercial, technical and organisational (human resources and cultural).

The CSFs are determined by analysing the objectives in a critical and creative manner. Objectives are usually stated within a short paragraph densely packed with information. The CSFs may have to sweep up implicit as well as explicit requirements. If we take the first Pravka objective, we can define some explicit and implicit CSFs. The characteristics of an ideal service provider can be determined through explicit statements. They include:

- Company with a presence in our target markets.
- Service standard at least equal to our current standard.
- Cost no more than 5% above current levels.

They may also include implicit CSFs:

- Will support our business goals in new markets.
- Provide Pravka with advice and guidance in markets.

While the process sounds simple, it rarely is. In writing an outsourcing book, we can be selective about example objectives. The outsourcing team will not have that luxury in real life. The objectives they will work with may be less explicit about the outsourcing driver. They may have to scrutinise objectives carefully and check that the CSFs they identify are consistent with the objectives, and later that the criteria remain consistent with the CSFs.

One useful source of CSFs is the implication analysis of objectives mentioned in Chapter 1. The implications often drive out the CSFs because they usually state what the requirements are for delivering the objective, which are almost analogous to CSFs. The team should also check that the CSFs they specify cover the areas identified by the Balanced Scorecard. For example, using the perspectives promoted by Kaplan and Norton, we can check that the example CSFs provide a rounded picture of the provider (Figure 3.1). It may not always be possible to do this. However the discipline of attempting to have at least one CSF for each of the categories is worthwhile.

Filling in a blank template based on Figure 3.2 provides an excellent check that the goals, objectives and CSFs are decomposed adequately. A useful approach is to draw the template on a large whiteboard and then populate it. Label columns as "Customer", "Process", "Financial", "Growth" and "Learning", and ask the team to identify appropriate measures. The presence of the boxes seems to provide a considerable motivation to not leave any blanks.

Customer: Company with a presence in our target markets.

Process: Service standard at least equal to our current standard.

Financial: Cost no more than 5% above current levels.

Growth: Will support our business goals in new markets.

Learning: Provide Pravka with advice and guidance in markets.

Figure 3.1—Using CSFs to provide a picture of the provider

Defining selection criteria

It may seem obvious that the selection criteria should be based on objectives and their CSFs. Yet companies often break this critical link and set out a list of selection criteria that read like a list of noble business virtues, for example:

- The service provider must demonstrate good corporate ethics.
- The service provider must have a commitment to teamwork.
- The service provider must adhere to equal employment opportunity principles.

Valuable and virtuous as these criteria are, they are often meaningless. No sane service provider is going to respond that they are unethical individualists using discriminatory hiring practices. If they must be included, then:

- justify their inclusion
- weigh their importance

Goal: *Pravka will become a global player within the next five years, leveraging other organisations' competencies and skills to achieve its goal.*					
Objective: *Pravka will outsource IT to a global company in order to leverage our market presence in countries listed in our future development plan. This objective is based on the premise that by doing so we will pay no more than a 5% premium over opening and operating our own global network.*					
CSFs	**Customer**	**Process**	**Financial**	**Growth**	**Learning**
1. Company with a presence in our target markets	●				
2. Service standard at least equal to our current level		●			
3. Cost no more than 5% above current levels			●		
4. Will support business goals in growth markets				●	
5. Will provide Pravka with advice and guidance in new markets					●

Figure 3.2—CSF decomposition diagram

- determine measures for evaluating these criteria
- position them in an appropriate part of the RFP.

The majority of selection criteria should derive from the CSFs. A warning: not all selection criteria can be linked to the CSFs. Some will fall outside the realm that the CSFs cover, either explicitly or implicitly. Examples of criteria that may fall outside the range covered by the CSFs include such items as a requirement to meet national registration or government regulations.

What differentiates selection criteria from critical success factors?

The key differentiation between selection criteria and CSFs is that the selection criteria define the *evidence* to be produced by the service provider that they are able to deliver on the CSFs.

It is clearly possible to skip steps in the breakdown of goals to objectives through CSFs and criteria. The virtue in following the pedantic process is that it makes it possible for others to see why the outsourcing team selected these particular criteria. It also makes it possible to understand the relative importance attached to each criterion as it can be readily traced back to the goal it supports.

An intuitive process that skips steps is not so readily traceable. While the selection of the criteria may appear obvious to the outsourcing team, it may not be so as time passes, people move on and memories fade. To illustrate this point, the concept of breaking down goals, objectives, CSFs and Criteria is repeated.

The following CSFs were developed in response to the Pravka objective mentioned earlier:

- Company with a presence in our target markets.
- Service standard at least equal to our current standard.
- Cost no more than 5% above current levels.
- Will support our business goals in new markets.
- Provide Pravka with advice and guidance in markets.

This led to the following criteria in support of those CSFs:

- Offices in Belgium, China, India and Japan.
- Four reference sites with service standard equal to or better than Pravka.
- Ratio of experienced network staff to users of at least 1:50.
- Deploy Tier 1 network management tools.
- Desktop total cost of ownership (TCO) at $3000 per seat or better.
- Contractual commitment to support our business plan in above countries.
- Induction plan to familiarise Pravka staff with new markets.

Some of these attributes then need to be defined to another level of detail. Some may wish to further define some of the criteria, for example: *Experienced network staff are defined as holding a Microsoft or Novell Certificate of Competency and at least two years' experience managing a network of 100 seats or better.*

Weighing selection criteria

All selection criteria are not equal, for example most new car buyers would probably rank colour choice as less important than number of seats or engine capacity. The most common way of denoting the difference in importance is to use a numerical scale. A range from 6 (mandatory) to 1 (least important) serves most purposes. Use an even-numbered range so that it is impossible to select a mid-point. Broader ranges, say from 10 to 1, can be more confusing than helpful.

You must always define each weight, as the challenge in allocating weight to criteria is to keep the allocation of weight consistent (for example, see Table 3.1).

One major advantage of using a numerical scale is that it makes it easy to use a numerical scoring system to compare responses from the prospective providers. Other systems of weighting exist that accommodate quantitative and qualitative data, for example verbal and graphical systems. A pair-wise assessment scheme might include comparing the relative importance, preference or likelihood of the two elements with respect to the data. *Importance* is useful when comparing one objective with another, *preference* when comparing alternatives, and *likelihood* when comparing the probability of outcomes.

A useful tool for carrying out the first level of analysis is a relative value chart. This is illustrated in Figure 3.3, which also carries a more detailed explanation of the chart's construction and use. The relative value chart is a numbers-based comparative method.

Remember that selecting a service provider is not a mechanical exercise. The process of weighing and numerical evaluation should be treated as an *aid* to decision making, not a substitute.

Culling criteria

The idea is that less is more. This applies to criteria in particular. You will start by listing far too many criteria that then have to be culled to a manageable number. There are two things that help in culling criteria. The first is the ranking process. Resist the temptation to promote unimportant criteria. If criteria do not cry out to be in the RFP, then ditch them. Indications are that approximately 20% of criteria will prove to be unimportant on closer inspection.

The second culling tool is dependency. For some criteria to be met, other criteria must, by implication, also be met. Returning to our Olympic hopeful, let us imagine that under the CSF "top coach" we have a list of criteria that include:

- track record 100 metre dash
- experience in 100 metre dash
- trained 100 metre athletes
- trained gold medal winner in 100 metres in major international competition, e.g. Olympics, Pan Pacific Games.

If we select the fourth criterion, then we should be able to dispense with the other three. If we selected the first criterion, we should be able to dispense with criteria 2

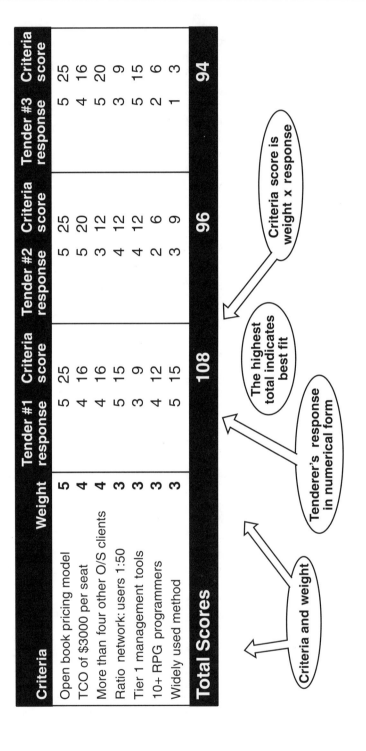

Criteria	Weight	Tender #1 response	Criteria score	Tender #2 response	Criteria score	Tender #3 response	Criteria score
Open book pricing model	5	5	25	5	25	5	25
TCO of $3000 per seat	4	4	16	5	20	4	16
More than four other O/S clients	4	4	16	3	12	5	20
Ratio network: users 1:50	3	5	15	4	12	3	9
Tier 1 management tools	3	3	9	4	12	5	15
10+ RPG programmers	3	4	12	2	6	2	6
Widely used method	3	5	15	3	9	1	3
Total Scores			**108**		**96**		**94**

Criteria score is weight x response

The highest total indicates best fit

Tenderer's response in numerical form

Criteria and weight

Figure 3.3—Relative value chart

and 3, and maybe 4 if the track record was defined further as having trained top-class athletes in international competition. To do that, however, we should define what we mean by "track record". This small exercise points to the importance of clear thinking and definition in our criteria. Criterion 4 is unambiguous.

Too many RFPs are cluttered with unimportant and dependent criteria, which can lead to poor outcomes:

- The sheer number of criteria masks those that are important. Proposers faced with the task of responding to every criterion lapse into "tick the box" mode, providing inadequate and poorly considered responses to the RFP.
- The host company winds up doing little more than mechanically processing responses. Simple mechanistic scoring processes supplant thoughtful consideration of the responses. Selection is numerically objective but lacking in any reflection or understanding.
- The cost of preparing the RFP and responding to it escalates as it grows into an unwieldy lump containing huge lists of criteria.
- The process of allocating weights tends to become "averaged" as the large numbers of relatively unimportant material overwhelms categories 3 and 4. To illustrate this point, consider that meeting two level 2 criteria (marginal) will be the equivalent of meeting one level 4 (Important) criterion.

Criteria should be soundly balanced. The following would provide a reasonable balance:

- Essential—5–10% of the total.
- Critical—25–50%.
- Important—10–15%.
- Preferred—5–10%.
- Marginal—5–10%.
- Low—less than 5%.

Ideally, you should dispense with all but essential, critical and important criteria. Focusing on how well a respondent meets 15 or 20 critical criteria is likely to result in a more thoughtful and analytical selection. If the host company has to process 400 criteria for each response to their RFP, of which the bulk are cosmetic, then they may not have time to thoughtfully consider what the scores are telling them.

If the objectives are clear, and the CSFs limited to the 5 ($\pm$ 2) things that are critical for the objective to be realised, then these should be few in number. Certainly if the RFP contains hundreds of criteria then the company has probably slipped into developing a wish list far removed from the characteristics needed to deliver the objectives.

Referring back to the car analogy, we can reduce the selection criteria to those things that are essential and critical to our choice. If we assume the person is

Table 3.2—Reducing the selection criteria

Item	Category 6 (essential)	Category 5 (critical)
Price	$20 000–$30 000	
Seating	Four	
Gearbox		Auto
Air conditioning		Standard

seeking a car to transport a family of four with a price between $20 000 and $30 000, then we can narrow the criteria down as shown in Table 3.2.

The following criteria were removed on the basis that they did not add real value to the selection process:

- Colour—a variety of colours are readily available.
- Radio—few cars today do not include a radio.
- Seat belts—legislation demands these in many countries.

Common issues with selection criteria

Noble criteria

Other common issues with criteria (and indeed objectives and CSFs) are the inclusion of *noble criteria*. For example, a company may rightfully set ethical business practices as a CSF, with matching criteria. Worthy as this noble CSF might be, no company is going to score themselves as a zero or non-complying organisation. Including these criteria is a waste of time.

Intuitive criteria

Another issue is *intuitive criteria*. For example, the objective, *Reduce the TCO of the local area network (LAN) by 30% within 18 months*, may be broken down as shown in Figure 3.4.

Unless the company knows why the total cost of ownership is high, they may misjudge the attributes. For example, if the root cause of TCO in your business is a nonstandard desktop image, obsolescent routers, decomposed cable and plant, and a proprietary network operating system, then the above criteria may do little to cure the problem. Certainly they will be useful in resolving the issue, but not without an understanding that the organisation will also need to allow for capital expenditure to replace the existing low-quality infrastructure.

> ## CSFs
> The service provider must have a high order of network management skills.

> ## Criteria (evidence)
>
> 1. Proven TCO at three other sites of $3000 per seat.
> 2. Average network uptime at above sites >99.0%.
> 3. Ratio 1:50 experienced network staff per seat.

Figure 3.4—Breaking down the objective

Nick Kovari, formerly of CSC, pointed out in an interview that "this failure to understand the root cause of poor current performance often leads to disputes when the service provider informs the client that they will need to spend on infrastructure to cure a problem." The need to "discover" the current state of the IT environment is discussed in the next chapter. It is absolutely critical that the criteria required to meet the objectives reflect the real need and not some intuitive belief that "doing these things will make it better". That is analogous to selecting a cure without knowing the nature of the illness.

Unquantified criteria

In many cases it is not enough to define the criteria; they may also need to be qualified. In our example, the company seeks experienced network staff at a ratio of 1:50 users. A common failing is neglecting to specify *how much* of the specified criteria must be supplied. The risk is that the service provider will give a positive but incomplete response to the question in the RFP. Unhappy times will follow when it is discovered later, after the contract is signed, that the "experience" is limited to one staff member who is committed to another site for 80% of their time.

Alignment

The RFP and the outsourcing contract must reflect the objectives, CSFs and criteria contained in the outsourcing project. Indeed, it is difficult to see how one could develop a useful contract without this alignment. The objectives and CSFs for outsourcing should be stated clearly in the RFP, and the contract (and service level agreement) should show how these are addressed.

It is also useful to group the criteria into at least three categories, namely commercial, technical and organisational. This will also make for a better structured contract, as the warranties, conditions and schedules of the contract will tend to group these matters together.

The alignment would normally follow the model shown in Figure 3.5. This shows the alignment of the above, including the suggestion that they are grouped into the categories described above.

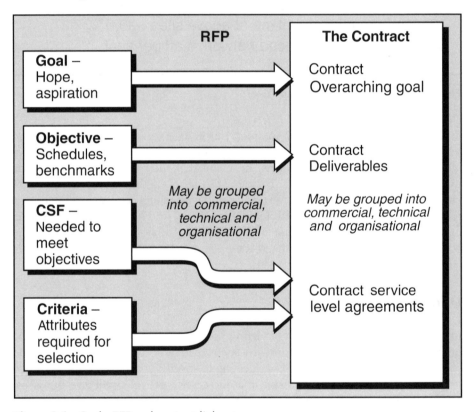

Figure 3.5—Goals, RFP and contract linkage

Prerequisites

If the objectives of outsourcing, and therefore some of the contract deliverables, include, for example, large-scale system development, the team may discover that these goals cannot be achieved unless certain foundation tasks or items are first put in place. Typically, these prerequisites will include training business staff in new methods and acquiring new hardware and software tools to support the development. It may even include some remedial work on existing systems so that critical staff with specific experience can be freed from maintenance and turned over to development.

Finally, do ensure that all objectives are time-bound. That means including a start and completion date in the statement.

The dating of criteria may be critical to the RFP issue or response. Further, the discipline of examining precedence and timing is useful and should flow through the outsourcing development process.

Arbitrary criteria

The biggest single issue in outsourcing is the failure to link objectives, CSFs and criteria. Too often the criteria are plucked from the air and at best connected only faintly to the objectives, which sometimes seem to have been developed in isolation from the goals. Even worse, some criteria set in this arbitrary manner wind up being in conflict with the goals and objectives. This is most likely to occur when the decision to outsource is based on a knee-jerk reaction to a black-hole project or is driven by an intuitive belief that outsourcing will improve things. Mountaineers, hikers and sailors are taught to trust their compasses, not their intuition in fog, white-out or darkness. Goals and objectives are the compasses of business.

Response weighting

This aspect of RFP response processing is covered in this chapter for the sake of completeness. When working to develop the criteria, it is worthwhile to have clearly in mind the nature of response you wish to get from proposers. Try to avoid the traditional "comply" and "not comply" model because this form of answer is uninformative. Few respondents will comply absolutely or fail totally to comply. In truth, most will comply to some extent with the majority of the criteria. The challenge is to understand the *extent* to which they comply or do not comply.

The RFP should include an instruction to proposers to respond using a numerical scale. Define the scale in plain English, in the same way as weights were defined. This keeps the approach consistent with the criteria weighing process and helps avoid self-serving interpretations of the relative score given by the proposer.

A suggested scaled response is shown in Figure 3.6. It includes a baseline that relates it to the current status of those criteria within the host company. It is a matter of judgement whether this information is shared with the candidate service

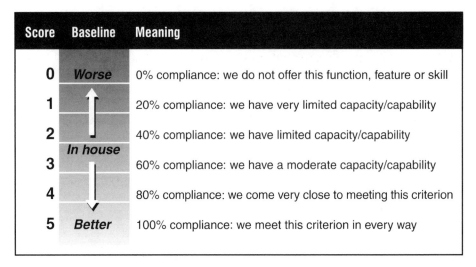

Score	Baseline	Meaning
0	*Worse*	0% compliance: we do not offer this function, feature or skill
1		20% compliance: we have very limited capacity/capability
2		40% compliance: we have limited capacity/capability
3	*In house*	60% compliance: we have a moderate capacity/capability
4		80% compliance: we come very close to meeting this criterion
5	*Better*	100% compliance: we meet this criterion in every way

Figure 3.6—Scaled response form

providers. However, as a general rule, the more information you make available, the better informed responses you will receive.

Highlight the fact that these responses will form part of the conditions and warranties in the final contract. This will encourage reality in the responses provided by the proposers. An example of a response scale is given in Table 3.3. Include such an example in the instructions to bidders on completing the RFP.

The benefit of the numeric scale is that it facilitates processing of the responses in spreadsheets or decision analysis tools. Some alternative methods are explored later in this chapter.

Encourage the candidates to explain their scores. Few things are more frustrating than to be a bidder and find responses limited to a simple (and ultimately misleading) response rule. This usually manifests itself with a requirement that one must respond to criteria with a yes or no answer, rather than providing an opportunity to suggest an alternative or explain why the service provider does not comply with some irrelevant measure.

Table 3.3—Sample scaled response

Example criteria	Example fit	Example score
Provide 10 "C" programmers	Have 10 or more available	5 (fully compliant)
- ditto -	Have 8 available	4 (80% compliant)
- ditto -	Have 6 available	3 (60% compliant)
- ditto -	Have 5 available	2 (50% compliant)
- ditto -	Have 2 available	1 (20% compliant)
- ditto -	Have 0 available	0 (Noncompliant)

The reasoning behind the drive to cull criteria and reduce them to those items critical or mandatory to the host company's needs should be starting to become clear. Careful, analytical research into candidates' abilities to perform on the key criteria is likely to give a better selection outcome than simple numerical ranking of respondents based on processing hundreds of largely irrelevant criteria.

Too often RFPs are issued with far too much emphasis placed on the processing of the responses and far too little emphasis on uncovering the best service provider for the task in hand.

Worksheets

A worksheet for recording and responding to criteria is shown in Figure 3.7. The end column refers to the note number, which is any written explanation from the proposer on their rating of fit to the criteria. The worksheet is largely self-explanatory, though you should note the following observations: *Business goals* may be so vaguely stated as to have little obvious direct connection to the objectives. If this is the case, then explain the linkage. *Objectives* must follow the guidelines defined in Chapter 1, and must be explicit measurable performance commitments, i.e. quantified, measurable, time-based and achievable. *CSFs* are the few key inputs or characteristics the service provider must have if they are to help you meet your objectives. *Criteria* are those attributes used to measure the quality and quantity of key inputs or characteristics (CSFs) of the service providers who may bid for our business.

Software tools

Decision making is often difficult because trade-offs need to be made amongst competing objectives. If a team uses appropriate tools, then it can leverage its decision quality in the face of complexity. The tools that are described in this section are used for rating the extent to which service providers' claimed offerings match your criteria. The tools are introduced at this stage as you may find it useful to develop your criteria in a way that best fits the tool of your choice.

Relative value chart

The relative value chart (RVC) is recommended as a tool that can be used for second-stage processing of submissions. The first stage is an "eyeball check" to

Criteria Worksheet

Goal: Xylog's aim is to remain a virtual corporation focusing on our core competency of interim management of IT. We will outsource all other functions where suppliers offer greater economies of scale or efficiency.

Objective: Xylog will outsource the provision of all information technology if it can be shown that a service provider can meet our goals of achieving a level of service in desktop and network operations 10% better than we can ourselves, at an equal or lower cost.

CSF: Demonstrated ability to provide a satisfactory level of service and desktop TCO of $3000 per year or less for a company of 50 people.

Criteria	Quantity	Dates by	Weight (1–6)	Response (1–6)	Note number
1. Desktop TCO of $3000 per year or less	50 desktops	31 Dec 2003	5		
2. Proof that 90% of critical help desk calls are resolved within 20 minutes	20 per month	30 June 2002	4		
3. Proof that resolution of 95% of noncritical calls are resolved within 4 hours	60 per month	30 June 2002	4		
4. Proof that network up time for other customers now meets or exceeds 98.5% between hours of 07:00 and 19:00 Monday to Friday	Mon–Fri	28th Feb 2002	5		

Figure 3.7—Criteria worksheet

cull and discard any tenders that fail to meet essential criteria. From this, you understand the essential must be defined as indispensable and that failure to possess this attribute means instant rejection.

The RVC is a well known process. Robbins and Mukerji[26] give a comprehensive explanation of the process. An illustration of the model is given in Figure 3.3, which includes a description of each column, and how it is used.

Commercial decision analysis tools

There are a wide range of PC-based decision analysis tools. These are not normally stocked by the average computer store; it may be necessary to seek out a specialist supplier of scientific and mathematical software. Many publish excellent catalogues of mathematical, statistical, risk-analysis and decision-making tools. Good products I have used to advantage include *Expert Choice, Data 3* and *BestChoice3*. Make your own choice, as there is a wide range of specialist tools available, including add-on applications for some of the industry standard spreadsheets.

Figure 3.8 shows a useful flow diagram for complex decisions.

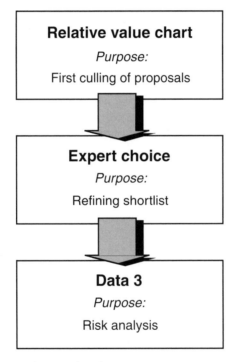

Figure 3.8—Flow diagram for complex decisions

The section that follows describes some of these tools in more detail. The extracts have been published with the kind permission of the developers.

Expert choice

Expert Choice Pro is a product of Expert Choice Inc., Pittsburgh, USA.

Expert Choice is based on the analytic hierarchy process (AHP), a multicriteria or multiobjective decision-making process that was developed by mathematician

Thomas L. Saaty at the Wharton School of the University of Pennsylvania. The AHP makes it possible for you to deal with both tangible and intangible factors. You can organise your data, thoughts and intuition in a logical, hierarchical structure. You can express your understanding and experience with pair-wise comparisons about the relative importance, preference or likelihood of all relevant factors. The AHP accommodates uncertainty and allows for revision, so that individuals and groups can grapple with all their concerns, and the results are easily tested for sensitivities to changes in assumptions and judgements.

Decision Analysis by TreeAge

Decision Analysis by TreeAge (DATA 3.5™) is a product of TreeAge Software Inc., Williamstown, USA.

DATA 3.5 has been designed to implement the techniques of decision analysis in an intuitive and easy-to-use manner. It transforms decision analysis into easily applied and highly visual means by (1) organising the decision making process, (2) analysing the problem at hand, and (3) communicating both the structure of the problem and the basis of the decision reached.

In decision analysis, the problem is disaggregated into components small enough to be readily understood and analysed, and then some components are used to model the problem's possible elements. Under this methodology, the possible events (decisions, uncertainties and final outcomes) and the relations among them are identified.

By itself, this clear identification of the sequence and linkage of events would be of great benefit in clarifying complex decisions. But decision analysis as implemented by DATA 3.5 does much more. By calculating the value of each possible chain of events, and by weighing uncertain results by the probability of each possible outcome, the decision maker can evaluate each intermediate part of the model and identify the sequence that will maximise value, or minimise costs, depending on the objective.

DATA 3.5 reduces the complexity of decision analysis, both in the initial stages of formulating and structuring the problem, and later in calculating and testing the analysis.

BestChoice 3

BestChoice3, from Sterling Software, is powerful and easy to use paired comparison processor. The product outline is shown in Figure 3.9.

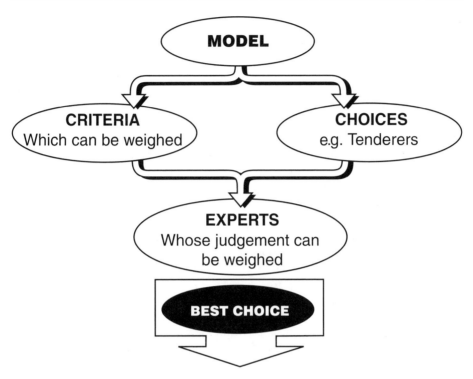

Figure 3.9—Outline of BestChoice 3

Conclusion

The decision to outsource is generally as significant as any major engineering or other project decision. Yet there is often a surprising lack of rigour and decision analysis applied to evaluating responses and selecting the preferred service provider. What is more, the decision, once made, is not easily reversible. The CEO of RDC, a benchmarking company is quoted as saying, "Once control of technology operations has been relinquished, it may not easily be won back . . . When you give away your data centre, it is very difficult to get it back, because you lose the infrastructure and the people."[27]

Similar views were expressed by Suh when he said, "Companies that abandon control of their systems . . . can find that their knowledge of the business and their systems are permanently disconnected."[28]

Outsourcing is a big and risky decision. Examples abound of optimistic ventures winding up in disaster. Anyone doubting that should refer to Lacity and

Hirschheim's book[29] on the experiences of more than 20 companies. Other examples of unfortunate outcomes can be found in Domberger and Hall's *The Contracting Casebook*.[30]

The host company cannot be too careful in selecting its service provider. One method used by PA Consulting Group has been to divide the selection team into three distinct groups. Each group was assigned the task of evaluating the proposals from a single viewpoint. One group independently reviewed the commercial, another the technical and the third the organisational sections of the proposals.

At the end of the evaluation process the three teams were brought together to explain and justify their rankings. This helped ensure that the technical selectors were not influenced unduly by the commercial considerations, and vice versa. It also ensured that the critical human factor was investigated in appropriate depth by the team.

At this point, it seems worthwhile to note that the host company may like to note Greaver's five reasons for using outside advisers or consultants to assist you in selecting your service provider. Greaver included the following:[31]

- To help manage risks.
- To level the playing field with provider expertise.
- To assist the project manager in focusing on outsourcing issues.
- To act as a paradigm buster (challenge established thinking).
- To offer independent observations on the outsourcing environment.

A consultant who achieved the above targets would make a very worthwhile contribution to the outsourcing project.

In the next chapter, we will discuss discovery, i.e. the process of ensuring you know and understand your own IT. The discovery process may require you to alter some of your CSFs and criteria if you find that the root cause of some of the obstacles to achieving your objectives is not as you thought.

Checklist

1. Can you trace upward from criteria to CSFs and objectives?
2. Have you defined the weights you will apply to criteria?
3. Have you defined the distinctions, such as "essential" and "critical" in plain English?
4. Have you defined the response scores in plain English?
5. Have you provided an example to the bidders of a proper response score?
6. Have you baselined your current position against the criteria?

7. Have you grouped the criteria into categories, such as technical, organisational and commercial?
8. Have you culled all unimportant criteria?
9. Is the distribution of criteria sensible (see p. 6)?
10. Are the remaining criteria unambiguous?
11. Has everybody on the selection committee agreed the criteria?
12. Are noble criteria included or excluded from the critical selection tables?
13. Have any numerical quantities been checked and tested by a third party?
14. Is each criterion based on a factual understanding of the environment?
15. Have you allowed for explanations in tender response forms?
16. Have you tested the RVCs required to process the criteria?
17. Is the weighting and scoring system compatible with the chosen decision support tools?

4 Discovering your environment

Discovery is the process of documenting the totality of the host company's IT environment. IT departments will often have entered into myriad maintenance and support agreements and volume-based purchasing agreements, and hold a large number of licences for operating systems, software, utilities and programming or development tools. The testing question is whether you can produce a list of all your maintenance and licence agreements signed over the past 20 years. It is difficult but important to do so.

GartnerGroup reported: "Companies who abdicate a proper discovery process go to the negotiating table without being able to accurately describe the dimensions of the deal within a desirable 5% margin of error . . . some clients have miscalculated distributed computing assets by more than 50% while their business cases assumed a 20% worst case variance."[32]

If you underestimate, your company may discover that the $10 million a year outsourcing cost has suddenly increased by another $2 million. The discovery issue is exacerbated further by the existence of unofficial or feral IT units. At the risk of being repetitive, I reiterate Strassman's comment: "According to a survey by the Diebold Group, user spending on information systems outside IT budgets was equivalent to another 64% of the IS department spending in manufacturing and 27% in service firms."[33]

This chapter should be read in conjunction with Chapter 10 on due diligence. There will be significant overlap between these two processes. Discovery is the process by which the host company prepares for the later due diligence search by the service provider. In discovery, the primary research is carried out by the host company with the aim of knowing their IT in order to properly prepare the RFP and to come to the negotiation table well prepared.

During due diligence, the service provider seeks to confirm the environment, baseline measures and issues that they are about to enter into a contract to operate and manage. Discovery must be done. Its value is maximised if it is done early—producing a better business case, a better RFP, a better set of responses and a better outcome.

Scope

The scope of discovery depends on the scope of your intended outsourcing agreement. However, it is prudent to make the scope as wide as possible, as few areas of IT operate in isolation. LAN bandwidth or quality may influence mainframe application response times. Back-up and recovery windows may be influenced by back-up software tools or hardware. The truth is most IT assets may overlap from one area to another. The existence of staff, equipment, contractors and consultants may be "hidden" outside the IT budget, and these can have a significant effect on the success of the outsourcing agreement.

The task is often immense. Tracking down long lost agreements is often a difficult and lengthy process. Requests to the vendors to supply copies of agreements will show their record keeping is equally poor. New contracts and maintenance agreements may have to be agreed in advance of the outsourcing tender. Internal difficulties may arise in the business if there are "hidden" IT costs that need to be incorporated in a new IT budget. Business people previously supportive of the outsourcing project may react adversely when the realisation strikes that IT is about to come under a more rigorous and searching regime, bringing to an end some of the autonomy that a business unit may now enjoy.

The following checklist gives a sense of the possible scope of discovery. It is not complete, but it does include many of the less obvious search points in the task ahead.

1. Human resources
   - annual leave and sick leave entitlements
   - corporate benefits
   - fringe benefits, such as car leases, mortgage support, child care
   - contracts with independent contractors
   - shadow costs of IT absorbed through staff employed in business units
2. Software licences and agreements
   - development tool license and maintenance
   - transfer fees for assignment to third party (outsourcer)
   - maintenance and support costs for utilities
3. Other licences and agreements
   - disaster recovery
   - telecommunication contracts
   - databases
4. Hardware
   - telecommunications equipment
   - switches, hubs, routers
5. Non-IT assets
   - mobile phones

- pagers
- furnishings, fittings

The number of people required to carry out the work may be substantial. Klepper and Jones noted, "As Dupont [USA] evaluated its IT services needs prior to its $4 billon sourcing arrangement with CSC and Andersen Consulting . . . the project team consisted of approximately 25 full-time people and an additional 300 from all parts of the company who served on various supporting teams."[34] This is not a spare-time task for one person.

The team may uncover unfortunate truths. One such is that your company will probably uncover a number of things that have been successfully hidden for many years. These are bound to result in internal disputes and acrimony, and may well delay the project while they are resolved. However, it is wiser to deal with these behind closed doors than have them surfaced by the service provider during due diligence or later in the contract.

A second unfortunate truth is that some current vendors will seize the opportunity to review existing contracts. This is particularly true of older maintenance contracts that have been blindly renewed for years at a (now) outdated price structure.

The third unfortunate truth is that the company will often discover that the true cost of information technology in the business is substantially higher than the annual budget has indicated.

The final unfortunate discovery is that the company often has a substantial amount of unlicensed software running on desktop PCs. The cost of purchasing licensed copies of office automation products to remediate the situation may run into substantial figures.

However, these discoveries are best made before the business case is completed or an outsourcing agreement is reached. One thing you may be absolutely sure about is that the service provider will discover these issues and costs. The second thing you may be sure about is that you will pay the service provider a "margin-on-services" to resolve these issues.

Unpleasant discoveries during due diligence or post-contract tend to swing the balance of power to the service provider, and undermine the credibility and standing of the host company.

Purpose

We undertake discovery because the contract or price agreement is sensitive to the composition, complexity and number of items in the deal. If the service provider bases charging on supporting 1000 desktops and then discovers the true number is 1200, then the host company will face an embarrassing renegotiation over price early on in the contract, and from a position of weakness.

Anand Barry of Fujitsu spoke of an outsourcing project that he had been involved in, where "a large national organisation was getting prepared for outsourcing, and as part of that exercise was putting together a list of equipment to be supported. Believing that there were about five mid-range systems, the team nevertheless sent out a message to all business managers, indicating that if a full listing was not provided, no support would be available once the outsourcer had taken over. A few weeks later, the list had increased to over 50 systems and they were still counting."

The desktop PC is a prime indicator of misjudged numbers. Estimates based on a ratio of PCs to employees are consistently incorrect, even when a ratio of 1:1 is used. In two recent studies of comparatively small organisations, the number of PCs outnumbered the staff by 20%. One case uncovered over 480 PCs for 380 staff.

A second major reason is to appreciate and manage issues such as licence transfers to the service provider. Software vendors have shown a remarkably opportunistic streak in seeking "transfer" fees from host companies that shift their IT to a third party. The transfer fees quoted in some instances amounted to hundreds of thousands of dollars for database management systems and the like. If this issue is not dealt with in advance, then the surcharge may be unavoidable. Few companies are going to undo a multimillion dollar outsourcing contract because a software vendor has slapped a two hundred thousand dollar invoice on the table. Paying up—after some bitter argument—is often the only choice left.

A third reason is to estimate the host company's contract management requirement. The effort required to manage an outsourcing contract is, in some way, proportionate to the scale of the deal. A surge in the outsourcing service provider's scope and scale required to handle previously "hidden" IT may well be met with some corresponding growth in the host company's service management team.

This third issue is likely to be most troublesome when discovery is made of several previously undocumented IT projects or units within a business. These groups may masquerade on payroll as "business analysts" or "maintenance engineers", or in one company as "warehousing specialists" (they were building a logistics management system). These IT units often work outside the disciplines and process that is expected to surround corporate IT. Incorporating them into an outsourcing contract is likely to bring a number of tensions over cost and management processes. These are better dealt with before the contract is entered into.

The fourth reason is to prepare for the due diligence process. In the period between the selection of the service provider and signing the contract, the service provider should carry out a due diligence on the human, physical and software assets and environment they are committing to support. Ideally, this task should be carried out in a cooperative fashion by both the host company's outsourcing contract team and the service provider's outsourcing contract team working in harness.

In short, the host company must catalogue all in-house services and determine how well they are delivered at present. Otherwise it does not know what it is asking the service provider to steward.

Approach

If the process is to be effective, then at least five specialist skills must be assigned to the team, along with other IT and business skills as required. The specialist skills are:

- Project management for planning and oversight of the task.
- Audit skills and experience in identification and tracking of business assets and information.
- Records management to create the repository and index for the discovered material.
- IT infrastructure sizing skills so that the current infrastructure and its limitations are documented properly.
- Performance measurement skills, preferably provided by a consultant to make an independent assessment of the current measures of performance.
- Financial analysis skills to ensure that the business case and costing models are properly framed and robust.

If the company elects to appoint individuals to carry out these tasks, then the role descriptions should clearly define the accountabilities and responsibilities. None of the roles are trivial. Below are some of the major accountabilities and responsibilities of each of the roles.

Project manager

- Define the scope of the discovery process.
- Prepare the schedule of work required to carry out the process.
- Organise resources to execute the process.
- Manage the process.

The project manager may require support to organise travel, security access, procurement and recruitment of other members of the team.

Auditor

- Identify and record the location and condition of all assets.
- Resolve issues with missing licences and assets.

Auditors may require application software to support their role. Again, the role is not trite and may well require additional support staff if asset management has not been disciplined in the past. The effort required identifying and documenting many hundreds of desktop software licences and identifying, tagging, valuing and registering thousands of PCs and peripherals may be very large.

Auditors may also have to deal with issues of valuation and licence negotiation with third parties. These issues are important as the condition and valuation of assets is a source of potential irritation and dispute as the programme of outsourcing moves forward. Auditors may well identify other issues in the discovery process and their professional training will be useful in a number of areas.

Records manager

The records manager will, in discovery, take the first step in forming the new IT library. All businesses embarking on outsourcing should establish a proper library covering:

- staffing records (some of which may be confidential)
- licences
- maintenance agreements
- purchase orders
- service agreements
- contracts and variations
- project statements
- project reports
- budgets
- plans
- design documentation
- user documentation
- correspondence to and from the service provider
- meeting agendas and minutes
- assets and inventory

Ideally, a qualified librarian should be used to set up the library and index methods and assist in establishing archiving and destruction rules. This library is a critical risk management factor in disputes and disengagement processes. A software package can improve the process of managing and recording records.

The outsourcing contract should assign ongoing accountability and responsibility to the service provider for maintaining the library on an ongoing basis and for the quality and completeness of content.

Infrastructure expert

The infrastructure expert is required to investigate the state of the current infrastructure. He or she is responsible for:

- defining the level of maturity for key components, ranging from state-of-the-art to obsolescence;
- documenting the limitations of the current infrastructure, e.g. disk space constraints, bandwidth utilisation, CPU usage;
- making a prognosis of the effects on planned projects of all types on the current infrastructure.

The infrastructure expert will have to work closely with the performance measurement expert to ensure that current measures are understood within the context of any current infrastructure limitations, and that future performance goals include an appreciation of changes that may be required to the infrastructure.

The infrastructure assessment appears to be a common blind spot in discovery. Many companies appear to delude themselves that they have state-of-the-art technology. Sadly, this is not true. However, years of promoting this myth to potential customers and staff has often led to this almost religious belief. Unhappily, the outsource service provider will not subscribe to the myth, and the company may find itself under tremendous pressure to upgrade obsolescent plant at short notice as the service provider rolls out the deliverables.

Performance measurement consultant

The last specialist in the team is the performance measurement consultant, who is responsible for establishing current service benchmarks and resource consumption. Performance measurement is visited twice in this book. Within the scope of the discovery process, the aim is to establish the current level of performance, against those measures you intend to use to measure service provider achievement. Tasks include:

- identifying all things that are to be measured;
- establishing the current measures;
- documenting the environment in which those measures are achieved;
- noting any infrastructure or other impediments to measure improvement;

- comparing the measures against best practice where possible.

It is important to make every effort to establish current levels of performance at this stage. In most cases, the contract will require the service provider to deliver improvements. The incoming service provider is likely to demand to know the current state of play before committing to delivering a better level of performance. Leaving this process until due diligence can put the host company on the defensive, as they will have entered the RFP process without adequate understanding of the current state.

If possible, appoint an independent third party, as it is unlikely that in-house staff have adequate access to:

- templates and tools for measurement
- benchmarks from peer organisations
- expertise of the type held by the likes of Gartner Measurement.

An argument can be made for bypassing the process of assessing current benchmarks, on the grounds that the only thing of interest is the delivery of the future and contracted levels of performance. This approach has merit, particularly so if the service provider is not obliged to inherit a legacy of poor process, documentation, suboptimal skills and poor management structure. However, if the host company does not have a long history of performance measurement, then some hard work is in order to establish those current benchmarks.

However the task is done, it is critical to decide *what* is to be measured and *why*. Do not make the mistake of selecting an arbitrary set of yardsticks against which to measure performance. Companies often pick very technical parameters for measuring the success of their outsourcing venture. Frequently, these criteria are of such a low level that the impact of failure on the business is insignificant. Further, they in themselves are so swamped by other associated criteria that excuses abound when performance standards are not met.

The key to selecting appropriate measures is to challenge them until there is no doubt they are valuable and acceptable to the business. The suggested method is exhaustive questioning:

- Why is this measure important?
- What does it tell us?
- What can affect it?
- Can the service provider control this performance measure?
- How can the service provider control it?
- Who else or what else can control it?
- What will happen if the service provider exceeds the measure?
- Will anyone care?
- What will happen if the service provider fails the measure?
- Will anyone care?

Ideally, pick a few (5 ± 2) key business outputs that will indicate if the service provider is moving towards delivering the objectives of outsourcing. According to Vince Graham of the National Rail Corporation, "Success does not come from managing inputs, it lies in delivering outputs, in our case cost reductions, service quality, and safety performance."

These key business outputs must be tested for acceptance by the business. It would be appropriate to insist that the future "output" measures be defined and agreed in a workshop attended by the key executives of the business.

A common failure is to have IT decide the performance measures without business input. Karpathiou and Tanner observed, "End user involvement in IT outsourcing decision making is only about 15%, although the study does indicate that the involvement of end users does have a positive effect on the achievement of desirable outcomes."[35] The term "senior executives" could be readily substituted for end user.

There appears to be little point in measuring response times, packet collisions or function points delivered per programmer day unless these are in some way germane to the delivery of the business objectives. Generally speaking, the best measures are business outputs, which may be successful and timely process runs on which the business is highly dependent. If they are working well, then it may stand to reason that the infrastructure, operations and response times must be sound.

All indications are that this task of establishing the current measures of performance is lengthy, tedious and prone to significant error. It also frequently overlooks the constraints on improved performance, so contracts are reached that require improvements that cannot be achieved without the removal of unforeseen constraints, in particular hardware-bound constraints.

One sound approach is to employ a consulting group to undertake the performance measurement task, such as GartnerGroup, who have much experience in benchmarking and measurement. This is what Howard Morris of CBA did: "CBA assigned a dedicated project manager to oversee the due diligence. Gartner Consulting provided financial and resource consumption templates. Gartner Measurement provided benchmarking studies to compare CBA against representative peer groups."

The task is complex and an inexperienced company may find it cheaper and faster to use an appropriately skilled consulting group to undertake this task.

Financial analysis

Modelling the costs and money benefits of outsourcing is often a complex process. It calls for expert financial skills to accurately forecast and describe the effect on the business. Issues will arise over the treatment of assets in the business case and transfer agreements. Are they to be recognised at book value or market value? What are the taxation implications of outsourcing? How will net present value be calculated? Does the business require a discounted cash flow table? What rates will be used to account for inflation or return on investments? Can leveraging new financing models lower costs?

Indeed, it is prudent to involve corporate taxation planning specialists, external auditors and the whole range of financial expertise in undertaking analysis of the financial model for outsourcing.

Discovery issues

The process of discovery may surface a number of issues that need to be dealt with. Amongst these are:

- The scale and required effort are seriously underestimated. This is a common issue and has been reported by a number of practitioners.
- Licence and maintenance agreements may need to be renegotiated with suppliers to ensure that the transfer of management responsibilities or asset ownership to a third-party service provider is not obstructed or costly.
- Corporate assets may need to be revalued, either up or down, depending on number and condition of undiscovered assets.
- The need to address the transfer value of assets whose book value may be well above market value and so distort the business case.
- Surplus assets may need to be disposed of. They may be large in number. (Just where did all those old PCs and printers go?)
- The company may discover a lot of unlicensed software that needs to be "legitimised". This may incur considerable expense.
- Some assets may be difficult to identify properly. This is often true of software, where the original supplier cannot be traced.
- The process may generate large second-order tasks, such as updating or rationalising subsidiary registers, e.g. help desk asset records.
- The company may also discover that the cost and effort of establishing current performance measures is beyond its reach.

Needless to say, the legal counsel and financial units of the business may find themselves involved in sorting out the issues that arise from the discovery process.

The task of discovery is tedious, lengthy and frequently disheartening. It must be done. If not, personal and financial embarrassment will follow as surely as night follows day. If the host company does not discover the state of its IT before it outsources, it surely will afterwards: the service provider will see to that.

Before dealing with preselection, there is one further structure that companies should have in place before they move further down the outsourcing path: the management framework. In the next chapter, companies are urged to develop principles that define in advance the template for information management in the new regime.

Checklist

1. Current environment:
    1.1. locations
    1.2. location budgets
    1.3. location business IT plans
    1.4. hardware assets:
        1.4.1. mainframe computers
        1.4.2. mid-range, such as UNIX, OS/400 and other
        1.4.3. Intel servers
        1.4.4. PCs
        1.4.5. LAN hardware (e.g. routers, switches, hubs)
        1.4.6. LAN cabling
        1.4.7. other telecommunications (e.g. modems, multiplexers)
        1.4.8. printers
        1.4.9. scanners
    1.5. software assets:
        1.5.1. operating systems
            1.5.1.1. mainframe
            1.5.1.2. mid-range
            1.5.1.3. Intel server
            1.5.1.4. desktop
            1.5.1.5. laptops
        1.5.2. applications:
            1.5.2.1. mainframe
            1.5.2.2. mid-range
            1.5.2.3. Intel servers
            1.5.2.4. PCs
            1.5.2.5. laptops
        1.5.3. utility assets:
            1.5.3.1. mainframe

          1.5.3.2. mid-range
          1.5.3.3. Intel servers
          1.5.3.4. PCs
          1.5.3.5. laptops
      1.5.4. tools
      1.5.5. systems design
      1.5.6. systems development
      1.5.7. change management
      1.5.8. systems management
   1.6. telecommunications:
      1.6.1. equipment (e.g. modems)
      1.6.2. lines (e.g. data/phone, cable, X.25)
2. Library/reference materials:
   2.1. user manuals
   2.2. technical manuals
   2.3. vendor correspondence
3. Furnishings, fittings and office equipment:
   3.1. computer room (environment)
   3.2. workstations
   3.3. desks
   3.4. telephones
   3.5. mobile phones
   3.6. fax machines
   3.7. photocopiers
   3.8. shredders
4. Management processes:
   4.1. budget preparation
   4.2. planning preparation
   4.3. existing strategic, tactical and operational plans
5. Moribund assets:
   5.1 hardware
   5.2. software
   5.3. utilities
   5.4. tools
   5.5. non-IT assets
6. Human resources:
   6.1. HR files complete and up to date (including contracts and confidentiality agreements)
   6.2. skills register, which may be separate from the HR files
   6.3. benefits (pensions, bonuses, discounts, stock options)
   6.4. turnover rates
   6.5. training commitments
   6.6. equipment provision (phones, office equipment)
   6.7. subcontractors

7. Existing service contracts:
    7.1. operations management
    7.2. application maintenance
    7.3. systems development projects
    7.4. procurement
    7.5. inventory management
    7.6. strategy and architecture
    7.7. security management
    7.8. disaster recovery
8. Current performance records:
    8.1. back-up/recovery
    8.2. database management
    8.3. upgrade management
    8.4. fault reporting
    8.5. problem resolution
    8.6. software distribution
    8.7. transaction monitoring
    8.8. customer satisfaction
9. New performance measures:[b]
    9.1 key outputs
    9.2 agreed baseline
    9.3 target improvements
    9.4 measurement:
        9.4.1 milestones
        9.4.2 benchmarks
        9.4.3 adjustments
10. Intellectual property agreements:
    10.1 contracted development
    10.2 purchased software and tools
    10.3 vendor supplied manuals
11. Payments status:
    11.1 outstanding
    11.2 disputes
    11.3 payment cycles
    11.4 purchase commitments:
        11.4.1. hardware
        11.4.2. software
        11.4.3. contractor staff
        11.4.4. services
12. Audits:
    12.1. audit letters

[a] The details can be documented in schedules that attach to the contract. This method can also be used for inventory, human resource, environment and other key details.

12.2. current compliance status
13. Confidentiality agreements:
    13.1. staff
    13.2. contractors
14. Insurances:
    14.1. hardware
    14.2. disaster recovery
    14.3. public liability

This list is not complete. It should, however, serve to illustrate the scope of discovery and hopefully stimulate the organisation into considering the scale of the task in gathering, recording and indexing the discovery materials.

5 Setting management principles

Principles are broad guidelines issued by the host company to the service provider for the proper governance of outsourced IT. They are set at a high level, and I am indebted to Paul Strassman for his observation that "the simplicity of the US Constitution has much to offer as a template for information policy guidance. It represents a point of view that addresses the governance of complexity by concentrating only on the fundamentals while leaving everything else for resolution by means of due process wherever that is deemed appropriate."[36]

Principles are a very important part of the outsourcing agreement. They give the service provider a broad framework in which to manage the delivery of services. They set out in advance how the business expects key aspects of the programme to operate.

Outsourcing redistributes responsibility and accountability, and "when you redistribute responsibility and control to others, you must also reallocate accountability and expertise for taking action."[37]

I have chosen to use the word "principles" rather than "policies". The two words carry quite different connotations: a principle is defined in the Oxford English Dictionary as "a general law as a guide to action", and comes from the old English word for foundations. Principles define the foundations of acceptable behaviour in the agreement. Policy is a word more often associated with contract, as in "insurance policy", and is associated with the French word *police*, which carries with it rigidity and exactness that we do not seek to achieve with principles. Put simply, principles provide a guide to action and incorporate the concept of flexibility and adaptation to circumstances. Policy suggests detailed and precise instructions from which deviation is not permitted, and indeed non-adherence will result in punishment. A failure to define principles leaves the host company open to "the opportunistic acts of a transient administration".[38]

Yet companies frequently either hand over their staff and assets to strangers without any policy guidelines for the ongoing management of the service, or are equally negligent in issuing old policy manuals originally developed for use within the business, without regard to their appropriateness for the outsourced environment. This is not uncommon among larger bureaucratic entities, including public service units. Inappropriate policies are probably worse than no policies at all. In the absence of policy, there is a reasonable probability that someone will ask what the appropriate standard is for acting on a requirement.

You cannot outsource effectively without issuing the service provider with the rules of the game. You must develop principles that define *in advance* the template for information management in the new regime.

Principles are usually defined in short statements, as shown in the two examples below:

> All systems development projects, regardless of scale, will be developed consistent with the outsourcer's proprietary methodology.

> Xylog has an agreed IT blueprint. All systems development must be consistent with the blueprint.

Principles should be the outcome of clear and rational thinking, and for this reason each principle should be developed within a standard framework or template. Principles should be defined and agreed by the same group of senior executives that developed the outsourcing goals. According to Strassman, "the most senior executives, as a group, should conceive of and preferably author the fundamental statements of information policy themselves."[39] Strassman goes further to advise against using consultants for this important task, as they will be seen as a proxy for the hirer. However, do use consultants to *facilitate* the process—they bring with them no baggage of the past. Do not delegate this task to lower-echelon staff because they lack authority and are more likely to create obstacles that hinder progress.

The host company might also wish to consider this as an opportunity to introduce the concept of principles on a broader scale within the company as well. They can be developed and applied for any area of the company, for example:

- marketing
- distribution
- short-term projects, where they can be used to nail down in advance how key issues will be addressed.

Scope

Principles should be developed to cover at least the following five areas:

- *Organisation*—laying out the general rules on organisation, accountabilities, employment, human resources, and adherence to host company house rules where appropriate.
- *technology assets*—procurement, vendor relationship management, discounts, commissions and disposal.

- *Software assets*—licensing and licence management, maintenance agreements, renewals and terminations.
- *Service levels*—authority to vary, compliance, dispute resolution and change management.
- *Data*—ownership, management, standards and archiving.
- *Software development*—project accountability, approval processes, issue recording and resolution, change management and intellectual property.

Principles should form part of the outsourcing contract. It is useful to include them as a schedule to the contract. This gives the principles additional weight and authority.

Template

The template consists of several sections, explained in Figure 5.1.

Issue: A statement, usually in the form of a question, of the scope of the issue that the principle seeks to address.

Options: Alternative means of addressing the issue, any of which could be selected as the principle.

Principle: The selected option, which is now a principle.

Rationale: The justification for selecting the particular option as a principle.

Implications: A short list of the potential positive and negative implications of the adopted principle.

Approval: The signature of the authorising body.

Figure 5.1—Elements of a principle template

Figure 5.2 shows a template for a sample principle.

Process

Our preferred approach to developing principles is:

1. Define the areas that principles need to span. These could include management processes, hardware, projects, operations, network, reporting and staffing.

Principle #1

Issue
What methodologies and standards will apply to systems development in the outsourced environment?

Options
1 We will use our existing methods and standards.
2 We will adopt the service provider's methods and standards.
3 We will mix and match to suit each individual situation.

Principle
(2) We will adopt the service provider's methods and standards.

Rationale
The task of training the service provider's staff in our standards will be greater than the task of training our staff in their method. The service provider's methods are an industry standard. Our methods and standards are unique and have previously failed us.

Implications
Our systems development will be to industry standards.
+ Our systems development should be of a higher quality.
+ We limit dependency on in-house expertise and the service provider by adopting an industry standard.
− We will have to purchase licence rights to use the methodology.
− Staff may find the new methods more onerous than the in-house methods.

Approval: (signature)

For the Executive Committee   07 Oct 2000

Figure 5.2—Sample template for a principle

2. Populate the templates:
  2.1. State an issue that will arise with outsourcing, e.g. How will we ensure that the outsourcer does not run our critical applications on substandard hardware?
  2.2. Offer options to control the issue, e.g.
    • Option 1: We will control all hardware purchases.
    • Option 2: We will instruct the outsourcer to only purchase from tier one suppliers.
    • Option 3: We will ignore the quality of the hardware used by the provider so long as the service standard is met.

3. Circulate the templates to the senior executive.
4. Workshop with the senior executives to select the preferred option (see below).
5. Document the rationale behind the decision in one or two sentences.
6. List the 5 ± 2 positive and negative implications attached to the selected option, e.g. if option 1 was selected, then the implications could include setting up and staffing a hardware purchasing unit within the business.
7. Detail the principles in the RFP.
8. Include the principles as a schedule in the outsourcing agreement or contract.
9. Circulate the selected principles for final ratification by all those who attended the workshop and, if appropriate, the chief executive.
10. Circulate the principles to the staff in both the host company and the service provider's organisation.

This last point is critical. The principles are of no use as shelfware, and should be available and known to all that use them. As Strassman explains, "to manage information technology successfully, policy makers must set forth explicit policies for information governance and secure cooperation by engaging everyone in a discussion as to their implications."[40]

If the workshop is to be effective, then the senior executive should both understand the purpose of the meeting and have given the issues and options some consideration before the meeting. It is recommended that:

● A briefing paper be issued with the agenda, including photocopies of the first three pages of this chapter.
● The templates be prepopulated with issues and options. All else should be completed at the workshop.

I subscribe to Strassman's view that "the most senior executives, as a group, should conceive of and preferably author these fundamental statements of information policy themselves."[41]

Benefits

The benefits of principles extend beyond protecting the business from the "opportunistic acts of a transient organisation". If you fail to set out the principles under which the service provider is to deliver the service, then the company gives permission to the provider to adopt any method they choose. For example, cost reductions may be achieved by purchasing low-quality, substandard equipment or staff. Projects may be developed without adequate documentation, systems may be built outside the corporate architecture, and the outsourcer may encourage the growth of "feral" IT in recalcitrant departments.

Principles also:

- ensure that decisions are made within a considered framework;
- ensure that the framework itself is usually internally consistent, which leads to better decisions;
- remove the need to micromanage the service provider on every decision;
- allow the host company to focus on controlling the broad strategy and direction;
- communicate the rules of engagement to all in the service provider's domain;
- communicate the same rules to all in the host company;
- reduce the probability of issues and disputes;
- protect against arbitrary decisions;
- bring cultural differences between the two organisations into the foreground;
- support the proper execution of the contract;
- inform the peripherally involved, e.g. lawyers, auditors and consultants of the management framework;
- provides a framework for future contract variances or increases/decreases in scope.

Developed properly, they will be limited in number yet cover the whole scope of management. Principles are key, if not *the* key to a successful outsourcing agreement. The contract warranties and obligations do not provide a sound basis for making management decisions. Principles do.

Drawbacks

Principles do have their limitations, although many of these can be avoided by appropriate high-level supervision. Drawbacks include:

- Danger of abrogation, substituting principles for oversight and supervision.
- Overdevelopment, so they become a form of constrictive micromanagement.
- Inconsistencies between principles, e.g. between quality-based and cost-based principles.

- Overly liberal interpretation, as they do not define policy in tight, restrictive terms.
- Blind adherence in circumstances where the principle is inappropriate.
- Abrogation by the service provider of their responsibility for supervision of the activities of their staff.
- The service provider may find the principles onerous and seek additional compensation.
- The development of principles may generate as much corporate discord as unity.

The benefits far outweigh the limitations. The drawbacks can be limited by adhering to good practices. The key is to keep them at an appropriate level, as described in the analogy at the beginning of this chapter on the model of the US Constitution as a guide for developing IT policy guidance

Good practice

- Define a principle only when there is a clear issue to be addressed. Do not define principles for which there is no issue, and where the correct path is clear and obvious to all.
- Keep the principles focused on the few fundamental things that need to be defined in advance.
- Limit the principles to a small manageable number, so they can be front of mind. Keep them at a high level.
- Ensure the principles are developed at the highest level in the organisation. Do not delegate the responsibility to a junior staff member, or worse still a consultant.
- Include the principles in detail in the RFP, as they provide critical insight to candidates on how the host company expects them to deliver the service.
- Circulate the principles widely before the contract is entered into. Include staff on both sides of the outsourcing divide.
- Review the principles at least once a year for relevance and currency.
- Develop a framework for changing principles and settling disputes or doubts about the application of a principle.
- Ensure the principles do not conflict with the contract terms. This requires particular care for alterations and amendments made after the contract was signed.

Change control

This should be considered from the outset and can be incorporated into the contract change control framework. The primary considerations in change control for principles are that they are the considered opinion of the senior executive on how the IT service should be managed. It goes without saying that the same people who made the decision to adopt the principle should in turn be asked to approve any alteration or amendment.

The second consideration is that the principle may be linked to warranties and obligations within the body of the contract document. Changes to principles should be vetted by the legal department to ensure they do not inadvertently create waivers or negate other important obligations within the contract.

The third consideration is that the change control process must be undertaken with sufficient rigour to ensure:

- all copies of the obsolete principle are retrieved and destroyed;
- appropriate staff receive copies of the revised principles;
- the reasons (rationale) for modifying the original principle are recorded.

The rationale on the new template must also inform staff *why* the change was made.

Disputes

Disputes will arise. Some people may make well-intentioned decisions to sidestep a principle. Others may find it convenient to ignore a principle to further their own objectives. Staff turnover and ordinary human frailty and forgetfulness will ensure that some, but hopefully few, occasions will arise when the principle gives rise to a dispute.

Every company is different and some have well-established procedures for dispute resolution. It is not possible to offer a single prescription for setting a dispute resolution process. However, the following aspects should be given proper consideration. First, remember the most frequent source of disputes may be within the host company. Those that made the rules are usually those who feel most free to break them. This aspect must be considered within the dispute resolution process. It will normally be an internal dispute rather than an external dispute. The internal politics and lack of an arm's length commercial relationship makes internal disputes more difficult to resolve.

Second, and for the above reason, always favour an honest broker or independent third party to oversee contract adherence and dispute resolution. Dennis Wood of Cathay Pacific Airways said, "We used an independent third party and found it very valuable. It provided a buffer between ourselves and the contractor and removed the emotion from the issue."

Third, both the host company and the service provider should ensure their dispute managers are trained or at least well acquainted with the process of commercial mediation.

Finally, remember the dispute may arise many years after the principle was developed. The managers who set and agreed the principle may well be long gone. This is why it is important to record the rationale for setting the principle in the first instance. As Strassman says, "Any conflict resolution process must have a legitimate forum for interpreting the *original* intent of the approved policies [principles]."[42]

Rationale can prove exceptionally useful at a later time when someone seeks to understand the thinking that lay behind the adoption of the preferred principle. Those that still doubt the value of the rationale should consider the US Constitution's provision to allow the "bearing of arms" and the self-serving arguments that have been advanced for this provision by those supporting and those opposing gun control.

Conclusion

DMR Consulting, a large international IT consultancy business, admonishes its consultants to remember "corporate management are looking for the policies and principles which will ensure IT has a major impact on financial performance. The power of establishing such strategic statements is that they define clear direction without stifling the innovative proposals for IT which typically come from lower in the organisation."

I encourage you to consider this and produce a framework that encourages both sound management and innovation.

Checklist

The template in this book includes three components to help minimise the issue of future interpretation. Listed below are three supports for defining principles:

1. Scope checklist to help you ensure all appropriate issues are covered.
2. Process checklists to ensure those things are done properly.
3. Examples of principles in Appendix F.

Scope checklist

You may wish to check you have developed principles for the following:

1. responsibilities and accountabilities at the executive
2. responsibilities and accountabilities of operating managers
3. responsibilities and accountabilities of planning and finance
4. responsibility and accountability for IT strategy
5. subcontracting by service provider
6. problem resolution
7. help desk management
8. data management
9. geography (centralisation and decentralisation)
10. personnel development
11. systems design and construction
12. technology advancement
13. telecommunications
14. risk management
15. technology acquisition
16. security
17. administration
18. asset management
19. human resources management
20. planning and scheduling
21. network management
22. performance monitoring
23. capacity planning
24. preventive maintenance
25. software upgrades
26. software licensing
27. inventory control
28. media and storage control.

The list is indicative, not comprehensive. Many of the ideas in this chapter come from the work of Strassman: companies intending to outsource could do worse than refer to his work.

Process checklist

1. Have the issues been defined?
2. Are the answers self-evident? If so, this is a self-evident truth and does not need a principle.
3. Has more than one option for dealing with each issue been proposed? If only one option is offered, then this is probably a self-evident truth and does not need a principle.
4. Has a briefing paper been prepared for the executive so they understand the concept of principles?
5. Has the rationale been defined for each adopted principle?
6. Does the rationale still seem sound three days later?
7. Have the implications been considered and documented?
8. Do any of the implications suggest that the rationale is weak or the principle wrong?
9. Have all staff down to the level of supervisor, in the host company and the service provider's organisation, been handed a copy of the principles?
10. Has the legal department reviewed the principles?
11. Have the principles been detailed in the RFP?
12. Are the principles incorporated in the contract?
13. Has a change control process been documented and agreed by the executive?
14. Has the change control process been agreed with the service provider?
15. Have you checked the principles do not conflict with business goals?

Outsourcing of telecommunications saves millions—A global composite insurance player

The situation

The group IT director was concerned about the levels of expenditure on telecommunications and the service that was provided to the organisation. The company, a global composite insurance player, was, at the same time, intent on moving a significant amount of its business to electronic distribution channels.

The problem

The challenge was to develop a global telecommunications strategy to improve service levels, reduce costs and facilitate the introduction of new technologies such as the Internet.

The solution

The insurer appointed a major consulting group whose recommendations included using outsourcing to escape the legacy of networks that needed further significant investment. A further benefit from the solution adopted was that headcount levels could be reduced by around 10%, which together with economies on network charges would lead to significant savings which were estimated to be around £1 million per annum for the organisation.

Focusing implementation for maximum payback

The challenge for the consulting group was to set up and manage the project to realise major savings within a year in the company's largest operation in the UK. Within this operation there was an immediate opportunity to improve the telecommunications network using outsourcing as the cornerstone.

The key stage in the project involved drawing up a requirements specification that allowed the client to invite competitive bids for the solution required. The consultant's role was to project manage a mixed business/consulting team through this process, from the preparation of bid documents, to selection and contracting with the chosen supplier.

Realising the benefits of successful delivery

At the end of this initial project the insurer had hard evidence that the strategy would work well and plans to roll out the strategy in its remaining operations in Europe, the US, South Africa and Asia. The payback for the UK project is predicted within one calendar year, with estimated savings of around £1 million per annum.

Case Study reprinted by kind permission of PA Consulting Group.

6 Preselecting service providers

Preselection is a process whereby the host company gets to know the market of candidate service providers. Domberger and Hall agree that this is a useful process: "It is generally a good idea for contracting organisations to get to know the market—establish the identity of contractors that meet the 'pre-qualification' criteria."[43]

However, no company will attempt to sweep every possible provider into the candidature net. The normal practice is to get to know only those companies that have a good probability of winning the contract. One method used to sift the market for those few companies is to establish prequalification criteria. Preselection criteria are a subset of the essential criteria described in Chapter 4, but they are nearly always based on readily available public information, such as company size, revenues and financial stability.

What differentiates preselection criteria from other essential criteria is that they are usually based on publicly available information. For example, preselection criteria for the New South Wales government's Corporate Service Group's contract to outsource the government's cleaning service included:[44]

- annual turnover greater than $15 million
- more than 500 employees
- capable of funding [payroll] of more than $5 million per zone.

Companies that did not meet these measures were not permitted to tender.

Essential criteria may also consist of yardsticks on which information is not readily available, such as staff skill mix, technical facilities, and project management record, and will only be given out in a response to an RFP.

Preselection is usually done in one of two ways:

- Issuing a request for information (RFI) to the market and evaluating the responses lodged by interested service providers.
- Carrying out covert market research into known candidate service providers.

Both processes may be combined and indeed this is common.

Objectives

The objective of preselection is to inform the host company about the market in order that they may:

- be better informed about market offerings and tailor the RFP to best advantage;
- be better informed about the real capabilities of individual service providers and so make better judgements about the veracity of claims made in the proposal response;
- refine other mandatory criteria to further limit or broaden the number of potential responses to the RFP.

Benefits

Benefits can accrue to both the host company and the service provider.

Host company benefits

Once the RFP is issued, it is difficult, if not impossible, to change it so that it does not accidentally exclude desirable candidates or embrace the undesirable. If the host company does not carry out some preselection research, then:

- the host company may well discover that some of the criteria they have selected for the RFP may exclude otherwise excellent candidates;
- the RFP may encourage responses from unsuitable organisations. The host company may find that tightening up some of the criteria will exclude unsuitable candidates who submit responses that take time and resources to process and analyse;
- the RFP can be modelled to build on known strengths and protect against known weaknesses in the field of candidates. The outsourcing team has an opportunity to study candidate's strengths and weaknesses before they issue the RFP;
- the RFP can be tailored to encourage responses from the right providers. The top tier of service companies are selective about tendering on RFPs. Costs to respond may run into hundreds of thousands of dollars, which represents a financial loss for the unsuccessful bidders. The bidders need to know they have a real chance of winning the contract. If they know the field is limited,

and they therefore can make some judgement about who the competitive bidders will be, then they are more likely to bid.

The outsourcing team is also better informed about the true abilities of the respondents and can better judge the veracity of the candidate's responses during the selection process.

These are significant benefits. Issuing an RFP and analysing the responses can make huge demands on time and cost on the host organisation (and the candidates). A well-tailored RFP can significantly reduce the cost of issuing the RFP and evaluating responses.

Excluding otherwise excellent candidates can happen accidentally. For example, the RFP may stipulate a scale or financial position that may exclude the small local branch of a larger and ideal candidate, or it may ask for a commitment that will not be countenanced by any major provider.

The second issue is one of encouraging responses from a large number of unsuitable organisations. This can occur if the preselection criteria are too broad. This is the more common issue. I have seen bids for multimillion-dollar public projects submitted by companies with very limited asset backing and financial strength.

The third issue of capitalising on strengths and protecting against weaknesses is critical. A well-focused RFP written "knowing the reader" can better inform potential respondents about the host company's requirements.

The fourth concern is to ensure that the appropriate providers respond. As mentioned earlier, the larger and more sophisticated and professional service companies are reluctant to waste time and money on tenders unless they believe there is a reasonable chance of success. From the service provider's viewpoint, RFPs are expensive and tiresome to respond to. It frequently costs tens of thousands of dollars to respond to an RFP.

Typically, a service provider will have to pull a number of their best staff back to base to respond to a large proposal. During that period, the service provider's staff are not earning fees, and this may represent a significant loss of revenue. Even those service providers with staff dedicated to business development, including proposal response, face a choice between gambling on a large proposal or continuing their incremental business development though normal channels.

It can not be emphasised enough that the more sophisticated and better managed companies judge their chances of success *before* they respond to an RFP. If they think the risks are high, then they will not respond. It is in the issuer's interest to get the right companies to respond. Issuing a limited proposal, letting them know they stand a 1:3 or 1:5 chance of success, is more likely to encourage the top-tier service providers to respond—and respond well.

Ann Harding of Budget-Rent-A-Car speaking at a conference mentioned that she had even considered "paying a fee to the final round of bidders to offset the costs of providing a thorough proposal". This radical thought is a good indicator of just how hard it may be to get a good-quality proposal from a major provider when the risk is high.

There can be no more disappointing an experience for the intending outsourcer than to sift through 40 responses from a wide range of hopefuls, only to find that no serious player has responded to the RFP.

The fifth benefit is that the outsourcing team is better informed and better able to judge the veracity of the responses when the RFP is finally issued. Staff whose remuneration is dependent on the outcome prepare responses to RFPs. In the pursuit of victory, truth can be an early casualty. A senior executive of a service provider put it thus:

> The risk component of the negotiating teams remuneration is usually tied to the sales effort, so they are inclined to win the contract at any cost. The sales people don't have to live by the commitments they make on performance or budgets . . . many outsourcers are making commitments knowing they cannot be met, and relying on a combination of miracles and post-contract waivers to get them through.

This is not limited to second-tier providers either—we know of cases where market leaders responded in a similar fashion, and the dollar value of the sales commission may well run to 10% of the value of the proposal! Doing your research in advance can help you pick those miracle commitments.

The sixth benefit is achieved through limiting the field, which will flow through into reduced cost and improved quality in the process:

- Cost is reduced, as the number of proposals to be processed should be much smaller than would follow an unrestricted RFP.
- Quality of process should be improved when you are able to concentrate effort on selecting from those who have the capacity and capability to do the job.

The basic cost of issuing an RFP of any significance is unlikely to cost less than US$100 000. If the costs of discovery, the initial business case and other preliminary activities are factored in, then the cost can jump rapidly towards the half-million-dollar mark depending on the complexity and specificity of the response required. The host company also faces significant cost and effort in evaluating responses. This can be a very expensive and time-consuming business.

Those without experience of the process may be overwhelmed by the effort required to handle enquiries from 40 or 50 candidates and distribute information updates to such a large field. The process of sifting through dozens of responses and dealing with 49 disappointed suppliers is neither fun nor good management. Preselection can reduce the cost and effort for all concerned and lead to significantly better analysis than would be expected with a larger, undifferentiated field.

The final benefit comes from keeping the RFP focused. Real estate agents list three important criteria for selecting an investment property: location, location and location. The RFP, tender and contracts drawn up for outsourcing agreements need three similar important criteria: focus, focus and focus.

The process of preselection should also enable the host company to keep the RFP focused on the selection criteria critical to delivering the business objectives and meeting the CSFs.

Service provider benefits

The service provider can also benefit from the preselection process. Depending on the degree of interaction with the host company, it should achieve some or all of the following benefits:

- Receive an RFP that is written by a well informed team that knows what it wants.
- Establish with some certainty its probability of success, therefore being able to make an informed decision as to whether to bid or not.
- Be better informed of the underlying issues surrounding the decision to outsource.
- Receive pre-advice that allows the service provider time to undertake some market research of its own into the host company's business practices and IT environment (the veracity argument cuts both ways!).
- Limits the time and cost in preparing a response. Costs can escalate if the bid team has to disband and regroup continually while further information is sought.
- Be better informed of the strengths and weaknesses of the host company and so tailor its responses to capitalise on the host company strengths and mitigate the weaknesses.

It would embarrass companies that issue RFPs to hear the discussion that takes place around the bid team table.

RFPs frequently seem to have been issued by people that do not know what they want or what the requirements are for delivering what they want. This should not surprise readers of this book. Chapter 2 provided several references to research that indicated the goals and objectives for outsourcing were either not present or were lost along the way. An RFP issued by a well informed team is cheaper, faster and much more satisfying to respond to—and you have some hope it will also be evaluated properly.

If the host company has carried out a good preselection process, and a service provider is invited to tender, then it should be possible to make some judgement about the probability of success. Certainly you are past the first hurdle and should see the RFP as the second interview.

The third benefit is that the service provider can carry out some market research of its own into the decision to outsource. The underlying reasons for outsourcing may be unpalatable or, for competitive reasons, the host company may not wish to make them public.

Knowing the host company is in the market gives the service provider time to talk to the host company's team and other suppliers to establish background. There should be time for research into past history, and an opportunity to investigate the company's modus operandi with regard to suppliers, and the truth of its commitment to words such as "partnership" and "gain sharing". Wayne Saunders made the observation in an interview that "a lot of service providers talk 'partnership' with no idea what this means. If you quiz them on their interpretation you may find they mean something quite different."

The fifth benefit is that the service provider may be able to limit the time and effort required to prepare the RFP. This foreshortening of time comes about because the bid team is well informed, background information has been read and digested, and the aim of various criteria are better understood and easier dealt with.

The final benefit is that the service provider can inform itself about the strengths and weaknesses of the host company. This investigation into strengths and weaknesses should not be limited to IT issues. It is critical to understand how the company you intend to service stands with regard to its culture, market, financial strength and position on the business maturity scale. These issues will all affect the stability of the proposed outsourcing agreement and its objectives.

For this reason, it is in the interest of all potential candidates to cooperate to the fullest in preselection reviews with the host company. Bitter as it may seem, it is far better to get knocked out of the race in the preselection process than to spend thousands of dollars on a bid that is going nowhere.

If you have to call open tenders

Many organisations, particularly in government or in receipt of public funds, are legally required to call open tenders. But this does not mean that you cannot preselect. Far from it! Preselection can assist by documenting the professionalism, rigour and fairness of your processes. It can pre-empt protests to regulators and politicians, because those eliminated will or should understand why they have been crossed off the list. If they are equally professional, then they will appreciate your input and either go away to get on with the things they are good at, or make the changes required to get back on the list. If there are informal or formal protests, you will be able to respond quickly and devastatingly.

At the end of the day, when you have to place an ad in the newspapers saying "Tenders invited (following earlier request for information)", if a candidate you have previously eliminated chooses to spend time and resources on tendering, that is their decision. They should be aware of their chances.

If you are in the position of having to call open tenders, go through the processes and be absolutely scrupulous about documenting all your communications with candidates, and all your decisions. Keep your processes open—you may need to seek advice from regulators, auditors, ombudsmen etc. If you do all this, preselection will bring just as many advantages as it does to those not bound by tendering requirements.

Process

This section suggests how you might go about creating a short list of desirable respondents.

First, define the preselection criteria, remembering those are the limited, set criteria that define the population of desirable respondents. They are probably the essential criteria described in Chapter 3. They may be simple, quantitative measures related to financial strength, organisational strength or location, e.g.

- annual revenue greater than $100 million
- profitable trading for past three years
- staff numbers greater than 350
- location: Chicago and Los Angeles.

Second, prepare an RFI. The RFI may include other criteria or information that you may find useful in this preselection phase. A possible structure is:

- brief statement on why the RFI is being issued
- brief set of critical information required
- preselection criteria
- other criteria
- process timetable for the outsourcing project.

The host company may find it useful to issue the RFI anonymously through a third party, such as an outsourcing consultant, their auditors or legal advisers. This subterfuge can help protect against the host company, its CEO and board members being besieged by service providers anxious to peddle their wares in advance of the RFP process.

Next, prepare a list of all outsourcing service providers in order to identify those you would prefer to respond to the RFI. Mundane as it may seem, the local business directory is a good place to start. Reviewing the entries in a public directory such as this helps protect against oversights and omissions. Another good source is companies that have already outsourced, and consultants such as the PA Consulting Group.

The fourth step is to sort the list into three categories. This step is based on limited information and precedes detailed information gathering:

- *Rejects:* those companies that we already know fall well outside the preselection criteria. These candidates are immediately discarded.
- *Doubtful:* those companies that may or may not meet all the preselection criteria. More information or research is needed before you can decide whether to include or eliminate them.
- *Candidates:* those companies who, without doubt, are capable of providing the service required.

The final step is to issue the RFI, or alternatively to carry out detailed information gathering without the RFI.

If direct market research is preferred, then as a minimum the research group should obtain annual reports and carry out online company searches. The objective of the RFI and/or desktop search process is twofold:

- To obtain enough information on "Doubtful" to decide whether or not they graduate to the "Candidates" category.
- To obtain enough information on "Candidates" (and those "Doubtful" that graduate) to build your background library and so inform both the development of the RFP and the later review of proposals for consistency with background information.

Regardless of whether the RFI or market research method is selected, it is important that the evaluation and elimination process be done with some formality, and proper notes made as to why certain companies were *not* included. The host company must protect itself against allegations of impropriety and be able to show that the process of selection was fair and open.

Every hour put into precontract discovery, benchmarking, research and preparation will pay back a hundred-fold over the life of the contract. Too often, the "homework" is rushed and incomplete and contracts entered into without adequate preparation.

Once this step of evaluating RFI responses or market research is complete, you may find it useful and necessary to interview the preferred candidates before moving to the RFP stage. It is unlikely that a company could include this interview process unless the field of desirable candidates is small, say less than 10. However, the interview process does have a number of direct benefits, including:

- obtaining deeper knowledge about the candidate's organisation, culture and capabilities;

- seeking opportunities to interview some existing clients and so establish some factual data on delivery capabilities;
- eyeballing premises, people, processes, methods and standards to gauge potential fit;
- establishing each candidate's interest in providing outsourcing services.

The ultimate aim is to use this information to refine your RFP so that it seeks the right information and commitments, and elucidates more information on areas that are of concern. The second aim is to build the library of information on candidates so that the host company can lift the level of judgement on responses and fit to observed reality, and so make a better decision in selecting its ultimate provider(s).

Be cautious about being unduly influenced in this preselection process by cosmetic and cultural issues. The information and observations made during the preselection period should not be allowed to overwhelm or undermine the objective RFP selection process.

Those companies that choose to interview preselection candidates will find a possible agenda at the end of this chapter. If this interview and follow-up approach is selected at the RFI stage, then you may also find it useful to interview the following groups:

- Current customers of the service provider—interview those obtaining an outsourcing service similar to the one you plan to obtain.
- Past customers of the service provider—these may provide a more critical analysis. Remember, however, there usually is another side to the story.
- Peer review—ask those you know in the broader IT community about their opinions of the companies on the short list, especially those who have gone through the RFP process.

Remember that the aim of the preselection process is to limit the issue of the RFP to companies that are, on the surface, competent and capable of delivering your objectives, and to ensure the RFP is taken seriously by those companies you would prefer to deal with. By limiting the issue, you keep the evaluation process controllable in scale and complexity. By informing the right people in the market of your interest in their service, you improve the likelihood they will respond to your RFP.

An argument can be made that the elimination process is what the RFP is about. Although this is true, the post-RFP weeding process tends to suffer from the following faults:

- too great a reliance on what was written by the self-interested candidate;
- the workload and sheer drudgery involved in eliminating unsuitable candidates limits the extent of critical thinking and research;
- the RFP itself is too broadly scoped, which rules out penetrating questions and focused intelligence gathering.

Put simply, one or two weeks of interviews and personal research will pay back a hundred-fold in obtaining critical information and knowledge about the candidates, their strengths and weaknesses.

The careful researcher may also turn up new or critical information about the way various contracts have been structured. For example, pricing information and other material that will not normally be available through the RFP process.

Candidate interviews

Interviews with the candidate service providers should be arranged at the shortest (polite) notice. This goal should be to see the company in its normal work-a-day mode and not to fall victim to a parade ground presentation of their best and most glamorous. However, it is not necessary to barge in unannounced, and that is not what is suggested.

Do give the service provider an agenda listing the topics for discussion. A suitable agenda might include:

- corporate goals
- corporate history
- financial reports for last three years
- organisation structure
- location
- staff composition (technical, programming, management, etc.)
- methodologies
- standards
- hiring practices
- customers—current
- customers—past
- perceived strengths and weaknesses
- three- (or five-) year plan
- progress against last three- or five-year plan
- outsourcing approaches
- preferred pricing models
- preferred baseline approach
- outsourcing customers
- issues with outsourcing (their perspective)
- What if?

The last point is worth exploring. Greaver[45] provided the trigger to this concept. He proposed a number of open-ended questions, including:

- What happens if we double in size through growth or merger during the contract period?
- When problems arise, how do we solve them?
- What functions or processes do *you* outsource, and to whom?
- What happens if you determine our contract is not profitable?

Other questions might include:

- What are your objectives in providing us with an outsourcing service?
- What internal performance standards do you apply to outsourcing agreements?
- What will happen to our contract if you are taken over?
- What arrangements do you typically put in place for client management and measuring satisfaction (as distinct from technical performance)?
- What process have you followed in previous contract terminations—for whatever cause?

Clearly there are many other questions that can be asked. Remember, the aim is only to gather information and validate the service provider's inclusion in the candidate population. Do not fall into the trap of trying to make the selection at this stage. Limit the interview to one or two hours to avoid slipping into too much detail in this preselection process.

The aim of the interview is only to test preconceptions that the service provider has the capacity and capability to deliver the outsourcing goals. This is *not* the selection process. It is also to test whether the approach favoured by the host company is likely to receive sufficient bids from the market, and to gather ideas for improvement.

Ask to see, and observe everything. Ask for an office tour. Is the organisation and condition of the office consistent with good management practices? Ask to see the service provider's methodology documentation. Check its age and version control. Ask a question to test staff familiarity with their own material. (And don't be surprised if the answer reveals that it is shelfware, rarely read or acted upon!) Talk to the staff and gauge morale—one recommendation given to me was to go to the toilet and read the graffiti!

Examine staff profiles and CVs to get a measure of their recruitment standards in terms of qualifications, skills and salaries. If possible, ask for the employment history list and check the average employment time and the range. Ask the service provider to arrange interviews with their major customers *without* them present. Ask them for the names of five former customers so you can find out why they are "former".

Customer interviews

If time and opportunity present themselves, interview some of the preselection candidates' customers. This will be impractical unless the preselection candidate list is very small, e.g. if the list is 10 or more, and the host company interviews three customers, then it will be necessary to interview 30 organisations.

If there is an opportunity to sound out preselection candidates' customers, then the interviews could cover some of the following topics:

- outsourcing drivers
- service provider selection—method
- contract structure
- types of pricing models in use, e.g. fixed price, cost plus (open book), transaction-based, combinations of any of these
- reward and punishment mechanisms
- quality control processes in use for ensuring staff quality and ensuring software development quality
- systems operations management
- budget and cost control processes
- contract termination clauses
- planned disengagement processes
- Transition quality

These contract-specific questions can be followed by some open-ended questions that can often be revealing, for example:

- What would you do differently if given the time again?
- What are the dangers you think we should avoid?
- What tips can you give us for getting the best out of our agreement?
- Would you outsource again?
- Do you intend to renew the contract, and why/why not?

Summary

Preselection can help focus the RFP selection criteria back to a selection amongst equals. It can help eliminate a lot of otherwise redundant criteria that exist only to weed out no-hoper bids entered by organisations that are long on bravado but short on substance.

One of the objectives of this book is to encourage the development of specific criteria that derive from goals and objectives. The RFP should reflect those specific criteria and encourage an open and specific response to them by the service provider.

The RFP has the potential to be more focused when it is written with the known competencies, strengths and weaknesses of candidate target service providers in mind, using the technique taught at school of "writing the letter with the recipient in mind". With a limited field of potential candidates, it should be possible to develop a highly specific RFP targeted at extracting knowledge critical to your decision process.

The risk faced with more general RFPs, issued to the world at large, written without the benefit of knowing the market, is that the selection criteria may prove to be little more than a list of noble business virtues that have limited connection to the task at hand.

The potential service providers will also welcome receiving an RFP that has been written by a well-informed team that seems to know clearly what it wants. Service providers will also be more inclined to respond to RFPs when they know they are in a small field.

It is a mistake to think everyone wants your business. Those that want it most may well be those you least want or need. You must encourage the "right" companies to respond—and they may not respond unless they believe there is a reasonable possibility they may get the proposal, or part of it.

Checklist

1. Can the preselection criteria be measured against public information?
2. If not, then will you issue an RFI?
3. Have you identified your list of potential suppliers?
4. Have you culled the list as suggested?
5. Have you prepared a list of interview questions for candidates?
6. Have you prepared a list of interview questions for the providers' customers?
7. Have you researched public databases (e.g. Internet) on candidates?
8. Have you checked magazines and periodicals for stories on candidates?
9. Do the criteria defined in Chapter 5 need revision in light of the research?
10. Do the candidates know the size of the field?

7 Preparing the request for proposals

This chapter covers a number of aspects of RFP preparation, including:

- approach
- ownership
- guidelines
- structure
- criteria
- pricing models

We will also cover some common faults in RFP drafting.

Approach

The first philosophical belief is that the RFP should provide the bridge between business objectives and the outsourcing contract. This is illustrated in Figure 3.5 in Chapter 3. The failure of the RFP to meet this bridging role may be the root cause of failure for many outsourcing contracts. John McNally reiterates this: "Align the contract with the RFP. The RFP should fit snugly into the contract."

However, Domberger and Hall state: "Experience and the case studies in this book show that formal specifications often do not exist prior to contracting."[46] This is astounding. It seems almost impossible to imagine that businesses would enter into a contract without first defining the objectives or requirements.

The work to date in this handbook has been directed towards defining the specifications that need to be stated in the RFP, committed to in the bid and locked in through the contract. The RFP must be preceded by the definition of objectives, critical success factors (CSFs), and criteria that specify the aim of the outsourcing contract and the factors and criteria that are required to achieve those outcomes. Without these, the RFP may turn out to be little more than a wish list of attributes for a perfect IT department.

The failure of many companies to follow this basic logical path may be explained by the observation that a substantial number of outsourcing contracts are entered into in a knee-jerk reaction to a real or perceived black-hole project in IT. If the outsourcing project is based on a intuitive belief or a reaction to a recent IT issue, then it is probable that the RFP will be based on unsuitable, short-sighted criteria that will later lead to frustration.

It is critical that the RFP is derived from the decomposition from goals, through objectives and CSFs to criteria.

Ownership

It is also important that those charged with defining objectives and selecting the provider take ownership and accountability for the development of the RFP. This is not always the case. In some companies, RFPs and tender documents are developed and issued through a contracts department following a standard template. This template may be suitable for the selection of capital equipment or raw materials, but it is more often than not poorly suited to the less tangible aspects of providing a technical or management service. Contract departments often have limited experience in issuing RFPs where the intellectual content is high and the measures of performance are less tangible than in goods and materials procurement.

One good approach is to use a consultant who has done this before, and has a sound approach to the task. PA Consulting Group has managed the outsourcing process on behalf of host companies, and they have developed a model of best practice for the development and implementation of strategic outsourcing. PA named their process "SMART sourcing" since (they say) it signifies the nature of the result you are trying to achieve (for an outline of the SMART model, see Appendix G).

It is comparatively easy to let an outsourcing contract for fleet maintenance, office cleaning or print management. The criteria are often clear and objective. The areas covered are often far from mission-critical, and poor service represents at worst a serious inconvenience rather than major business damage. In comparison, IT outsourcing contracts often encompass a wide variety of services ranging from help desk to strategic planning. Deliverables are often goal-based, and it can be difficult to measure performance. The structures, models and concepts are often foreign to contracts departments.

That is not to say that the contracts department should be ignored. The team charged with the selection should take direct control of the content and process, and not abrogate their responsibility. Use the contract department's skills and resources, but leave the direction and final control in the hands of the selection team.

The other key organisational unit involved in RFP issue and contracts is the legal department. This plays a number of important roles:

- ensuring the RFP is worded so that it can support your intended contract. Too often RFPs are issued that call for the respondents to adhere to criteria or commitments that cannot be incorporated or supported in the later contract, or worse are in contravention of business law;
- ensuring the subsequent contract is unambiguous and reflects correctly the needs of the business and the capabilities of the service provider. It is important to involve the legal department early on in the development of the RFP so that when the time comes for contract formulation, they are well versed on the business needs;
- ensuring that the host company takes cognisance of case law and the litigation experience of companies who have entered into similar forms of agreement, or issued similar RFPs;
- supporting the negotiation process. Most solicitors today have extensive training in conducting negotiations. They can be very useful advisers during the bargaining process.

Do not abrogate responsibility to either the contracts or legal unit. Use them instead to provide expert advice in forming the RFP that you intend to send out. To reiterate:

- Use the strengths of the contract department, if you have one, for advice and guidance, but do not abrogate responsibility for the structure and content of the RFP.
- Use the lawyers to ensure the RFP is sound, consistent and provides a substantial path to the later contract.

If the host company does not have a contracts or legal department, then:

- inform yourself on contract case histories and issues. There are a number of books available on the formation of contracts, and the issues that surround them. Many of these issues stem from poor RFP specification, which in turn leads to poor selection and weak or misdirected contracts;
- appoint a firm of lawyers with previous experience in the outsourcing field, particularly IT. In any large city, there should be a number of lawyers who have drawn up IT outsourcing contracts. Find out who they are: talk to companies that have used them, and bring them into the process before the RFP is issued.

The model that should be emerging now is one where business goals have a strong thread through the objectives to the criteria, the principles and the RFP. The RFP will in turn link through to the contract, service level agreements and contract management process.

Guidelines

Below are 15 good rules for developing an RFP:

1. Don't lose sight of the purpose of the RFP. It exists to extract information on the capacity and capability of candidates to deliver your business needs. It does not commit the candidates to anything that comes later. That is the purpose of the contract. Remember that the RFP is the bridge between the business objectives and the contract.
2. Make it readable. The RFP should have a coherent structure and be easy to read and refer to, both for your own sake and the candidates'.
3. Group the commercial, technical and organisational criteria to facilitate evaluation and ensure that each aspect is given proper consideration.
4. Make it easy to answer. Use simple self-scoring systems that can be processed easily by the candidate and the host company. Where possible, supply candidates with electronic score sheets that they can return.
5. Define words such as "essential criteria".
6. Explain and give examples of acceptable bid responses.
7. Allow explanations on answers. The RFP is there to extract information, not to repress it with a binary yes–no limit.
8. Make it easy to process the responses. Providing electronic score sheets that are returned can remove much of the drudgery and dramatically shorten the time and effort required to establish the winning candidate.
9. Avoid criteria that are no more than noble virtues and to which you will always get a "fully compliant" or 10/10 score.
10. Focus, focus, focus on what you are trying to achieve with the RFP.
11. Take ownership of the RFP and do not abrogate responsibility for its content or style.
12. Use lawyers to ensure consistency, legality and correctness.
13. Incorporate the principles that will control the execution of the future contract.
14. Validate the proposed financial model using an independent expert.
15. Finally—despite the advice in point 7—do not fall into the trap of treating the evaluation as a mechanistic exercise where the correct selection can be based solely on a quantitative evaluation.

The point on financial analysis is also critical. For an example of how badly accountants can get numbers wrong, refer to Domberger and Hall's case study of the Sutherland (Australia) Council's miscalculations on nett present value.[47] Contract savings varied from AUD0.2m and AUD6.9m, and nett present value costs from AUD17.5m to AUD22.7m, depending on who did the calculation.

CBA were more cautious and "as a final quality assurance . . . assigned a CBA employee who was not on the RFP team to research all numerical values in the

RFP and receive sign-off on their accuracy and margin of error from the providers of the source data." (Howard Morris, Commonwealth Bank).

Do not forget to include recurrent costs in the RFP financial model and to set out your expectations for those costs, their growth and control.

The proposed principles that will govern the operation of the outsourced IT unit should form an essential section of the RFP. The RFP should specify more than mere criteria: it should indicate clearly why those criteria are important (they allow the host company to meet its goals) and the framework (principles) under which the successful proposer must operate. Most service providers will probably greet the inclusion of principles with welcome relief as it gives them a sound basis within which to frame their response.

Structure

The typical RFP suffers from an excessive emphasis on:

- a glorious and noble company history, leaving out disagreeable memories;
- RFP timetable and process; it is often overly bureaucratic and seemingly designed to minimise the information that the intending respondent can provide. Appendix H gives some indication of the time that may need to be allotted to each task in the outsourcing process;
- misleading and self-serving explanation on why the RFP is being issued (you will never see an objective for issuing the RFP state "Because we lack the competence, capability and resolution to do this work properly ourselves");
- a large number of quasi-legal clauses that belong in the final contract and serve only to constrain the ability of the candidates to put forward novel or creative solutions.

The typical RFP is also lacking in business goals and outsourcing objectives, or based on criteria that do not link to business goals or are irrelevant to the exercise. There is often no reference to the principles that guide the day-to-day execution of the RFP, and so only inform the service provider of what is to be done, ignoring the how.

The structure should include at least the following:

- relevant background on the host company
- brief explanation as to why the company is outsourcing
- company goals
- company strategic plan (relevant extracts)
- relevant objectives

- required outcomes
- selection criteria tables
- response definitions and guidelines
- principles that will apply
- pricing models that will be considered
- existing budgets
- existing IT strategy or tactical plans
- existing human resource/skills inventory
- existing assets and condition
- contractual requirements
- duration
- intellectual property
- warranties
- performance management
- relationship management
- baseline measures or approach to measuring
- target measures and timing
- reporting and correction
- rewards and punishments
- RFP process management
- timetables
- contacts
- rules of conduct.

This is not a complete checklist of all the facets of the RFP. Please refer to Appendix C for a more complete reference to what you may need to cover in the RFP. As a general rule, the RFP should provide as much information as possible that will enable the bidder to submit the highest quality proposal.

Company goals

These should be stated in the RFP. They provide intending respondents with the framework within which the outsourcing agreement will be expected to operate and deliver benefits.

Objectives

These are a critical component of the RFP. They are indeed the reason why the RFP is being issued and an outsource service provider is being sought. Here the message should be loud and clear—the aim of the project is to deliver business outcomes. It is probably useful to also indicate the importance that the assessing group will place on flexibility, performance and quality, rather than lowest cost, in selecting the provider.

I turn to PA Consulting Group for reiteration: "To enable outsourcing to deliver the benefits that are used to justify it, each of the project documents, from the statement of requirements to the service reports, needs to be derived from the business case."

This applies to the service provider as well as the host company. The service provider should have developed a business case that is based on a realistic appraisal of the costs and revenues that will come from winning the contract.

Sadly, many service providers rely on a distant pot of gold at the base of an ephemeral rainbow. The business benefits are often quickly lost from sight as the emphasis switches to functions and procedures and how they will be delivered and managed. The expected outcomes must be stated clearly. Never lose sight of the big picture.

Criteria

The typical RFP often differentiates poorly amongst criteria, making it difficult for the respondent, or any other reader for that matter, to distinguish between the relative importance of the selection criteria.

The traditional RFP implies differentiation through the use of word cues, such as "must comply", which is meant to define a mandatory criterion, and "should comply", which is meant to define a highly desirable criterion. While this method differentiates, it gives little useful information about the relative importance within a set. All "musts" are not equal. Avoid this weakness by defining the importance levels of criteria (see Table 3.1 in Chapter 3).

Some may question weighing requirements and argue that the definition is sufficient. However, in practice not all "mandatory" are equally important and further distinction is often required. Our language does not offer such precise definitions. We soon run out of words to distinguish across a scale greater than three.

It is important that the candidate knows the relative importance of the criteria so they can provide an appropriate level of detail in response. It is also important to be able to distinguish at a fine level in selecting between closely matched candidates. For this reason, it is important to ensure that the responses given by bidders allow them to give their level of fit to the criteria.

Responses

The standard RFP limits bid responses to words such as "complies" or "does not comply". These answers often tell us very little. It is not clear whether the bidder failed to meet the criteria completely or by a tiny margin. These one- or two-word responses fail to tell us the degree of compliance or noncompliance. Give the bidders the opportunity to score their fit (response) on a scale from zero (totally noncompliant) to five (totally compliant). The scale must be defined clearly so that the scores given are reasonably accurate and consistent. A clear definition should curtail subjectivity in bid responses (see Figure 3.7 in Chapter 3).

It may be necessary to provide three or four such examples. The objective is to ensure that responses are given using a numerical model that is easily understood and processed. Numerical responses for subjective or less easily measured criteria are more problematic. However, they can be defined and specified, and they still provide a much better degree of accuracy in response than the simple "comply" or "not comply" method. For example, see Table 7.1.

This method will encourage accuracy in bid responses, because respondents have an opportunity to bid based on a level of fit rather than an absolute true-or-false response. Accuracy will be enhanced further if respondents are allowed to include a short note to clarify their answers. This is the purpose of the Notes cross-reference column in the scoring sheets.

Table 7.1—Numerical responses for difficult-to-measure criteria

Example criteria	Example measure of fit	Example of appropriate score
Sound systems development methodology	Covers: 1. IT planning 2. Requirements analysis 3. System design 4. System construction 5. System testing 6. System implementation 7. Benefits realisation	5 (fully compliant)
	Covers 4 of above Covers 3 of above Covers 2 of above Covers 1 of above Covers none of above	4 (>75% compliant) 3 (>50% compliant) 2 (>25% compliant) 1 (<25% compliant) 0 (Noncompliant)

Testing

The host company should carry out a simple bench test of the RFP before circulating it. This can avoid market place embarrassment. Simply prepare a mock bid and bench test it through the RFP evaluation models. This process may be familiar to IT people who should be experienced in preparing test packs and testing software. It will be embarrassing and painful to recall the RFP and re-issue it if you discover later that the document or the electronic response sheets give incorrect results. Do remember, however, that this only tests the mechanistic side of the RFP evaluation process.

This may also be a good time to consider what methods will be used to test the less tangible aspects of the evaluation.

Pricing models

Pricing gets both too much and too little attention in outsourcing contracts. There is often too great a concentration on nailing down a tough deal on present-day pricing, and too little emphasis on:

- modelling alternative pricing models and their impact;
- longer-term impact analysis of the adopted pricing model;
- the implications of the adopted pricing model.

Pricing models are often driven from a current context perspective. If the business is about to embark on a major systems development project, then the pricing model adopted tends to be skewed towards that need. Alternatively, if the help desk is the issue, desktop total cost of ownership (TCO) models tend to dominate.

Appendix A provides some guidance on the important task of future proofing the agreement. In essence, each party should define what their business environment is like today, considering competitors, suppliers, technology change and customers. Then develop a similar simple model of the future, and finally review the changes that will occur in the business as the company moves from today to the future.

These models are very useful in selecting your pricing model, as they help to identify what technology change, support and cost type you will encounter over the life of the outsourcing agreement.

For example, the host company may regret skewing an outsourcing pricing model towards managing a global private email system in a world moving to the use of public email systems. The service provider may regret adopting a fixed-price model in an environment where there is widespread evidence that companies are expanding IT growth as a proportion of revenue.

The selected pricing model will bring with it a number of implications, both positive and negative. These implications should be documented and discussed with the financial analysts and legal departments of both parties.

Below we discuss some of the implications that attach to each pricing model. However, these are not universal and each organisation should develop those implications to suit their individual circumstances. PA Consulting Group provided significant advice in this area and the sections on fixed price, cost plus, schedule of rates and hybrid solutions were provided by Andy Zaple of PA.

Fixed price

This model is based on cost recovery plus management fee, and a schedule of rates, either as units of input or units of output. Fixed-price contracts are most suited to situations where the volume and nature of the required outputs, and the price and volume of the inputs, are stable. Such contracts tend to require the service provider to assume the risks of service provision. If the service provider is unable to recover satisfactorily the cost of carrying this risk, they may have cause to cut corners in order to achieve a commercial return from the provision of agreed services.

Cost plus

These contracts are most suited where the desired output is subject to change, and the inputs are unknown. Under such conditions, the customer tends to assume all risk associated with uncertainty. In addition, cost-plus contracts are adversarial in nature, since for a given service level agreement:

- the only way a service provider can increase its total profit is by increasing service costs;
- the only way a customer can reduce service costs is by reducing the service provider's total profit;
- there is no incentive for the two sides to work together to discover smarter ways to provide the required services since a win–win situation is impossible.

Schedule of rates

This is a variation on the fixed-cost approach, fixing the price of inputs (e.g. person hours) or outputs (e.g. completion of a known task). With fixed-input prices, the customer bears the risk of uncertainty in terms of volumes and costs. With fixed-output unit prices, the customer bears the cost of volume risk, while the service provider carries the risk of unit cost variability.

Open book

This approach provides visibility over the cost of providing the service and the outsourcer's margin over that cost. The typical structure is that the host company and the service provider strike an agreed mark-up on cost for inputs (staff). For example, to mark up the salary, government taxes and allowances of the outsourcers staff by 15%.

The challenges that need to be addressed in this model include determining the true cost for each category and level of staff member. In addition to the base salary, the service provider may incur:

- state and federal taxes for the employee
- health or salary continuance cover, and professional indemnity insurance
- pension contributions
- training and development fees
- management and infrastructure costs.

Determining what these costs are per employee is often debatable. Some costs, such as taxes and pension contributions, are objective and testable. Others, such as management, training and infrastructure, are derived and arguments over apportionment or costing methods are to be expected.

Another issue that tends to cloud the open book approach is finding agreement on what constitutes a "reasonable" margin. Differing industries have different volume and margin expectations for product or service sales. Typically, high product turnover businesses work on volume with low margin per item. Low product turnover businesses tend towards the sale of few high-margin items. The management of a supermarket chain that has a high-turnover low-margin business may feel challenged by the margins expected by the service provider that has a low-turnover high-margin business. The service provider may view the host company's margins as ludicrously low. The host company may have to make a concerted effort to understand the service provider's cost and risk environment if they are to find agreement on an appropriate margin on sales that takes the form of the provision of human resources.

Other implications of these models include:

- Any significant shift in the service provider's costs will trigger an immediate shift of those costs towards the host company's business. For example, a 5% increase in base cost triggered by a local tax on payroll will pass through directly in billing.
- Any cost increase has a multiplier effect on the total cost. A cost of $100 with a margin of 15% amounts to a $15 margin. A cost increase to $110 with the same 15% margin amounts to a $16.50 margin.
- Annual salary increases in the service provider's organisation will flow through to the host company. This can become contentious when the service provider

gives more generous salary increases than have been given to the host company's staff.
- Bonuses and other performance-related rewards to the service provider's staff
  cannot only find their way to the host company's account, but also may do so
  with a margin. For example, the service provider grants a bonus to one of their
  staff, and charges the host company the bonus plus 15% for the privilege.

Some of the strengths of the model include:

- The host company has visibility over true cost and the provider's margin. This
  can eliminate concerns about unfair pricing.
- The host company can make a true judgement about what it would cost to
  return the operation in house. (It may surprise the host company to find that
  they cannot meet the operating cost achieved by the outsourcer, despite the
  margin they take.)
- The host company can manage costs up or down with comparative ease, by
  removing staff from the contract or adding staff to the contract, or varying the
  mix of staff quality (typically measured by level of education, years of experience, skill range and employment grade).
- The service provider can operate sure in the knowledge that costs will be
  covered and a reasonable margin obtained. This removes much of the element
  of risk associated with some other models.

Open book offers advantages and disadvantages. It provides great flexibility and
control over the quality and quantity of staff providing the service, identifies the
true cost of operation, and protects against unfair pricing. However, it requires that
both parties agree within the contract what constitutes reasonable costs, salary
increases and bonuses. It also demands agreement on when these will occur, what
will trigger them, and how they will be determined. There is also scope for agreeing what service provider costs will *not* pass through to the host company.

Companies that adopt the open book model are strongly advised to analyse the
potential impacts of this model over the life of the outsourcing contract. Failure to
do so, particularly in a period of high inflation, could result in surprise or even
shock in the future.

Joint venture

This model has been used with success in a number of organisations. Each version
of the joint venture model has a number of unique variances. However, the
approach involves shared equity between the host company and the service provider, either directly through stockholding by the host company in the service
provider's organisation (CBA and EDS) or joint stockholding in a third entity that is

established especially for this purpose, such as National Rail and Railtek in Australia.

The benefits that the joint venture model brings are:

- Stronger governance and control by the host company.
- More open management as the host company will typically demand a seat at the board.
- Simpler approach to sharing the financial upside and downside of the venture.
- Provides substance to the much vaunted "partnership approach".

It is probably worth reminding the host company again that the service provider is a commercial entity with its own economic objectives, motivation tools and culture. No matter how much "partnering" words are used, there will always be some underlying friction caused by these disparate goals.

Hybrid solutions

This may be an appropriate solution in some instances to allow a collaborative approach to service delivery and management. PA Consulting Group told of one UK IT outsourcing contract that was based on the cost plus model with open book accounting to protect the customer from vendor abuse. Service levels were poor, and costs were increasing. Recognising that this was a recipe for customer discontent, the forward-thinking vendor promoted a hybrid approach:

- The service costs for the next planning period (12 months) were fixed a certain percentage below the current period's costs when refined to account for the input costs and output volume increases.
- Four key outputs were selected, which all required improvements in delivered levels of service. Challenging but achievable targets were agreed for each output. Continual achievement of existing service levels would require the service provider to refund a certain percentage of the total service charge, while meeting improvement targets would earn bonus payments.

At the end of the next planning period, the whole process could be repeated as appropriate. The customer was guaranteed lower service costs if the levels of performance did not improve, and had motivated the service provider to seek to improve its performance in those few areas that were most important to the customer at that point in time. At the same time, the service provider was incented to find smarter ways of providing the required services, by reducing service costs as much as possible, but not at the expense of delivered service levels.

In this particular example, a significant proportion of the service provider's service delivery manager's remuneration was linked directly to the customer's satisfaction with the service delivered. This was an important contributing factor to the success of the outsourcing agreement.

Conclusion

Each model has its drawbacks and its benefits. No model meets all needs. Aspects the host company may wish to consider are:

- the risks with models that give host company no view of the service provider's cost base. This leaves the host company open to unreasonable margins. This is not a problem at the outset when bids are competitive, but there is a need to protect against this in the future;
- models that force the service provider to contain changes in the service provider's cost base. If the contract does not allow for cost variations based on internal cost increases, it can lead to the service provider downgrading service and quality as it struggles to maintain their margin;
- ensuring the service provider does not overlook recurring and unavoidable costs, such as salary increases or bonuses. If the service provider fails to reward staff for their efforts, they will usually seek alternative employment. This may lead to a high turnover rate amongst staff, with continuity and quality issues for the host company.

The service provider is there to make a profit on the service provided to the host company. However, in moments of tension or conflict, this underlying friction can surface in surprising ways.

Finally, let both parties develop their own implication lists for the model they adopt. These implications will be specific to each party. Understand them *now* before entering into the contract, not later when hands are tied and the parties face five or more years of unrelenting problems that could have been avoided in the first place.

The checklist at the end of this chapter poses a number of questions that both parties should ask themselves about why they have chosen a particular pricing model.

Contractual requirements

Clearly, the RFP should state the expected duration of the agreement and the current position on renewal. Some companies may prefer to have a roll-over date on which renewal is automatic. Others may not wish to contemplate these issues at this stage. The RFP may also call out other key dates, for example:

- due diligence commences and ends
- contract signing
- project review cycles
- renewal/termination timetable at contract end.

Intellectual property

Intellectual property (IP) is often the most debated item in the RFP and contract. In practice, it may well count for nothing or be of little consequence. Undertake a three-phase check on IP before you write the RFP requirements and enter the IP debate:

1. Find out what other companies have done and why.
2. Question the motives and intents of the IP clause.
3. Understand the practicalities of the IP ownership issue.

It is no overstatement to say that service providers are generally paranoid about protecting their IP and astoundingly overreaching in their demands to own work that they do for the host company.

Conditions and warranties

Traditionally, the law has classified contractual terms as either conditions or warranties. Generally speaking, conditions are essential terms of a contract; breach of that gives the innocent party a right to terminate the contract and claim damages for loss of the bargain captured by the contract. To determine whether a particular contractual promise is a condition, test whether the promise is of such importance to the promisee that they would not have entered into the contract unless they had been assured of a strict or substantial performance of the promise.

It is not possible to describe in any great detail the exact contractual promises that would be considered conditions in an outsourcing contract, as this will vary from contract to contract; but it may include a promise, for example, that the outsourcing provider will perform the services, acquire certain assets of the customer, and employ customer staff. A condition that is also implied into most contracts is that neither party will refuse to perform their obligations under the contract without just cause.

It should be noted, however, that even if a particular contractual promise is not sufficiently important itself to be a condition according to the test described above, the parties to a contract will always remain free to determine for themselves what obligations they will accept. This means that they may declare that breach of certain terms, regardless of whether they are conditions or not, will give a party the right to terminate the contract.

In contrast, warranties are representations recorded in the contract, breach of which may give rise to a right to claim damages, or more commonly in IT contracts a right to have product defects remedied, but not a right to terminate the contract. For example, an outsourcing contract might contain the following warranties given by the outsourcing provider:

- The services will be delivered in accordance with the agreed service levels, escalation procedures and quality assurance methodologies.
- The outsourcing provider will comply with its obligations under the agreed responsibility matrix.
- The services will be carried out in a proper, competent and professional manner by appropriately qualified personnel.
- The goods supplied or used in connection with the services will be fit for the purpose for which they are being supplied.
- Provision of the services will comply with all required consent, registrations, approvals, licences or permits.

In addition to including these warranties in a contract, the parties will often set out the precise remedies that are available to the customer if the outsourcing provider breaches these warranties. This is particularly important in an outsourcing contract, because the customer is often locked into the relationship, and requires continuity of service from the outsourcing provider irrespective of the breach. The agreement may therefore require the outsourcing provider to reperform the services, or to pay damages to the customer in accordance with an agreed formula.

Performance management

Make sure the following facets of the performance measurement component of the outsourcing agreement are made clear:

- The extent of the discovery undertaken by the host company.
- Current baseline measures (where these are not a commercial embarrassment).
- Key outputs that will form the basis of future measures.

- Method of measuring and who will do it (host, provider or independent third party).
- The extent to which there will be an opportunity for verification in due diligence.

Relationship management

This section should call out the expectations for client management by the service provider. Be precise about the organisation structure the host company intends to set up to manage the contract and performance. Make sure the host company stipulates the organisation structure it will provide to manage the relationship as well as the technology. Define the authorities, accountabilities and responsibilities of the key relationship management staff on both sides. Neither organisation can expect dynamic management if all decisions of any consequence must be referred up through an endless series of managers. Ideally, the host company manager and the service provider's manager should have sufficient authority to deal with all day-to-day issues and expenditures.

Target measures

State the desired new performance levels, including the timeframe in which these measures are expected to be delivered. If possible, state the obstacles that currently exist to achieving these measures and tie them back to the criteria listed in Chapter 5. Consider the fact that you may wish to move service levels up or down. Some services may prove to be overly expensive for the benefit they produce, and more than one company has found it can survive with less-than-ideal PC support services in return for savings of thousands of dollars in help desk salary costs.

Discovery

State in summary the current status of the host company's IT environment. This should be the catalogue of all major IT services and the current performance status and resource consumption. Again, a balance must be struck between "opening the kimono" for all to see the state of the host company's IT, and misinforming the bidder about the environment they are about to acquire

Due diligence

Explain the opportunity, scope and extent to which the service provider will be permitted to carry out due diligence on the host company's environment. It may be judicious to include an outline of how disputed findings will be resolved. It is also useful to include timing and duration, and inform the proposer what support or materials will be provided for them to undertake due diligence. Clearly, if the outsourcing decision is covert, and staff in the host company have not been informed, then due diligence may well be limited to a "data room"[c] review of reports and schedules, with little opportunity for the service provider to view "real life". However, we repeat again the general rule: the RFP should provide as much information as possible that will enable the bidder to submit the highest quality proposal.

Principles

Ensure that principles are included in the RFP. The bidder must be informed properly about the framework within which they are contracting to deliver the results. A failure to do this is likely to lead to bidders making commitments they intend to deliver in a manner that differs significantly from that envisaged by the host company. For example, a service provider's bid may be built around lowering costs by replacing high-cost, top-of-the-range hardware with second-hand or grey-market hardware. If this is not acceptable to the host company, there will be major problems later.

Reporting

State the required reporting regime for the agreement and the performance measures. Frequently they will not have been measured previously and the host

---

[c] In mergers and acquisition parlance, the "data room" is the place where all material on the target company's structure, financials, assets and staff are made available to potential acquirers.

company may well be surprised and unhappy at the projected cost of measuring and reporting on the project. Domberger and Hall suggest that "provided performance evaluation can be implemented in a systematic way, the cost of monitoring need not be higher than monitoring in house operations . . . the reason why it often appears monitoring costs are so high after contracting is that either little or no monitoring was previously undertaken or that its costs were not fully assessed."[48]

Rewards and punishments

Outline the proposed approach to providing incentives for performance above certain levels, and state the preferred approach to remedial action and retribution. The proposer needs to know the host company's underlying attitude to this specific issue. Surprisingly, many agreements have no reward or punishment mechanism. An executive of a service provider offered this view: "When the shit hits the fan, we have to provide resources the best we can. We usually rob those customers [no reward, no punishment] because we have least to lose. They may shout and scream but they can't put their hand in the till. We can stand shouting, we can't stand losses."

Rewards and punishments are discussed in further detail in Chapters 12 and 14.

Conclusion

The idea behind this section has been to encourage the host company to clearly communicate its needs and the relative importance of those needs to the population of bidders. It is also important to give those bidders the opportunity to provide more discriminating responses.

The ultimate aim of the RFP is to encourage proposal responses that provide the host company with sound and adequate information on which to base its all-important outsourcing decision. The idea is to elicit information from candidates on how well they can meet the objectives and provide the bidders with the chance to suggest alternative means of achieving those goals.

If the host company has carried out the preselection process outlined in Chapter 3, then the RFP should (hopefully) be issued to a small number of candidates, preferably somewhere in the order of 7 ± 2. A small number allows for careful analysis of proposal responses and should lead to the finer tuned selection of the most preferred candidate.

Checklist

The checklist that follows deals first with the pricing model, then with other facets. The pricing model checks are positioned first as they often have a significant impact on the overall RFP structure and contract management programme.

No doubt there are many other questions that can be asked by the perceptive manager. You must subject the chosen model to the most rigorous questioning you can. The host company must also ensure that every aspect of the model is considered within the contract, and that adequate flexibility is built into the contract for dealing with aberrations and change

1. Why have we chosen this model?
2. Why did we reject the other models?
3. What are the yearly cost projections for the term of the contract?
4. What are the 10 most positive implications of this model?
5. What are the 10 most negative implications of this model?
6. What are the legal issues surrounding this model?
7. What are the financial issues (cash flow etc.) surrounding this model?
8. Will this model be affected by significant changes in our business?
9. Have we projected technology changes that may affect the model?
10. Have we allowed for these changes to be accommodated in the model?
11. What benefits does the service provider gain from this model?
12. What drawbacks will the service provider face with this model?
13. Who (see short list interviews) else is using this model and why?
14. Who is not using this model and why?
15. What problems have others had with this model?
16. What benefits have others enjoyed with this model?
17. Are all the implications of the model controllable through the contract?
18. Have we informed the proposer of the meanings of our weighting criteria?
19. Have we illustrated appropriate response methods, and defined our view of various degrees of compliance?
20. Have we included expected key dates for reaching contract consummation?
21. Have we included the principles or guidelines within which service is to be delivered?
22. Is the current environment, as "discovered", described properly?
23. Has key baseline and target measure information been included?
24. Have the rules, timing, support and information base for due diligence been described adequately?
25. Have we outlined potentially costly service requirements, such as reporting and measuring?
26. Is the framework for reward and punishment included?

Don't forget the financials: an accountant's view

All outsourcing will involve significant financial considerations. Integrate the financial team with the technical team from the outset. If you want your outsource process to fail, forget the financials.

This process should be no different from any other business decision. Remember that the outsourcing considerations are prospective. There will be many longer-term cost/revenue assumptions. All this will involve the financial analysts.

Here are some illustrative areas.

- *Pricing models*—the way the outsourcing will be structured drives most of the financial considerations. There may be several models or combinations. Potentially, technology developments, efficiencies, growth and new services will all impact the operational models.
- *Cost reduction*—the way costs will be controlled and measured over time, including any incentives, needs to be addressed early in the process.
- *Profitability*—in seeking cost minimisation, the need for the service provider to achieve a reasonable return cannot be ignored. Some mutual appreciation of the respective objectives in this area needs to be understood.
- *Taxation*—taxation in its various manifestations is pervasive. Income tax, VAT, employment taxes and stamp duty are some examples.
- *Billing and contract management systems*—lack of efficiency in these areas will potentially undermine the effectiveness of the ongoing operation.
- *Personnel*—a major cost component with the potential for significant escalation. Employment costs are wide-ranging including salary, benefits, taxes, and training.
- *SLAs*—consider whether financial key performance indicators (KPIs) are appropriate, and plan accordingly. All SLAs will cost money to administer, which you need to assess.
- *Risk management*—all parties need to undertake a fully costed risk assessment.
- *Retention of expertise*—any retained expertise and contract administration need to be addressed.
- *Costing*—costing for outsourcing decisions involves complex accounting and costing issues. The choice of costing methods and the assumptions underlying the estimates are fundamental. Valid and full cost assignments need to be made against all the components. Remember that the different parties may have different approaches to the identification and accumulation of costs. There is no right or wrong way, and costing models should consider the full-cost method, marginal costing, discounted cash flow (DCF) analysis, and a sensitivity analysis.

Integrate the financial and technical teams from the start of the process. Ensure a fully absorbed costing approach is followed, otherwise unanticipated costs will emerge. Contractual relationships should ensure financial issues are addressed and documented. Establish robust billing and ongoing financial recording and reporting systems. Ensure an open, professional partnership between all the parties and don't forget the financials.

Ron Switzer BCom
FCPA

8 Issuing the request for proposals

This chapter covers the issue of the RFP. This will differ according to the type of document that is being issued, ranging from the formal style of proposal, to the informal and involved approach that can be adopted with a restricted RFP. Each process requires that consideration be given to managing:

- change control
- communications
- records

Each of these is explored before the discussion on the benefits and drawbacks of each form of tendering.

Change control

Change will occur regardless of the type or form of issue chosen for the document. Two common causes of change are:

- the issuing company picks up errors or omissions after the document has been issued;
- bidders raise questions or issues that cause the issuer to alter the document.

Change control must be managed tightly, and the following points must be checked before the change is implemented:

- Is the change acceptable to the host company executive team sponsoring the outsourcing agreement?
- Is the change acceptable to the legal department who may need to incorporate it within the contract?
- Does the change have a knock-on effect on other requirements in the RFP?

If the change is agreed then it must be communicated to:

- all organisations that intend to respond. This to ensure probity and fair play. Clearly this requires that a process be put in place to ensure that the host company knows who is going to bid;
- appropriate staff within the host company who are affected directly or indirectly by the change.

Tight management is vitally important if the host company is to avoid accusations of impropriety or bias in the process. Take the following three steps if you wish to strengthen any communication process:

1. Demand all companies that obtain a copy of the RFP inform the host company and provide a contact person and address for communication. Ideally, this should include phone, fax and email address.
2. Maintain a communication matrix similar to the example shown below.
3. Require that the proposers formally acknowledge receipt of changes and maintain their own change register so they can identify any gap in the (numbered) changes they receive.

An example change register is shown in Table 8.1.

Table 8.1—Change register

Change	Legal	Exec	Team	PA	IBM	CCS	EDS
001	●	●	●	●	●	●	●
002	●	●	●	●	●	●	●
003							
004							
005							
006							

Library management or document control is another important aspect of change control. The library should hold all details about the change, including:

- the original request, regardless of whether it was lodged by fax, letter, email or telephone. If it was lodged by telephone, then the change request should be in the form of a file note, which may be handwritten, but must be dated and include the name of both parties, the caller and the call recipient;
- background papers and minutes of meetings held to discuss the change and approve it;
- copies of the information communicated to both service providers and internal staff.

Resourcing

The extent of the job of managing the tender or RFP issue is large. Two recommendations are given to intending outsourcers: First, ensure that you have the right and sufficient staff to handle the workload during the issue period. One common problem is that a number of the outsourcing team will have planned holidays in this (imagined) quiet time between the completion of the RFP and the closing date for responses. There are few greater frustrations than discovering that the key people have planned time off while the RFP is in circulation. Unfortunately, they are precisely the people who need to be available as contacts and information givers during the RFP process. They alone are often privy to the deep-seated reasoning behind some of the requirements.

Second, allow both service provider and your company sufficient time to handle the process properly. It is easy to underestimate the time and effort required to manage ongoing communication with bidders responding to the RFP. VicRoads reportedly allowed six months for their RFI process, issuing their RFP in November 1993 and signing the contract one year later in November 1994. This was in the early days of outsourcing and VicRoads were pioneering. The duration was probably too long, and led to subsequent morale issues with IT staff.

However, the timetable should allow sufficient time for the intended respondents to examine the RFP, prepare their answers, have them quality assurance tested internally, and then checked by their legal counsel. It also needs to allow the host company and the intending partners to communicate and clarify ambiguities.

CBA set up a project office to provide a single conduit for communication about the RFP. "The project office provided a single point of contact for over 200 [service provider] questions and CBA responses. This provided valuable discovery as vendors [service providers] requested clarification."

The host company should also establish a project office with clearly defined roles. It can make a huge difference to a well-executed RFP management process. Appropriate roles include:

- *Project manager*—organises and coordinates all RFP activity.
- *Communication manager*—prepares responses, has them validated and checked, and then distributes them to all RFP participants.
- *Librarian*—manages the proper recording and indexing of the bidder questions and responses. This material may be crucial to forming a sound contract.

The project manager should oversee all ongoing communication with the bidding parties. The quality of responses to the RFP is critical to making a sound selection, and well-managed communication is necessary. Regardless of how precisely the RFP is written, some criteria or explanations may not be perfectly clear to the reader.

Some organisations try to discourage bidders making any contact on the following grounds:

- *Fairness*—all respondents are given precisely the same information.
- *Probity*—the process can be seen to be just and untainted.
- *Time*—the host company wishes to limit the time and effort required to deal with proposer enquiries.
- *Influencing*—the buyer wishes to limit sales activity during the process.
- *Objectivity*—all responses are equal and unambiguous.

These grounds are not to be scoffed at. They are, in some ways, reasonable and proper. Indeed, for some organisations the probity issue is so great that it will be impossible to adhere to the more flexible approach recommended in this text. However, the isolationist approach does itself hold dangers:

- Even the best RFP contains ambiguities and limited explanations. The service provider should be given the opportunity to clarify these in some detail.
- Service providers may wish to explore alternative approaches to meeting criteria and they should have the opportunity to explore the host company's readiness to consider these.
- The host company may discover additional information about itself that is needed to effect a strong and worthwhile contract.
- Discussion with intending respondents will often provide insight into their capabilities well beyond that contained in a careful, limited, written response.

It is possible to balance the competing issues of fairness, probity and objectivity with the need for openness and flexibility by ensuring all candidates are granted equal opportunity for contact and any significant new information or variation is communicated to all. This does entail more work and sound project office support. However, the decision that is about to be reached is a multimillion dollar one, and the effort should be commensurate with the scale and importance of the decision.

Finally, intending bidders should also be advised of the rules of conduct or protocols that will apply in managing the RFP process. These are normally well established and include:

- All enquiries and responses will be distributed to all (registered) participants.
- There will be no contact, except through the formal channels of the project office.
- No gifts, entertainment or other incentives may be offered.

Often, public service units and large companies will have boilerplate clauses to cover appropriate conduct.

As with so many things in the outsourcing process, putting the time and effort in now will repay itself time and time again during the life of the contract.

Drawbacks and benefits

A restricted RFP can provide a superior environment in which to select your long-term partner. Buying a house on the basis of on advertisement in the paper, a photograph and self-descriptions is risky: photographs can lie and self-description is always biased. Careful selection based on examination of the house and careful examination of the title deeds is more likely to lead to a good choice.

The process for handling a restricted RFP is covered in some detail, as is the formal RFP. Those organisations that are obliged to issue formal tenders will see that there is little difference between an open RFP and a formal tender. For this reason, there is no direct comparison with the formal tenders in this text.

The open request for proposals

The term "open RFP" describes issuing an RFP to the market at large. The normal process is to place an advertisement in the national press and allow any company to respond. The RFP may include criteria that rule against some bids, but the option to bid is open to all companies. The benefits of an open RFP are:

- It opens the opportunity to bid to all parties in the market, and ensures no one who is interested or capable is overlooked.
- The process is seen to be open and fair to all, and helps avoid the risk of unfair limitations.
- The process tends to be associated with much more rigorous limits on bidder interaction with the host company, and therefore reduces the amount of ongoing management.

The drawbacks include:

- The process opens the bid to all and sundry, as even unsuitable bidders will find novel ways of sidestepping preselection style criteria.
- The scope tends to bring with it limitations to open communication with bidders, and misdirections in the document are less likely to be corrected or refined.
- The task of communicating changes to the bidding population is often large and difficult to manage.
- Major service providers may not bid, especially if the host company is a medium-sized or smaller enterprise. Larger service providers may not be prepared to bid against an open field for a smaller contract.

- The evaluation process can become very large and mechanical, and can diminish in quality if there are a large number of bids to process.
- The scale of change management can become overwhelming, thus increasing the duration and cost of the process.

Public service enterprises may be very limited in their options with regard to issuing RFPs and tenders, and will be well aware of the issues. However, those companies that are not so rigidly bound may well wish to consider whether this style of RFP bid will provide them with good results.

The restricted request for proposals

The term "restricted RFP" is applied to RFPs that are issued to a limited and defined market. Only selected companies are invited to bid. Bids cannot be made by other organisations. The restricted RFP can provide a better process, and limit the time and effort that goes into making a superior selection.

The benefits and drawbacks of the restricted RFP differ from those of an open RFP. Even if your organisation is not able to issue a restricted RFP, for policy or other reasons, you should read this section.

Benefits

A restricted RFP:

- limits the field of potential candidates to those that have been preselected or are known to have capacity and capability;
- limits the potential workload in change control and communication;
- entertains an open and ongoing liaison between the host company and the bidders;
- offers the opportunity to improve the quality of the selection process by limiting the scale of the task;
- controls the dissemination of important company data that may otherwise fall into competitor's hands (RFPs contain much information about your business, and the criteria may be sound pointers to issues and weaknesses in your business);
- encourages responses from those service providers you would prefer to have running an important part of your business;

- eliminates responses from "chancers". These are organisations that lack the capacity or capability to support the proposal but are optimistic enough to believe that they will miraculously find the resources if they win.

Drawbacks

There are a number of drawbacks:

- Risk of impropriety as the open and constant communication may favour one candidate over another.
- Risk that candidates will have a greater opportunity to offer illegal incentives to host company staff.
- Risk that competitive candidates may have been unfairly excluded by the preselection phase.
- The possibility that the restricted RFP may not encourage an appropriate level of competition amongst the proposers.

These issues are very real and should not be underestimated. Nevertheless the decision on outsourcing is difficult and potentially hazardous, and will affect the company for many years to come.

An open and complete dialogue between the seller and the potential buyers should improve the quality of the process. Despite the dangers listed above, a preselection process and managed distribution and response process will most likely lead to better outcomes in most instances.

Issuing a restricted request for proposals

A suggested first step is to invite the preselected candidates, one at a time or together, to a briefing at which they will be given the RFP. The invitation should include a short briefing paper that outlines:

- the nature of the RFP (restricted RFP for outsourcing IT or other services);
- the objective of the briefing session—to inform the potential or preselected candidate about the RFP in more detail;
- information on the staff from the host company who will be giving the briefing;
- the timetable and agenda.

The actual briefing should be formal and controlled. The host company needs to ensure that all candidates are given the same information, and that the briefing is complete and consistent. The aim of the briefing is to encourage your preselected candidates to put adequate time, money and effort into developing a complete and proper response. Follow the tips below:

- Ensure one standard agenda is used for all the briefings.
- Present the material at a high level, elaborating on any special issues.
- Record any discussion as minutes of the meeting and distribute as appropriate.
- Let the recipients know how many of their competitors are being invited to respond.
- Let the recipients know why they have been preselected and their probability of selection (i.e. if you intend to select only one company for all services, but have invited six to tender, then their chances are 1 : 6).
- Brief the recipients on your expectations about the quality and depth of responses. Remember that they are only familiar with standard RFP criteria and responses.
- Arrange a follow-up meeting some days later to clarify any issues they may have about the RFP and its contents.

This should lead to the submission of sound, well-constructed and complete responses to the RFP. The next issue to be covered is evaluating those responses.

Checklist

1. Have you established a suitable change-control mechanism?
2. Have you set up a suitable communication management system?
3. Have you devised a suitable records management system?
4. Have you checked vacation arrangements for team members?
5. Have you allowed enough time for respondents to prepare quality submissions?
6. Has an appropriate RFP management team been set up?
7. Have the drawbacks and benefits of the various approaches been considered?
8. Has proper consideration been given to the issue of propriety?
9. Have standards been set for all briefings and external communication?
10. Are all relevant business staff aware of the ground rules surrounding the management of the RFP process?

Applying sound practice and method: BASF plc

The UK headquarters of BASF plc, one of the world's largest chemical companies, drew upon experienced outsourcing consultants in order to have its outsourcing strategy designed and implemented successfully within seven months.

The solution to finding the right supplier

SMART (PA's strategic approach to outsourcing) provided the framework for project timings, commencing with the identification of a short list of appropriate IT suppliers. This was followed by negotiation and contract completion, and clarification of the multitude of IT activities performed by the internal staff. The responsibility was then transferred to the new external supplier, and SLAs were put in place.

The consultants also assisted BASF in building a new internal IT organisation to operate closely with the business and helped BASF to demonstrate the effectiveness of its outsourcing decision.

Delivering business benefits

This initiative was introduced on time, according to the original seven-month schedule, a tremendous achievement that caused minimal disruption to business operations. Good communications between consultants and senior management ensured that decision making was prompt and all members of the team were working in unison.

The new IT service is able to deliver business benefits through IT, providing high-quality, cost-effective, directed services. From an internal IT department of 70 people spread across three sites, BASF moved seamlessly to a 25-strong team of focused IT professionals, with a new manager to oversee this important change in business practice.

By following a proven methodology and by drawing on the consultant's experience in identifying and avoiding pitfalls, BASF earned the respect of suppliers whose performance was critical with such demanding timescales. The consultant's project management expertise became the bedrock for timely success. These skills, combined with the vision and determination of BASF management, produced a strong working partnership and an effective new business practice.

> No major milestones were missed and the outsourced IT service went into production exactly as planned. Without PA's help we could not have achieved the target completion date. There was excellent teamwork throughout the intensive seven-month project. The successful outcome speaks for itself.

David Shoesmith
IT Manager, BASF plc

Case Study reprinted by kind permission of PA Consulting Group.

9 Evaluating request for proposals responses

The evaluation of responses is a challenging task. It may be best to divide it into a number of discrete steps:

1. An initial cull to eliminate the obviously unsuitable.
2. A detailed evaluation of the remainder to select the short list. This process can be broken into four stages:
   - Qualifying ambiguous responses.
   - Quantitative analysis based on numerical evaluation of responses.
   - Qualitative analysis based on opinion and research.
   - Customer and vendor site visits.
3. Follow with a risk/consequence analysis of the short-listed bidders.
4. As a last analytical step, model the financials of the short listed bids.
5. Select the preferred candidate.
6. Seek endorsement of the choice by the senior executive group or the board.

Each of these steps is discussed in detail in this chapter.

Evaluation team

This book contains an earlier recommendation that, so far as possible, the contents of the RFP be separated into at least three categories: commercial, technical and organisational. The benefits of this are numerous:

- It simplifies the process of response by the bidder, who can conveniently pass appropriate sections of the RFP to the internal business units who are best placed to respond on these criteria, e.g. human resources, finance, technical services.
- It simplifies the process of evaluation by the host company, who can likewise pass appropriate sections to those sections within the host company best placed to evaluate them.

- It ensures that each facet is evaluated independently, and not swayed by responses in areas where staff may hold opinions but lack expertise.

At the conclusion of the evaluation process, these views and the *qualitative* view must be brought together to select the preferred bidder(s). However, there is much to recommend deep analysis by experts in each field, rather than the "group think" that can easily emerge from a group review.

Initial cull

The first step in this process is to ensure that all in the outsourcing team agree the criteria that will be used to sort the bids. These criteria would normally consist of the essential preselection criteria (if any) and other essential criteria. The process suggested is:

1. Read all the bids, cross-checking adherence to the sort criteria. You should end up with three groups.
   - *Rejects*—those bids that have serious shortcomings or fall far short of meeting the criteria. Record the reason for the rejection.
   - *Doubtful*—those bids that are marginal with regard to the criteria.
   - *Candidates*—those bids that clearly meet all, or the vast majority of, the sort criteria.
2. Have an independent third party or host company person external to the evaluation team check the rejects and confirm that the decision to cull them was appropriate.
3. Further investigate the borderline. This may require some initial contact with bidders. This task needs to be managed tightly if it is to not run out of control and overshadow the process in the later detailed evaluation. There also needs to be strong management to ensure the process does not unfairly advantage an otherwise ordinary candidate.
   - The outcome of the process should be that some bids are demoted to rejects and others promoted to candidates.
   - The independent party should again cross-check and certify the decision to demote or promote. This is required to protect against later charges of impropriety or favouritism.

It is not wise to inform service providers that their bids have been rejected at this time. Hold the status of all bids confidential and within the bid team until the final choice is made. Otherwise, the company runs the risk of having to manage disgruntled bidders before they have selected a clear winner.

Qualifying responses

Before moving on to quantitative analysis, it may be necessary to qualify some responses in the pool of candidate bids. Please note that this qualification can take place before quantitative analysis, during quantitative analysis, or both.

Qualifying the responses means checking them out with the respondent. This can be done before the quantitative process commences, or after the first cut at the process. Bids may contain responses that are not clear or are ambiguous. The host company must follow up and obtain clarification on unclear responses. Surprisingly, this is not often done and analysts guess what the respondent's ambiguous response may mean. Our motto is: "If in doubt, ask!"

It is not unusual for the answer to be quite different from the imagined or guessed intention of the response. Yet, time and time again, this important step of reviewing the responses with the candidate is not carried out.

Try following the steps below:

1. Identify all criteria where there is some doubt or ambiguity about the bidder's response.
2. Document these criteria and list the questions that need to be answered to qualify the response.
3. Organise a meeting with the bidder at which they will be required to clarify their response (advise them that no other aspects of the bid are open for discussion at this time).

These workshops or meetings should be properly minuted, preferably overseen by an honest broker, and subjected to a post-mortem scrutiny by a third party.

It can be worthwhile to add to the relative value charts or scoring tools a column for "adjusted scores". These are changes or alterations to the initial score or the self-score provided by the respondent. These adjusted scores, which can move up or down, reflect the additional information gathered through the qualification process and provide a useful yardstick for comparing against base scores.

Quantitative analysis

Before starting this process, it is a good idea to refer back to Table 3.1 (see p. 28).

Preselection criteria were discussed in Chapter 6. These criteria were described as a subset of essential criteria that were based on public information. Chapter 6 also discussed how bidder responses could be similarly quantified, and how this scale should be defined, just as the weights were defined (see Table 9.1).

Table 9.1—

Score	Definition
0	0% compliance: we do not offer this function, feature or skill
1	20% compliance: we have very limited capacity/capability in this area
2	40% compliance: we have moderate capacity/capability in this area
3	60% compliance: we can meet over half of these criteria
4	80% compliance: we come very close to meeting these criteria.
5	100% compliance: we meet these criteria in every way

The final recommendation in the earlier examples was that the potential bidders should be given some illustrations that define clearly the expectation that some rationale would underpin their self-rated response. Refer back to Table 3.3 (p. 40) for an example.

Other verbal and graphical systems of weighting exist that accommodate quantitative and qualitative data. Alternative approaches include a pair-wise assessment scheme that might compare the relative importance, preference or likelihood of the two elements with respect to the data. *Importance* is useful when comparing one objective with another; *preference* is useful when comparing alternatives; and *likelihood* is useful when comparing the probability of outcomes.

The next recommended step is to evaluate the responses using the quantitative process embodied in the RFP. The relative value chart is a useful tool here.

In processing the bid responses, it can be useful to introduce a refinement to the process, namely the use of a qualified score. A score is said to be "qualified" when it is adjusted, either up or down, by the host company. This will usually occur if there is some doubt about the accuracy of the service provider's self-score. The adjustment should be made only after the score has been discussed properly with the service provider.

The suggested steps for processing an RFP response are as follows:

1. Enter the respondent's bid scores into the relative value chart, either manually or electronically depending on how the responses were provided.
2. Annotate those scores that require further qualification. This is to identify those scores that are to be reviewed. These may also include a new category for qualification—scores where the company has reason to doubt the accuracy of the respondent's self-scoring.
3. Investigate those bid scores that are annotated with the service provider concerned, and adjust them up or down as necessary:
   - This process needs to be open and testable. It is important to keep appropriate records of why such changes were made, and who approved them.
   - The revised scores and records should be scrutinised by a tried and trusted third party to ensure that the changes have the imprimatur of an independent review.

The outcome should be a shortlist of candidates based on the quantitative review. Clearly, there may be some aspects of the rating that are not answered satisfactorily by a number-crunching analysis. For this reason, it is important to include a qualitative review before selecting the short list for risk evaluation.

Qualitative review

Not all aspects of the review process fit comfortably within the numerical scale. It is tempting to push everything into a mathematical model, and to try and incorporate judgemental features such as "cultural fit" and "innovation". Opinions vary, and cultural fit is a subjective judgement that may reflect personal comfort rather than corporate alignment.

One possible approach is to ask each team member to rate the subjective criteria for the quantified short list, and to sum and average their scores. If the team is to do this professionally, they will need to:

- research these areas properly, through public database searches, newspaper and magazine articles, or other public documents;
- interview organisations or people who know the short-listed candidates to build some information base on which they will make their judgements;
- visit customer and vendor sites. Guidelines for this process are contained in Chapter 6.

Do not rely on intuition. Each participant should be required to document why they selected a particular number in making their subjective judgement. They should also be required to include any material they obtained, such as interview notes or articles on which they based their judgement. These qualified scores should then be included with the relative value chart scores to select the most desirable candidate. The strength of this process is that it makes it clear what proportions of the "winner's" score came from objective and subjective criteria.

There are other methods and approaches to quantification, both of quantitative and qualitative data. The methods described in this book are simple and reasonably sound. They can not be relied on to produce the "right" answers— that is a more complex judgement. The aim of these methods is to support the process of decision making and ensure that some degree of rigour is applied to the process.

Risk evaluation

The outcome of these processes should be a short list, preferably of three or fewer candidates. The final analytical process is to carry out a risk evaluation of the short-listed candidates.

Risk management is a skill in its own right. Those organisations that employ risk managers should use their professional skills to evaluate the risks associated with selecting any of the short-listed service providers. Those without those skills can refer to some of the many excellent references on risk management.

The sorts of risks that the host company may wish to consider include:

- Economic change may have a negative effect on the pricing model.
- The service provider may be subject to economic hardship or bankruptcy.
- Key staff in the service provider's organisation may leave for whatever cause.
- Government regulation or taxes may restrict the provider's activity, e.g. constraints on immigration, work permits or other labour controls may inhibit the service provider positioning appropriate staff in a location overseas.

There must be countless other risks. Risk management is not my profession and I have limited experience and skill in the area. Nevertheless, it should be applied to all substantial projects. Chapter 6 discussed other tools that can be used to support these processes and encourage businesses to investigate and find the one(s) that best suit them.

Financial modelling

Each bid will differ to some degree in proposed pricing and terms of payment. Many host companies will regard the prices and terms as an opening gambit to be refined during contract negotiations. Nevertheless, it is prudent to model professionally the first proposals to test relative differences and to ensure that appropriate cost estimates can be put in front of the senior executive or board.

Aspects of the financials that may need to be modelled include:

- comparative models of pricing, e.g. fixed price, open book, time and materials;
- comparative price levels across these models;
- effect of payment terms on cash flow, which may be substantial over the period of the contract;

- impact of gain sharing or penalties based on some statistical probability of certain events occurring;
- effect of varying levels of inflation on the price models;
- effects of taxation changes or import costs (overseas pricing) on models.

This is a field for the professional and it should be undertaken with diligence. It is not enough to do a simple discounted cash flow and rely on that as evidence of appropriate financial analysis. The world today is harder and harsher than ever before on those who err in financial matters.

Business case review

Clearly, this is also the time to review the bids against the business case for outsourcing. Now is the time to see how the assumptions, risks and projected costs and benefits stand in comparison to the reality of the bids. Surprisingly, both anecdotal evidence and research suggests this is rarely done. It seems few companies revisit the original business case and compare it with the framework that is now shaping up from the RFP and proposals.

Selecting the preferred candidate

This normally occurs in two stages. The first selection is made by the outsourcing team; the endorsement or approval from the senior executive or board will follow. The outsourcing team needs to agree or disagree jointly on the preferred candidate. A unilateral selection by the project manager will almost certainly generate guerrilla warfare against the decision by those in the project team who do not agree with the choice. Clearly, there needs to be consensus or at least a sizeable majority in favour of the selected candidate. It is not enough to rely exclusively on the quantitative and qualitative analysis. The following steps can help manage the process to conclusion:

1. Prepare a briefing pack covering the selection. It should contain at least:
   - quantitative analysis summary showing the scores of the short-listed candidates;
   - qualitative analysis summary as above;

- risk analysis report;
- comparative financial models;
- comparison against the original business case;
- written justification, preferably in report or essay form, substantiating the choice (the project manager or most senior person on the selection team should prepare this).
2. Present the briefing pack and findings to the selection team in a workshop.
3. If consensus cannot be reached, then ensure the views of the dissenting are recorded properly.
4. If appropriate, analyse further the dissenting views, and reconvene if necessary.

The same process should be followed at senior executive or board level. Clearly, there is more formality and usually less time surrounding the process the higher up the chain it moves. However, following a sound process will help damp down recriminations and stone throwing later in the contract when things go wrong—as they almost certainly will.

Common failings

The most common failing is not allowing enough time for reflection and thinking about the information gathered, the evaluations processed and the possible scenarios that may develop over the life of the contract. In the rush to "do", too little time is set aside for thinking. George Bernard Shaw said, "Few people think more than two or three times a year; I have made an international reputation for myself by thinking once or twice a week." Alan Anderson at DMR, and one of the most gifted thinkers I know stated: "We take too little time for reflection, rushing in and processing with our keyboards rather than our minds."

The greatest dangers facing the host company analyst at this stage is that the pressure for a decision will lead to substandard analysis of the qualitative information provided in the RFP. The dangers of treating the selection process as a desktop number-crunching exercise are many. The numbers are for the guidance of wise men and the obedience of fools. The number crunching should be used to help make a better decision, to isolate areas of doubt that require further clarification, and to highlight the weak points (risk points) in the respondents' offerings.

It is the weak points that will need most attention during the due diligence and contract development stage. They are the rocks on which the good ship outsourcing may founder. And again and again, it is surprising how often these weaknesses, clearly apparent and well-evidenced in the candidate's response, are given no further attention by the host company during the due diligence and contract period. They lie dormant until the knot is tied and then reopened, like Pandora's box, to torment the host company. The respondent candidates are often on solid ground in defence, pointing out these weaknesses were stated openly in the RFP.

Checklist

1. Do all on the selection team agree the culling criteria?
2. Did the evaluation team divide and concentrate on their areas of expertise?
3. Has an independent audit been made of the rejects, and the reasons why been given?
4. Have ambiguous or vague responses been qualified?
5. Has the numerical accuracy of spreadsheets been tested?
6. Have qualitative scores been taken properly?
7. Were customer and vendor visits made?
8. Has a formal risk analysis been done?
9. Have appropriate financial models been prepared?
10. Has the original business case been compared with the likely outcome and discrepancies highlighted?
11. Has the selection team leader written a justification on selection?
12. Has the team given consensus or majority agreement?
13. Has consideration been given to notifying unsuccessful bidders?

10   Undertaking due diligence

Due diligence is the process by which the service provider reviews and confirms the condition of the environment for which they are about to take responsibility. It normally follows on immediately from notification to the service provider that they have won the bid and are to contract. The host company and service provider should enter a short-term agreement that gives the service provider a right of inspection into all aspects of the host's IT environment.

The two contrasting approaches that can be taken are:

- data room inspection
- on-site inspection

The data room option is usually chosen when the decision to outsource is being kept secret from IT staff. Documentation and reports are placed in a secure location, often off site, and the service provider is given a set period in which to inspect the data and so inform themselves about the condition of the host company's environment. This method does have drawbacks. Chief amongst them is that the service provider has to rely on the host company's view of the environment. This may be incomplete or inaccurate. In the longer term, it puts the host company at a disadvantage as the service provider can argue they relied on the host company's (misleading) data.

On-site inspection puts the onus on the service provider to verify data first hand. This method has two major disadvantages. First, it may affect morale amongst IT staff. Second, it may take more time, as data may not have been collected and collated, as it should have been, as part of discovery.

Due diligence is not discovery

Due diligence should not be confused with discovery. The two processes have quite different aims: Discovery is the host company's process for establishing the entirety of its IT environment. Due diligence is the service provider's process for confirming the state of the environment they are about to contract to manage. Due diligence aims to reduce the risk of future controversy over existing performance measures or business output.

The material gathered during discovery forms an important ingredient of due diligence. However, discovery is not a substitute for due diligence. If the data room approach is taken, then the service provider places great reliance on materials provided by the host company. If this is the case, then the service provider must not rely blindly on the information, and must search for the enlightening discrepancies and anomalies that may (and usually do) exist. Another difference is that discovery is a process carried out by the host company alone, maybe with the help of independent experts, whereas due diligence should be a joint task, with both parties working to agree on a common view of the IT environment.

It is probable that some changes will have occurred in the status of the IT environment in the time between discovery and due diligence. Staff may have resigned, hardware may have been replaced, or new software may have been introduced into the mix. Both parties need to work together to ensure that they accept the common benchmarks.

The two processes also differ in duration: Discovery is usually less time-critical than due diligence. It may well drag on from project conception right up to the time that due diligence has to commence. Due diligence is usually time-bound. The host company's plans will often call for a limited period between advising the successful bidder and signing the contract. Due diligence will take place against a background of contract negotiation and a sense of urgency from both sides who wish to close off the project. The limits on time are pressured by the need to resolve conflicting views on data.

Morale issues may also exacerbate the process: Discovery often takes place in a more positive atmosphere than due diligence. Staff emotions tend to deteriorate as the process progresses. Due diligence is more likely to be undertaken in an atmosphere of fear uncertainty and doubt. At the time of due diligence, the service provider is known and the contract is imminent. Morale may well have plummeted. Don't let this be an excuse to rely too much on hope and to assume that more agreement exists than really is the case. Lacity and Hirschheim pointed out, "In some cases, these participants were placed in awkward positions—they assisted the outsourcing effort although outsourcing would eliminate their positions."[49] Staff may be resentful and distressed. Careless handling of the due diligence process will exacerbate the situation as the area comes under critical assessment from an outsider.

Due diligence is not discovery and should not be confused with it. Likewise, discovery is not a substitute for due diligence. It is important to do both and to do them right, even if they cover much of the same ground.

Scope of due diligence

Due diligence covers much of the same ground as discovery. Discovery may be the first time the company knows the true cost of IT, and realises for the first time what service they are getting. The difference is that in due diligence, the process is now focused on validating that discovery and resolving any anomalies.

Due diligence should inspect, review and confirm the following, at least. This list does not pretend to be complete. It does, however, serve to indicate the scope.

Human resources

- staff numbers, qualifications and experience
- staff employment contracts and status
- annual and sick leave entitlements
- corporate benefits
- fringe benefits, such as car leases, mortgage support or child care
- contracts with independent contractors
- shadow costs of IT absorbed through staff employed in business units

Software licences and agreements

- application licences, including maintenance and upgrades
- database management system licences
- utility, system and network tools and licences
- development and modelling tools and licences
- licence transfer fees, if applicable

Other licences and agreements

- disaster recovery
- telecommunications contracts

Hardware

- PCs and peripherals
- mid-range systems and peripherals
- mainframe equipment
- telecommunications equipment
- switches, hubs and routers

Non-IT assets

- mobile telephones
- pagers
- furnishings and fittings

The focus should be on those things that are critical to contract cost and execution. These are likely to be:

- benchmarks that are critical to achieving objectives;
- the quality and number of staff to be transferred to the outsourcer;
- unofficial IT expenses and staffing;
- procedures and documentation for operations and software maintenance;
- asset registry accuracy.

The review and confirmation process may well raise issues, including:

- benchmarks may vary from those taken in discovery;
- the service provider may make a different judgement about staff quality;
- there may well be asset mismatches;
- procedures and documentation may be lacking;
- reporting requirements may be little more than figments of the imagination;
- issues may arise over licence transfers;
- the service provider may uncover further unofficial IT expenses.

Benchmarks

The issue with benchmarks is that they may well have changed between the time they were taken and due diligence. IT is dynamic, and there may have been improvements in hardware or software in the interim. New applications may have been loaded that have slowed down the previous response and back-up times.

Staff may have reacted to the initial benchmarks and brought about internal improvements. The outsourcer may choose to measure a different milestone. The host company should not be surprised that these differences now exist. The goal of both parties is to accept the current benchmark. These differences do not devalue the work done in discovery. Many of the earlier measures will be unchanged. It also behoves the host company to have established its view of its environment before it canvasses service providers to provide management services.

Staff

The issue with staff quality is that the service provider may well come to the measure from a different perspective. Many service providers are, or have their foundations in, professional service companies, such as IBM, Andersen, EDS and CSC. These companies tend to set higher standards for recruitment (of IT people) than most businesses. The typical consultant will hold at least a first degree in an IT-related area, may have a second degree, and will be able to demonstrate considerable experience. Their judgement of what is a "top gun" may well differ from the judgement made by the host company. During an interview, Nick Kovari explained it thus:

> Medium-sized companies that outsource often have only PC/UNIX environments that are completely lacking in method and discipline. GartnerGroup describes them as being run by blue-collar programmers without the knowledge and disciplines of white collar professionally trained IT staff. The outsourcer has to bring white collar skills to bear and this costs money, but you can't fix the problem by hitting it with a hammer.

The staff issue may also be tinged with issues over staff attitude. In the normal course of events, people select their employers and vice versa. In an outsourcing deal, people are transferred to the outsourcer and, unless jobs are plentiful, without much option. The service provider will inherit a large tranche of staff, who may be hostile, unsuitable and from a completely different business culture.

The service provider may be prepared to accept only a limited dilution of their average competence and capability, and so will judge staff quality more sharply than the host company. A senior manager at one company, who wishes to remain anonymous, said:

> We thought we had top IT staff. The service provider graded them in the lower ranks of the food chain. Naturally, [the staff] were unhappy. But the truth was when we went over the job requirements with the service provider, they had much higher employment standards [for IT staff] than we did. It was a real problem as we had planned our cost model on equivalent salaries to ours, but the service provider argued that we'd paid peanuts, got monkeys, and that was why our IT was in a mess. I hate to say it now, but they were right.

At this point, it seems worth reiterating the view that the whole area of human resource (HR) evaluation and transfer is a potent political and legal nightmare. It cannot be stressed strongly enough that it is critical to place staff from both the host company and the service provider's HR units on the negotiation teams. Early and detailed discussion should have taken place with both the companies advisers on employment or industrial relations laws. In many outsourcing deals, the issues over HR transfers and redundancies have made the technical and financial difficulties pale into insignificance.

Assets

Asset mismatches are a common problem, but much less so for those companies that carry out a thorough discovery. Asset mismatches fall into two categories:

- New assets that were added to the environment in the period between discovery and due diligence. This may have been a period of many months, even years. It is not unusual for there to be significant change in an IT environment over such a time.
- The other and more pernicious mismatch is the discovery of equipment that does not appear in inventory records.

Tales abound of huge mismatches. One New Zealand company discovered 90 extra PCs—in a company that had a staff of 360. The count difference is shown in Table 10.1.

Table 10.1—Asset mismatches for a New Zealand company

Equipment	Discovery (host)	Due diligence (service provider)
Mid-range	(1) HP K series	(1) HP K series and (1) HP 8000
PCs	245	325
Laptops	4	15

This issue with hardware asset inventory is pernicious. The service provider will base help desk and operations staff counts on some ratio between hardware asset numbers and people. Typically for PCs, this will range around 1 : 50 staff to PCs. Getting the number wrong will create significant budget and service problems later.

Procedures

Procedures and documentation is another tricky area. The host company may well turn up a number of procedures manuals and (less likely) systems documentation. The service provider will focus on their currency and completeness. Sadly, they will find that the documents are out of date, incomplete or plain wrong. Old, established shops may feel they have limited need for documentation. Procedures are well ingrained in the minds of long-serving staff, and many of the original software developers may well be around. Manuals that do exist will often be a legacy of the past, a reminder of some post-audit flurry of good intentions that died as quickly as they were born.

Reports and documentation

Reporting is rarely as complete as the host company data may imply. Periodic status reports will have died because adhering to them was too time-consuming and labour-intensive. The host company may get an unpleasant surprise at the cost of reinstating the reports and meeting schedules.

The outsourcing process tends to break this nexus between staff and systems knowledge. Long-serving staff disappear, and the replacements are much more dependent on the documentation. The service provider will probably, and quite rightly, dispute the quality of documentation. The task of bringing the documentation up to date before the contract is signed may be exacerbated by the poor morale and reluctance of the current IT staff to participate in the exercise.

Surprise costs

We discussed the issue of detecting the whereabouts of all the existing software licences in the chapter on discovery. We also drew attention to the common and disturbing behaviour of vendors who suddenly seek large "transfer" fees for the licences, as they will now be under the care and control of the outsourcer. The problems need to be addressed now, and head on. If a vendor is going to slug someone for a hundred thousand dollars in the process, then now is the time to decide who will bear that cost. The service provider needs to make sure all licences and agreements have been discovered, and that the host company has written agreement from the vendor to permit the service company to operate the software.

The final and unfailing irritation will be what has variously been called feral, shadow or unofficial IT spending. It may be no more than a management subscription to GartnerGroup (which is not an insignificant sum). It may be the existence of a complete IT department at a remote site. The service provider needs to identify and nail down all these. The prudent provider will write the defined environment into the contract. Few things have a more disastrous impact on the costing and budget than the sudden discovery of hitherto hidden costs. GartnerGroup analysts point out that up to 16% of the average IT unit is externally sourced workers. These rarely appear on organisation charts or head-count figures. If a 100-person IT shop maintains this average, that is 16 extra salaries to be met in the outsourcing budget.

Organisation

The whole process may well be coloured by the degradation of the current IT environment. Staff morale tends to plummet. The current contingent will see the due diligence process as a witch hunt, with the staff as the victims. Self-esteem will fall as previously cherished achievements are belittled. The top guns amongst the host company's staff will find the outsourcer's staff are the centre of attention. It is not a happy time. Some quotes selected from Karpathiou and Tanner[50] illustrate the point:

"Staff fearful of management intentions, despite assurances and past trust."

"Staff were jealous when they saw positions filled by outside staff."

"Staff await redundancy payments."

This demoralisation is likely to make itself apparent in a number of ways:

- Drop in productivity as staff spend time worrying over perceived threats.
- Decline in staff availability as they start to clock-watch and take days off.
- Careless work that manifests itself in poor software and missed procedures.
- Obstructionism as staff seek to protect knowledge and skills.
- Union involvement over comparatively minor issues.
- Business reactions as some feel their colleagues are being sold into slavery.

Additional problems that might arise include:

- confused lines of responsibility;
- additional cost as IT staff are drawn into the due diligence process;
- logistical issues in providing data and work space for the due diligence teams.

Lines of responsibility may get confused. The service provider's staff may be premature in giving direction or making demands on the host company's staff. They must remember that the contract is not signed yet and they are not yet in charge. Costs may rise as existing IT staff may be expected to help the service provider quarry for information. This will distract them from their daily routines and may thus lead to problems with workload and focus.

Logistical issues arise because the service provider will usually need to position its team in the host company's IT area. Few companies have an abundance of spare offices and workstations. You must think about this issue. The due diligence team may be as many as 10 in number for even a small contract.

Other benefits

The due diligence period provides a significant opportunity to involve the business as a whole in the coming contract agreement details before they are fait accompli. The business can participate in agreeing the performance measures at the outset. Now is the time to refine and agree with the business on:

- performance measures for service level agreements;
- management processes for project and expense approval;
- schedules and contents of reports and meetings.

Due diligence can also bring about a healthier appreciation of the current condition of IT, and can help manage business expectations of improvement.

Managing the process

First, ensure that the parties enter an interim agreement under which the preferred candidate will carry out due diligence. The host company and service provider working in unison should confirm the baseline. Some useful steps that can be taken include:

- Prepare a communication plan that covers host company staff, service provider, vendor and other involved parties, e.g. lawyers and auditors.
- Define the aims of due diligence clearly, and publish them so staff in the IT unit and the business as a whole are aware of the aims of the process.
- Develop a work plan for the period, outlining sequence, tasks, resources, timing and deliverables from each phase.

- Assign a person from each of the service provider's and the host company's HR units to undertake appropriate HR due diligence during this period.
- Agree a system of arbitration to cover disagreements about the accuracy or content of information or matters unearthed during due diligence.
- Agree the supply and logistics required supporting the due diligence period. This should cover offices, workstations, PCs, telephones, documents, security etc.

This list is a minimum. What else is done depends on the scope and nature of the outsourcing agreement. However, the behaviour between the two parties at this stage will set the tone for the contract and management of the agreement.

The following sections show some steps that can help ameliorate some of the problems that often arise during due diligence.

Project team

The service provider should allocate four disciplines to the due diligence team:

- *Project manager* to plan and oversee the task.
- *Auditor* to track and identify business assets and information.
- *Librarian* or records manager to organise and index the discovered material.
- *Performance measurement consultant* to carry out an independent assessment of the current measures of performance.

The due diligence process belongs to the service provider. This is the service provider's opportunity to validate the details of the environment for themselves, and satisfy themselves that they can deliver what they will be contracted to do. Nevertheless, the host company may wish to allocate a similar shadow group to support the service provider in their task.

Full cooperation and support should be given to the service provider's team in this process. The failure of the host company and service provider to agree on the status of the current environment before entering a contract is the Achilles heel of many outsourcing agreements.

It is important that the service provider respects this trust and is open about what is unearthed. The service provider's team will have their focus on unearthing "black holes". They may also discover "nuggets", i.e. opportunities to make windfall profit on aspects of the contract. These must also be shared if the future agreement is to be one of mutual trust.

The standards of behaviour shown by both parties during due diligence will set the tone for the contract and the success of the coming contract. Crucial to the swift execution of the project is a well-organised library, which should have been developed through discovery. Well-organised and indexed information can save countless weeks of searching and confusion over document versions and completeness.

Interim management

One company took an unusual but useful approach to the due diligence process. They entered a short-term interim management agreement with the service provider. Under the terms of the three-month contract, the service provider had to provide five essential managers to partner with existing IT staff. The service provider's staff were essentially there to learn the environment first hand. They participated in all meetings, planning and discussion, and while they could make recommendations, they could not make decisions or commitments. The strengths of this approach were:

- The service provider obtained intimate knowledge of the true state of IT.
- The service provider had the opportunity to observe many of the day-to-day interactions between IT and the business.
- The service provider was better able to judge the actual competence of employees.
- The service provider was able to gather due diligence information.
- The service provider was paid for due diligence and therefore had the opportunity to do it properly rather than trying to reduce it to minimal time and cost.
- The host company got to measure the competence of the service provider.
- The host company staff got to know future colleagues and company.
- The transition at the end of the process was less traumatic.

The weaknesses of the approach include:

- Initial hostility and suspicion amongst host company staff.
- Fear that staff being "understudied" were earmarked for extinction.
- Cost to the host company that had two "management payrolls" over the period.
- Service provider staff not concentrating sufficiently on the raw hard data, and basing judgements on day-to-day happenings in a now artificial environment.

Nevertheless, the model has virtue and should be considered where the stakes are high and a honeymoon period may allow both sides an honest judgement of reality.

Closing thoughts

The failure of the host company and service provider to agree on the status of the current environment before entering a contract is the death of many outsourcing agreements. The situation will be exacerbated if the contract sets out performance targets with incorrect data about current levels of performance, regardless of whether those measures are better or worse.

One of the great, if initially painful, benefits of discovery and due diligence is that previously hidden costs become visible. It is better to know what the real costs and processes are, and what the cost of achieving the target delivery will be, before signing the contract.

Due diligence is probably the single greatest insurance against entering into a contract based on misconception and myth. The dangers of doing so are real. The host company also gets a valuable opportunity to size up the service provider's capacity and capability. This insight can be used to protect against actual weaknesses that were not evident in the RFP, or alternatively build on hidden strengths. Finally, the host company may learn much about its own IT that will be of value.

The host company cannot be too cautious in ensuring that the service provider carries out a thorough due diligence. It is in the host company's interest to see that all issues and concerns are removed at this stage. The host company can be sure that any remodelling post-contract will be driven by Murphy's Law and will be to the detriment of the host company.

Checklist

1. Does the due diligence team hold the appropriate skills for the task?
2. Have steps been taken to manage and index the documentation?
3. Has the IT unit been informed of the process and the need for cooperation?
4. Have the appropriate business staff been advised of specific needs, e.g. HR, finance, audit?
5. Have business units been advised of the need to be open about any IT arrangements that may lie outside the normal IT budget?

6.   Have steps been taken to control decline in morale during the period?
7.   Have staff been advised of any interim changes to reporting and responsibility?
8.   Have key staff, including non-IT department staff, been "back-filled" so they may give adequate attention to due diligence tasks?
9.   Are arrangements in place to handle due diligence questions from the bidder?
10. Has a dispute process been agreed for resolving differences of opinion on findings?
11. Has all discovery documentation (if available) been indexed and made available to the bidder?
12. Is there an agreed process for signing off due diligence and acknowledging completion?

Outsourcing and mergers: BP

Following the merger of BP and Amoco Corporation in 1999, there was a need to harmonise business processes across the merged organisation. Both BP and Amoco realised that rapid and decisive action to align the two companies and eliminate overheads would be key in meeting stakeholders' expectations and vision of global success.

The situation

The strategy for the outsourcing of non-core services, such as telecommunications, had to be addressed rapidly. BP launched the Telecommunications Outsourcing Project (TOP) to place all of the merged organisation's core managed telecommunications services under the control of a single entity.

The vision of BP's Group Telecommunications Director was to drive towards unit-priced services, with each business unit paying only for what it uses. The cost control levers would be in the hands of business units, who would be able to understand immediately the relationship between their demand and their costs.

The solution—innovation in supplier selection

TOP began when a small, core team from BP launched a request for information to 36 of the world's leading telecommunications and IT service organisations. BP partnered with a major consulting group to complete a rapid and innovative competitive selection process. Following some hard bargaining, a global service agreement between BP and MCI WorldCom was signed to cover all core managed telecommunications services for BP around the world.

It was obvious from the beginning that the traditional supplier selection process would be too slow to meet the needs and expectations of BP's senior management. Realising that they would have to shave four to six months off the timescales without sacrificing quality and the necessary legal process, BP and consulting team took the elements of the traditional request for proposal process, and worked them in parallel and in reverse.

Following reference site visits in each continent and in-depth technical and commercial work-shops, the short-listed suppliers provided written proposals. These provided a summary and confirmation of the ground already explored in depth in both supplier and client workshops. The process was intensive and thorough, but by reaching a conclusion quickly, weeks or even months of uncertainty were avoided.

There was a high degree of business involvement in the process, as the core team solicited views and tested its conclusions with representatives from BP's four major business streams. The methodology used to score the suppliers and analyse their strengths and weaknesses allowed the team's conclusions to be readily shared and understood.

Striking the deal—external negotiation, and internal selling

Having been authorised by BP to proceed, the TOP programme manager re-shaped the team to address the demands of contract negotiation. BP involved fully the consulting group in the negotiations, seeking their advice on negotiation strategy and using them to facilitate the negotiation sessions.

Recognising that the deal would need the full support of BP's business units, the consultants also worked with BP on a communications programme to sell the benefits. This involved presenting the details of the programme to the business community, thus ensuring that they understood clearly the business benefits and impact of the arrangement.

To establish the extent of the financial benefits, the consulting group prepared a model of all baseline costs to analyse the impact of MCI WorldCom's pricing. The challenge for MCI WorldCom's team lay in gathering and assimilating due diligence information about 1600 locations in 85 countries.

On 30 November 1999, BP Amoco and MCI WorldCom were able to announce that they had signed a global service agreement.

Delivering far-reaching benefits to BP

Thanks to both the ongoing rationalisation work and the TOP deal, BP has reduced its overall group telecommunications running costs by almost 50% or some $100 million per annum. The team was also to show that unit telecommunications costs would fall in every country, gaining universal business support for the outsourcing deal.

Another financial benefit to BP is that its contracting arrangements, and associated overhead costs, will be reduced greatly. Previously, BP's procurement information system listed over 1000 suppliers of telecommunications products and services around the globe. The TOP deal results in just one major global partner, who will absorb or manage the many hundreds of existing contracts allowing extra savings from the streamlining of procurement arrangements. Use of a global consulting group was key in striking this innovative contractual arrangement, which is on the leading edge of outsourcing.

Case Study reprinted by kind permission of PA Consulting Group.

11 Forming the contract

Halvey and Melby wrote: "Given the wide variety of business issues and the many legal [and other] disciplines which are involved in even the simplest form of outsourcing contract, it should come as no surprise that one of the most difficult, if not the most difficult, stages of an outsourcing transaction is the drafting and negotiation stage of the agreement."[51]

The task will certainly be made simpler if the host company and service provider are well prepared for the task. Preparation will include:

- defining the scope of the contract
- discovery
- due diligence
- position paper preparation
- agreement on protocols and schedules
- dispute resolution process
- assigning the appropriate skills

The contract, after all, will be the only enduring record of the agreement between the service provider and the host company. Those without a legal background may be surprised to discover that the courts in many countries will usually not accept background documents or verbal representations as evidence. In fact, many contracts will explicitly exclude any representations from the scope of the contract, thereby limiting any evidence on agreements during a dispute to the contents of the contract.

Yet the host company and the service provider must toe a line between an overly specific contract and one that allows sufficient flexibility to accommodate changed environments and objectives. PA Consulting Group note:

> To be successful, an outsourcing contract must be sufficiently "tight" to protect both parties from operational and commercial risks that may result, yet at the same time be flexible enough to enable changes to be made to the scope of services provided, the service levels to be achieved, or the base upon which the charges are to be applied (including the payment of performance related bonuses or penalties).

In addition, a well-defined change management process is an important component of a good contract. The change management process should allow appropriately authorised staff to propose and manage contract change.

It should also come as no surprise to now find a recommendation that the host company be quite clear *in the contract* on its objectives for outsourcing, and that the contract is framed to achieve those objectives.

The host company should avoid any temptation to adopt the service provider's "standard contract" as the solution. Halvey and Melby state correctly: "One of the fundamental truths about the outsourcing industry: the standard form [supplied by the vendor] is invariably inadequate from the customer's perspective."[52]

The contract must reflect the host company's needs, business goals and objectives. It is tempting and easy to run with the service provider's standard, but this leaves the business open to the following dangers:

- Weaker negotiation stance as the service provider enters the negotiation phase from a position of power with a well-understood document framed to their own needs.
- The definition of the contract commences from the wrong angle and the wrong frame of mind. Instead of framing it to their needs, the host company may only seek out items that are contrary to their goals. Removing objectionable clauses is a very different process to that of stating corporate requirements.
- The process of negotiation over a pro forma contract is unlikely to explore the intentions and constraints that are embedded in the wording. This may lead to unpleasant surprises when disputes arise over issues, and the parties find themselves poles apart on interpretation.
- There will be little if any back-up material to the contract that shows how it was formed and what issues were debated and discussed. This absence of material compounds the interpretation issues.
- The pro forma contract may not provide sufficient cover over the scope of the works undertaken. It is surprisingly easy to overlook some aspect of scope in contract negotiations.

Gay and Essinger[53] used an analogy that suggested allowing the service provider to draw up the contract was similar to asking a hungry crocodile to draw up its suggestions for the lunch menu and promising to go along with them.

In short, the contract must be crafted to the individual circumstances. Avoid using a standard contract. As with so many things in the outsourcing agreement process, time and effort expended on this issue at the start will pay itself back ten-fold over the life of the contract.

Objective

Vince Graham, Managing Director of the National Rail Corporation, Australia, made the point that "an outsourcing contract that is a technical specification is doomed to failure. The contract must be a performance based contract . . . because unless the contract is performance based you wind up managing the minutiae of the contract and achieve nothing . . . managing inputs is a waste of valuable executive time that could be better focused on managing the revenue side of the business."

This handbook repeatedly stresses the importance of defining the objectives for outsourcing and ensuring that the thread is clear and visible through all parts of the outsourcing transaction.

Klepper and Jones[54] suggest that the process of forming the contract should be to "design the relationship". I can think of no better slogan to underpin the process and the focus of contract development. The contract is, after all, a sound means for both companies to communicate their expectations and capabilities. While this communication will be made more granular and precise in the service level agreements, it must rely on the central pillar of the contract as its foundation.

The two parties should also give considerable thought to plans for disengagement. Contracts are not entered into in perpetuity. The contract must end at some time, possibly in aggrieved circumstances. Both parties should spend considerable time and effort taking into account the possible triggers for disengagement and the scenarios that surround the triggers. These triggers might include termination for non-performance by either the host company or the service provider, termination as a result of merger or acquisition, and termination without cause. These are discussed further in Chapter 17.

Now let us move on to the importance of critical success factors in forming an outsourcing contract.

Critical success factors

Critical success factors (CFSs) include:

- Assembling a team with appropriate skills and disciplines.
- Defining clearly the scope of the contract at the outset.
- Undertaking adequate discovery and due diligence to ensure both teams are well informed about the state of the current environment.
- A well-prepared position on key issues.
- A complete meeting protocol, including dispute resolution.
- A complete and agreed schedule and time to do the job properly.
- The composition and skills of the contract negotiation team

Skills

The first step is to assemble the contract team. The contract will often cover the full gamut of business function. A sound contract team would have the same make-up as the outsourcing team; indeed, preferably it should be a continuation of that team. The appropriate skills to include are:

- contract team leader (project manager)
- IT specialists
- human resources
- finance
- legal
- audit
- performance measurement consultants
- logistics.

Other skills, such as taxation or merger and acquisition specialists, may also be required if a joint venture or similar structure is envisaged.

Finally, find a legal firm that is highly experienced in outsourcing contract work. Lawyers, like doctors, tend to specialise in certain fields. The depth of specialisation has long since moved beyond commercial and criminal law to much finer specialisation, such as industrial relations, professional indemnity, tax, insurance and others. Seek and ye shall find good outsourcing contract lawyers. A good way to start is to ask other organisations. Ask them who they used, how satisfied they were, what was done well, what was done badly, how the lawyers handled the process, how successful they have been in avoiding disputes, and so on.

A good legal adviser will do much more than write your contract: he or she will:

- bring insight and advice to the table based on their experience at other sites;
- mentor the teams and ensure that they are well prepared for the negotiation table;
- introduce high-level negotiation skills to ensure the contract meets the organisation's needs;
- produce some lateral thinking and innovative means to overcome obstacles;
- draft a document that is readable and manageable;
- provide post-contract management advice to keep both parties out of the courts when disputes arise.

The legal adviser should be chosen with the same level of care as you might choose any other critical business partner. List the criteria, weigh them, ask two or three firms to write a short bid for your business based on the criteria, and then go through a careful selection process. This requirement applies equally to the service provider. Nick Kovari, formerly of CSC, made the point: "Organisations [host companies] are getting better at outsourcing contracts. They are hiring good lawyers and consultants. They are probably better at it than the novice service providers who are getting themselves screwed into a corner."

It is generally not a good idea to use the company's normal legal advisers unless they have demonstrated competence in this area and the parties are comfortable that they possess the appropriate experience or skills.

The other team member that may need to come from outside is the performance measurement specialist. There are few practitioners in this field, which requires considerable skill and experience. For this reason, it will be important to find and contract that resource well in advance of the contract negotiation period. Indeed, if the recommendations on discovery and due diligence have been followed as outlined in this book, the resource will already be on board.

The rest of the multiskilled team is usually sourced from within the business. The benefits of a multidisciplinary team include that cited by Nick Thornton, of PA Consulting Group: "Multi-disciplinary teams encourage re-examination of 'boilerplate' clauses that are often used by default and can prove hopelessly inappropriate to specific service applications."[55]

However, it is important that each individual's role is specified clearly. Vague role definition will lead to duplication and wasted effort in discovery and preparation; at worst, it will lead to a free-for-all during contract negotiations, and place the balance of power in the hands of the opposing team. The role each member will play in the negotiation process must also be defined clearly in the role definitions. An uncontrolled approach may divide the team and compromise key positions. Assign a chief negotiator and ensure that the person selected has the skills and training for the role.

It may also be useful to agree on a set of signals that can be used between team members, which can be used in the negotiation room to denote concern, disagreement or the need for a break to discuss an issue outside the room.

The team's first task will be to define the scope of the contract and, by implication, the discovery tasks, materials and requirement specification each team member will bring to the negotiating table. Each of these items is covered later in this chapter.

The host company may also need to consider "back-filling" the normal jobs of the team members. As a rough guide, the company should allow one day of preparation for every hour to be spent in contract negotiation. Team members cannot do their temporary role justice if they are engaged fully in normal day-to-day management.

Service providers are often better off in this regard. The flexible nature of consulting often provides the opportunity to assign people to a key task without the distraction of other work. Even if the service provider's team is working on multiple concurrent bids, they are at least working in circumstances that are conducive to contract negotiation. They are also more experienced in outsourcing contract negotiations—they do it more often.

Upskilling

> The principle cause of the power imbalance [between host company and service provider] is that the typical customer does not view negotiating the contract as part of the outsourcing process. Instead he or she merely regards the contract as a necessary evil. The vendor, on the other hand, regards the contract as the final stage in the sales cycle and its representatives are schooled in how to close the deal.[56]

To complicate matters, staff whose remuneration is dependent on winning the contract rather than on providing the service, may populate the service provider's team. I repeat an earlier warning by a senior executive in a service-providing organisation:

> The risk component of the negotiating team's remuneration is usually tied to the sales effort, so they are inclined to win the contract at any cost. The sales people don't have to live by the commitments they make on performance or budgets. The problem for host companies is that competition is so fierce that many outsourcers are making commitments knowing they can not be met, and relying on a combination of miracles and post-contract waivers to get them through.

This observation is, unfortunately, true. The host company can remedy the imbalance by ensuring it upskills its own team. This upskilling can be done using internal or external resources. Some appropriate options include:

- Give the key negotiators training in mediation and dispute resolution. The company's legal advisers may be able to supply details on public mediation courses.
- Give training in sales and negotiation. This may be available internally (most larger companies have access to internal or external resources that teach sound sales and negotiation methods).
- Introduce training on the law of contracts. This can be delivered by the organisation's legal department or by a public institution.

Training should commence as early as possible, preferably at the outset of the project. Contract negotiation is a professional process. It is not a game for enthusiastic amateurs. Do not rely on personal powers of persuasion.

A well-trained group will conduct discovery, RFP preparation, evaluation, due diligence and contract negotiation in a more focused manner, aim their information gathering and preparation at material matters, and limit the effort expended on peripheral issues.

Scope

The first task of the trained team is agreeing the framework of the contract or the content list. The output of this process should be a document that sets out clearly the areas the contract will cover, at least to headings and subheadings. For example, a section on human resources should cover at least remuneration, vacations, transfers, pension transfer, redundancy payments and sick leave. Ideally, the document will be accompanied by some initial position papers on key issues. Position papers are discussed later. These documents set out the organisation's opening position on key issues that have been identified either in the proposal evaluation process or from known positions of the preferred service provider.

Each contract will differ in its scope. Appendix C provides a reasonably comprehensive contract checklist. However, the following should provide an indication of the scope of an outsourcing contract.

- definitions
- objectives
- principles
- term
- current environment
- ongoing management (including principles)
- assets
- human resources
- scope of services
- performance
- document management and control (library)
- intellectual property
- payments
- taxes
- audits
- confidentiality
- contract change
- termination plan
- dispute resolution
- indemnities
- damages
- insurance
- publicity and advertising
- representations and warranties
- miscellaneous

Once the framework is agreed, then final discovery can commence. At this point, you should refer to Appendix B to get a flavour of the depth that may need to be covered on each topic. The scope of the termination plan is worthy of special mention. Contracts may be terminated for a number of reasons, including:

- expiration of the contract
- breach of contract
- special circumstances, e.g. merger or acquisition
- convenience

The first three examples are common to many contracts. Termination for convenience occurs when the service provider or host company decides that it no longer wishes to continue with the contract in circumstances where there is no clear breach or contractual issue. Both sides will normally agree to a penalty payment to be made to the party injured by the termination for convenience. This payment may be significant, given that it will be framed to cover the potential loss to the service provider.

Discovery

By the time the parties reach the contract stage in the process, they should have carried out a discovery and due diligence. At the risk of overstating the case, the contracting parties are urged to carry out a last cross-check of information gleaned during those two phases to ensure that they are well prepared for the contract negotiation. Human memory being what it is, things may well have been forgotten in the often long-drawn-out march to the contract table. A quick cross-check of the earlier material may well prove worthwhile.

The professional service provider will normally do their homework and revision very well. Their staff may have been freed from other duties to concentrate almost exclusively on informing themselves to win the contract, and so it should be. They may have gathered additional details on the host company's IT unit through a number of channels, for example:

- sales representatives or relationship manager's records of previous contacts
- company Web pages
- online databases
- news cuttings and magazine articles
- conference presentations
- contacts within the company, including its IT department.

If there are conflicting opinions or issues of fact in dispute, then these should be resolved now before the contract formation process commences. The contract formation process should not be used as an arena for point scoring. For this reason, it is important to review the findings of the discovery and due diligence material to ensure that it is agreed and complete.

The review process is quite simple, and is based on filling knowledge gaps that may have become evident, either from information gaps that appeared during the RFP proposal evaluation phase or from reviewing the contract scope against the discovery information library.

It would be unusual for both the host company and service provider to have covered the discovery and due diligence processes so completely that there were no gaps or differences in each party's information base of the area to be outsourced.

It is at this time that contract discovery often uncovers new issues, such as:

- company precedents on damages, insurance or indemnities;
- human resource issues that were missed in the first instance;
- shifts in the outsourcing framework, as the host company becomes more aware of industry developments.

Information is power. The discovery and due diligence exercises inform a substantial part of the operative sections of the contract, especially the performance standards or service level agreements, as well as the final pricing model. The earlier discovery (Chapter 4) should have provided most of the information required for the contract, including existing contracts, staffing and remuneration, infrastructure, procurement and management processes. However, it is probable that some time will be required for the project team to sweep up loose ends that have risen to prominence during the later stages of the project.

The review process may be triggered by an enlarged scope or the need to determine company precedence or preferences on the more esoteric aspects of the contract, for example in the indemnity, security, confidentially or damages sections of the contract.

To go to the negotiating table without complete knowledge and understanding of the IT environment is negligent. Halvey and Melby draw attention to the fact: "It is not uncommon for the vendor to know more about the customer's IT department than the customer, thereby giving the vendor the upper hand."[57]

One of the common oversights in discovery is overlooking ancillary costs of the IT unit, such as training (HR budget), office services (corporate services budget), telecommunications (telephone budget), finance and administration costs.

Preparation

The final stage before entering the negotiating room is to ensure that the process management components are in order. These components are:

- position papers
- meeting protocols

- requirement definitions
- dispute resolution
- contract work schedule

Position papers

Position papers set out the organisation's position on key issues. These issues will have surfaced during the evaluation of RFP responses and during the due diligence phase. Typically, the host company and the service provider will find they have differences of opinion on some of the following issues:

- intellectual property
- indemnities
- Damages—direct and consequential
- remedial action for performance failures
- pricing

There is nothing in the outsourcing process that will provide more return for effort than preparing position papers. This applies equally to both host company and service provider.

A well-formed position paper is, in many ways, similar in format to a principle (see Chapter 6). Figure 11.1 shows an example of a position paper prepared by the host company.

The benefits of position papers are that they help to ensure that:

- the issue has been considered before it gets to the table, and the underlying rationale has been defined;
- the more obvious options have been identified and the implications of accepting them considered;
- consideration has been given to the fall-back position[d] so the chief negotiator is aware of the offsets that are acceptable;
- a record exists should disputes arise in the future over any contract provisions. While these may not be admissible in court, they certainly can sway the majority of negotiations, which, fortunately, never enter the courthouse.

Nothing is more devastating to a negotiation position than the all too familiar sight of the team arguing amongst itself over its position on a key issue in front of their opposing numbers.

---

[d] Students of mediation techniques may recall this as BATNA—best alternative to a negotiated agreement.

Position Paper: Highly Confidential.
1. Issue Service provider limits direct damages to US$1.0m and consequential damages to US$500 000.
2. Issue rating 2.1 Risk/consequence matrix: risk low/consequence high. 2.2 Issue criticality: Level 3 (highly desirable but not critical).
3. Options for dealing with the issue 3.1 Accept the limitation. 3.2 Accept the limitation provided consequential damages are lifted to US$1.0m. 3.3 Request an increase in direct damages to US$1.5m and forego consequential damages.
4. Preferred outcome 3.3 (increase to US$1.5 and forego consequential damages).
5. Reasoning Consequential damage is difficult to prove and probably unenforceable.
6. Implications If we have to accept alternative(s): e.g. If 3.1, then we accept a limit lower than other similar-sized customers have obtained. If 3.2, then we achieve coverage equal to the best the service provider has given. If 3.3, then we gain on direct damages, which are simpler to prove and more valuable to our business.

7. Trade-offs
Possible trade-off issues are:
    • Clause 3.7 Damages on termination for no cause. Position paper 17
    • Clause 7.2 Guarantee payment in escrow. Position Paper 24

Issue Owner Rob Aalders
Circulation SP, DS, BB

Figure 11.1—Example of a Positioning Paper

A sound method for developing and refining position papers is to use the workshop review process:

- The owner prepares the position papers. Typically, this is the person whose business unit is most affected by the issue, for example HR normally prepare position papers on staff issues in the contract.
- The position papers are circulated to the team, who are asked to review and particularly consider whether the position on the issue effects them, the risk and criticality rating, and whether they can offer alternative or better trade-in positions.
- The negotiating team then meets and reviews the issues, refines them and approves them as a group. The negotiating team review *must* include a review by legal advisers. They then pass to the lead negotiator, who incorporates them into the portfolio.

In some instances, it may be useful to give certain position papers to the opposing side in advance of the meeting. This gives them time to consider their responses, and either articulate their position more clearly or offer useful alternatives.

Few tasks in the contract negotiation phase offer so much lasting value for so little effort as the use of position papers.

Protocol definition

A number of good texts exist on managing meetings, and this handbook will not usurp them or repeat their contents. If the team is not familiar with efficient meeting management and protocols, then they would be well advised to consult a bookstore or good library.

However, both parties must still agree in advance to sound meeting protocols. Some specific inclusions are:

- *Maintenance of a circulation matrix* showing each person's name; and the documents issued to them and when (Table 11.1).

Table 11.1—Example of a circulation matrix

	Tom	Sue	Ahmed	Bardhold	Chun Wa	John
P- Paper 1,2	26/1	26/1	–	–	–	26/1
Agenda	30/1	30/1	30.1	Leave	30/1	30/1
Minutes	03/2	04/2	03/2	Leave	04/2	04/2

- *Agreement on reference numbering for all documents.* Typically, this will be associated with the clause in the contract.
- *Agreement on calling breaks.* During negotiation sessions, parties may wish to separate to consider issues and regroup. The protocol for calling breaks should be agreed in advance.
- *Agreement on location and provision of facilities* to the negotiating teams. Typically, this will require a meeting room and two break-out rooms. Both parties tend to bring a substantial amount of material to the main meeting room, and neither party will wish to vacate the room leaving the other party with access to their materials.
- *Agreement on circulation of material* and expectations on pre-reading before meetings. There are few more frustrating things than to receive a 50-page document 10 minutes before a meeting, or to sit in a meeting while someone reads through a document that was circulated 10 days previously.
- *Agreement on dispute resolution.* Both parties should be empowered to make appropriate decisions at the table. However, it is inevitable that some issues will arise that require resolution at another place, for example by the CEOs or boards of the two companies. The process for classifying this level of dispute and the framework for escalation must be agreed in advance. Failure to do so is likely to lead to unnecessary ill feeling if one party feels the other is always seeking outside approval on minor issues.
- *Agreement on a minute keeper.* This may be best done by inviting a neutral third party to maintain the minutes. The cost will soon be offset by the speed with which agreement is reached on the accuracy and content of the minutes. A bipartisan secretary is a necessary adjunct to successful negotiation. It is also useful to agree on the content and form of minutes. Will it be a comprehensive record of discussions or will they merely record decisions and action points arising?
- *Agreement on impasses.* There is little value gained in endless point scoring debate at the table. Ask each party to return to the next session with a position paper on the issue. Included in the appendices are some tools to help in this process. These include a content checklist, requirement state-ment (next section), a position paper pro forma, and a contract change control form.

Standard meeting agreements on agendas, meeting objectives, timing, chair-personship and politeness (interruptions and interjections, filibustering, etc.) should preferably be included in a briefing pack for all participants on both sides.

In closing this section, I would like to emphasise the value of stating *why* a particular contract meeting is being held. Too often, parties come to a meeting without a clear understanding of the aim of the meeting. Meetings should not be held to discuss issues; they should be held to resolve issues or deliver outputs. Define the objective of the meeting as the first entry on the agenda.

Requirement statements

The penultimate part of preparation for contract negotiation is to prepare require-ment statements for each contract clause. Halvey and Melby[58] remark that while no IT manager would undertake a systems development project without an ade-quate statement of user requirements, the same IT manager expects a lawyer to draft a contract without any statement of requirements.

Each business must clearly state their precise needs and aspirations for every clause in the contract. These should be drafted in plain English as statements of requirement. The lawyers can then turn them into appropriate legalese. This ap-proach should be familiar to IT professionals. They should be used to drafting user requirements while the IT team code the program. There is a strong parallel in a business stating its contract requirements and lawyers "coding" the contract.

However, it is rare for business teams to provide clear statements of requirement to their legal teams. Too often, the contract is developed without due consider-ation or based on vaguely stated needs that are voiced during the negotiation phase. An extract from a requirement statement for the host company is shown in Figure 11.2. Appendix E illustrates a pro forma requirement statement.

Clause: 7.1.2 Human Resources – Liability for Sick Leave
Xylog will have an actuary calculate the proportion of accumulated sick leave that is likely to be realised and pay this to the service provider as a lump sum. After that we will accept no liability for sick leave for any staff who are transferred to the service provider's payroll.
Owner: Rob Aalders **Date:** 12 Aug 2000 **Cross-reference:** Position Paper 32

Figure 11.2—Extract from a requirement statement

A requirement statement should be prepared for every clause in the contract. As with the position papers (which are reserved for issues) requirement statements bring benefits:

- Consideration by the business team of every clause in the contract.
- Clear direction to the legal team on the intent of the clause to aid them in drafting.
- A supportive plain-English interpretation of the clause to aid all participants to understand what is often an obtuse document.
- Clear thinking and appreciation by both sides in the negotiation on what the clause and contract are all about.

Requirement statements, like position papers, should be carefully indexed and filed within the outsourcing document management system or library, to support future interpretations or understanding of the aims held by the original contract team.

Those unfamiliar with the limitations of contracts may be surprised at the extent to which the parties will dispute the intent of a particular clause four or five years after the contract was signed. Requirement statements can pay dividends that well exceed the effort expended on preparing them.

Schedules

There is no doubt that a long drawn-out contract negotiation process is destructive. It has a negative effect on:

- contract team focus and energy
- employee morale on both sides
- productivity
- confidence in the process.

The things that help keep the window of negotiation short are those things outlined in this chapter: an appropriately skilled team, proper project role descriptions, adequate discovery and due diligence, well-considered position papers, clear requirement statements, sound meeting protocols, and lastly, a schedule.

Without a schedule, the contract negotiation phase will take as long as it takes. Many contract negotiations have dragged on for a year or more, severely damaging the existing IT department's morale and composition, and the company's overall productivity. Graham Bull of Telstra spoke of how on one project he was involved in "six weeks to write the contract became four months".

There is no magic to developing the schedule. However, it does require something better than a list of dates plucked from the air. IT managers are all too familiar with the unpleasant kick-back of project schedules based on a hopeful guess. The process is not straightforward, so the organisation should ensure it uses an expert in project planning to undertake this task. The expert will need at least the following information.

- A list of all the tasks that need to be undertaken by *both* parties.
- An indication of any dependencies between tasks, e.g. contract signing must be preceded by 80% staff acceptance of transfer offer.
- A list of the resources from both parties available and their availability preferably expressed in hours per day.

- Vacation schedules for the above staff if appropriate.
- An estimation of the duration of each task by both parties.
- An estimation of the effort required for each task by both parties.
- Any deadlines that have been (arbitrarily) set or are driven by tax or other financial implications.

An expert planner will work with both parties to develop a schedule, taking into account slack and float times, dependencies, resource availability and contingencies. This is the same approach recommended at the outset of the outsourcing project—plan and then execute the plan. This is a subproject within the overall plan. It updates the master plan drawn up at the outset of the project, and it is by its nature based on best guess for most of its tasks. John McNally spoke of the dangers:

> Driving the project, which is full of unknowns, to a strict imposed deadline is dangerous. The rush to the end will see things put aside to be fixed "after the contract is signed". You may be encouraged to do this by the service provider's team which is made up of people whose speciality is getting you to sign. Things that are to be fixed "after the contract is signed" are, in retrospect, the difficult and tricky stuff and it will come back to haunt you.

Tips

This section passes on some hard-won experience from earlier participants in outsourcing agreements. The tips are few but important:

- Remember contracts often need to be changed. Define a contract change protocol within the contract.
- Don't overlook the right of the host company to arrange professional audits of the provider's service, including disaster recovery, security, change control, and control processes, as well as the obvious issues of value for money and quality of service provision.
- Ensure the objectives of outsourcing are stated within the contract, and that the detail of the contract supports those objectives.
- Do not seek to overpunish the service provider for failure. This is further discussed in Chapter 14. In fact, the courts may void a punitive contract.
- Do define what you mean by "failure" to perform on a given measure; define it to cover both major instances and a cumulative set of minor instances that are damaging to the company.
- Put as much effort into considering termination scenarios as is put into the start of the contract.

- Remember that "representations" made outside the contract are not enforceable.
- Protect confidentiality of trade secrets and financial positions
- Focus on business outputs as a measure, not on controlling inputs
- Keep the negotiation sessions to two hours or less and break at least every 45 minutes. Research suggests that few people can concentrate effectively on one subject for more than 45 minutes, and boredom and fatigue lead to capitulation and mistakes.
- Preparation, preparation and preparation are the three cues for success.
- Get yourself a good lawyer.

The next chapter deals with service level agreements. Although essentially these form part of the discussion on contracts, with all the same rules applying to discovery, issue statements, requirement statements and protocols, the scope of discussion is so wide that the two topics are separate from each other.

Conclusion

A wide range of skills and a well-managed process are the two major requirements for developing a sound contract. Give yourselves the time to do the job correctly and be aware of the danger of putting matters aside.

Remember the words of Jill Klein (Riggs Bank, USA), who expressed the view that contract success lies in "knowing what really matters to your company. Winning every point is not your objective. You want to win those that truly matter."[59]

Finally, be prepared to walk away from the deal if you cannot structure what you want. Don't fall into the trap of entering into an agreement just because you have put a lot of work into getting to the negotiating table.

Checklist

The list below is not comprehensive.

1. Have you defined contract negotiation roles for each participant?
2. Have you prepared a contract contents list?
3. Have you prepared a statement of requirements under each heading?

4. Have you prepared position papers on key issues.
5. Is your chief negotiator a qualified mediation expert?
6. Have the other members of the team been adequately briefed on their roles?
7. Have you assigned a bipartisan minute keeper to the team?
8. Have you defined meeting protocols?
9. Do the protocols include impasse management and dispute resolution?
10. Has a set of signals been agreed for use in the negotiating room?
11. Do you have a schedule for contract development? (The process may last weeks. Setting specific meeting dates in advance should help ensure that appropriate staff are available to attend.)
12. Have contract dependencies been considered?
13. Is your legal adviser an expert in outsourcing contract development?
14. Have you included the principles as a schedule to the contract?
15. Have you defined terms and words in the contract?
16. Have you included objectives in the contract?
17. Have you included human resources, transfers and redundancy agreements?
18. Have you defined the human resources, qualifications, skills, and levels of experience required?
19. Have you set site staffing, base number, additions and subtractions, and removal rights?
20. Have you agreed on dispute management negotiation and jurisdiction?
21. Have you specified cost models, base costs, annual increases, audits and reviews?
22. Has consideration been given to acquisitions and mergers, contract transfers and assignments?
23. Has consideration been given to the often prickly question of limitations on advertising, publicity and press releases?
24. Has consideration been given to terminating the contract one day (see Chapter 17) and the possible triggers for this, i.e. convenience, breach, expiration or special circumstances?
25. Has consideration been given to the complications of turn back of software licences and third-party or subcontract agreements, which may be held between the service provider and software vendor?

Observations from the field: a line manager's view

You can outsource practically anything these days, and many organisations have been doing just that. Reception and security, kitchens, stationery and records management, mail handling, vehicle fleet management, travel, recruiting, or all of HR— the list goes on.

Errors and omissions

There is a bit more involved in performance management than just quantifying service requirements. This is particularly so in the early stages, when the partnership is settling in and the service supplier learning exactly what was meant by all those criteria and specifications. This must be an ongoing process, checking periodically not only on what the supplier has done, but on what they may not have done. Is there a report they did not send? Are there processes they did not run, or files they did not archive? Monitoring at this level takes time, a well-thought out strategy, and skill— the host company cannot afford complacency because the partnership is in place.

Informal communications

There also have to be mechanisms to include the service provider in the corporate grapevine. The service provider tends not to pick up informal information in the lifts or canteen, especially if they are not in the same building. So, you suddenly find that they are not aware there is a corporate restructure underway. Or they may have just signed $100 000 of annual subscription renewals for online databases that relate to a part of the business that is about to be sold off. The host company needs someone on their staff whose job is to feed that information to the service provider.

Hostage clauses

Any host company that off-handedly signs a supplier's standard contract deserves what they get at termination. Hostage clauses and pricing strategies are there because service providers rightly need to protect what can be a significant capital investment, in learning, staff and IT systems. However, it does neither party any good for hostage clauses or prices to emerge only at termination. Discuss them openly when negotiating the contract, and don't forget to allow for takeovers of either party.

Outsourcing these sorts of functions can work well, provided the host company knows why they are outsourcing and both parties take the time and effort to establish a well-defined and monitored partnership, with realistic, practical provisions for termination.

Glenn Sanders
Director, Sanders Information Management Services

12 Defining service level agreements

Introduction

According to a spokesperson for PA Consulting Group, "Service level management is the regular, systematic review of [service provider] performance against pre-defined service level targets."[60] This systematic review is difficult to achieve in practice and, in many respects, the most difficult to define. Few companies would claim to have developed perfect service level agreements (SLAs), measurement systems or remedial actions.

To complicate matters further, different outsourcing deals require different measures and corrective actions. This complexity is then overlaid with the structure under which the service is provided, e.g. arm's length, joint venture, best-of-breed, prime contractor, and the pricing model adopted under the agreement. This problem may be aggravated by the parties differing motivations, e.g. "If the service provider views success as revenue growth from your account, then there is no incentive for them to introduce efficiencies."

This chapter covers a number of practices that together should improve the parties' chances of getting it right. It suggests that you:

- scope the service level agreements
- set the measures
- agree reporting on measures
- define remedial or corrective action
- institute a change management process
- agree how issues will be managed.

The process of determining service level agreements should start at discovery, be refined during due diligence, and have reached a good degree of stability by the time contract negotiations start. Be mindful of the advice given by John McNally of VicRoads: "Catalogue all in-house services and assess how well each of these is delivered . . . understand the cost of these services."

Assessing and agreeing the current performance levels will often prove tricky and debatable. The host company may measure on one basis, the service provider on another. For example, the in-house systems development often lacks the methodical approach expected from a service provider. Host company measurements may be based on producing the output in a laissez-faire environment where limited time and effort are expended on documentation, change control or formal design.

Nevertheless, both parties need to accept the outputs to be measured, and their current baseline, before any meaningful discussion can take place on future targets. SLAs are, after all, critical to the service provider in informing them about the expected outcomes of the contract they are entering into.

Scoping the service level agreements

Experienced host companies are increasingly shifting to the view that the focus of SLAs should be on measuring a few essential business outputs. This evolution has taken place for a number of reasons, including:

- the realisation that the host company can compromise its position by dictating inputs to the service provider. The service provider cannot be held to account for failures in which the host company dictated the quality, quantity and management of the inputs;
- the growing appreciation that managing the inputs consumes a disproportionate amount of host company resources and is, in many ways, tantamount to managing the outsourced unit;
- the number and variety of inputs usually far exceeds the number of outputs. Experienced host companies now understand that if a few key business outputs meet performance criteria, then by inference the inputs are of proper quantity and quality;
- by focusing on business outputs, the business can concentrate on the "real" business rather than covertly managing an outsourced IT function.

To quote Vince Graham, Managing Director of National Rail Corporation:

> Success lies not in managing inputs. Success lies in delivering outputs, in our case service quality, cost-reduction and safe-performance . . . and unless the outsource agreement is performance driven you manage the minutiae of the contract and achieve nothing.

Graham goes on to observe, "Even if outsourcing is more expensive than an in-house operation it can still be worthwhile as it allows management to concentrate on revenue side changes."

Gay and Essinger reiterate this: "Organisations are more likely to meet their commercial objectives and maximise their success if they direct management control not so much towards controlling inputs, but rather towards focusing on the finished output."[61]

The scope of the SLAs should be those business outputs that contribute to business goals and objectives. It should be possible to trace a long unbroken thread from the business goals, through the selection process, and finally to the SLAs.

Charge the team tasked with developing the SLAs to ask the business users what they think are the important outputs. IT is poor at double-guessing the business, and frequently selects the wrong outputs.

There is virtue in isolating SLAs to measure those 7 ± 2 things that matter most to the business. It will not be easy to limit the SLAs. At the outset of the contract, there will be a large number of candidate areas for improvement. The one that often gets the greatest attention, but wrongly so, is the IT shop itself. SLAs may be set for internal IT processes that are no longer the direct concern of the business. The management of performance within the outsourced unit is the business of the outsourcer. The host company's concerns should be that the outputs are of appropriate quality and cost.

Here are some checks that can ensure that the candidate pool of SLAs is appropriate:

- Review the business goals and check they are linked to the outsourcing agreement. These should point towards the objectives and, by implication, the key performance measures.
- Decompose the objectives, seeking an important process or function that can be measured easily.
- Question the rationale for measuring each proposed item. This should separate the nice-to-know from the things that matter. Some further questions for testing the rationale appear in the next section.

To those that find the idea of a small number of SLAs challenging, consider an analogy with a car. The concern of most people is that the car works when they wish to use it. Some basic instruments give us a good appreciation of the vehicle's overall state. I do not demand instruments to report on current pressure and flow of the injectors, the fatness of the spark, or the status of the steering geometry. The same applies to the business perspective of much of IT. If the business process runs effectively, then it is usually reasonable to assume that the application, infrastructure, management and change control processes are also running effectively.

This view was explained well by John McNally of VicRoads:

> Instead of reviewing systems issues such as availability and response times it would have been preferable to have monitored things like the average time to process a licence. It appreciated this was challenging as non-IT factors could affect these outcomes.

Defining service level agreements

The proper time to start defining SLAs is at the discovery stage of the project. This is when the current performance standards should be first measured, preferably by an independent third party. Ask these questions of every SLA:

- What is being measured, and is it a business output? Users are not interested in bandwidth utilisation; they are interested in how long it takes them to issue an insurance policy or process a bank deposit.
- Why is it being measured? Give some rationale for selecting this particular item for measurement. This step is most useful as it usually leads to a vigorous culling of the list of potential SLAs.
- How measurement will be done? Many organisations have little history of performance measurement and the complexities and costs involved. It is important to define how measurement will be done at the outset.
- When will the measurement take place? Will the process or output be measured daily, weekly or monthly? Will the measure be made at peak times, or at random times during the period?
- What is the current performance level for the item? This should be based on a statistical method. Averages are dangerous. A set of measures that give ranges (lowest and highest measures), modes (most frequent measures) and means (average measures) is more likely to provide a sound basis for judging improvement or failure than a single percentage.
- What are target performance levels? How were they determined?
- When are these levels to be reached? Demand some statistical probability of meeting them.
- Have the accountabilities and responsibilities of host company and service provider been defined?
- Will remedial action be taken to correct a failure to meet an SLA or if a failure to meet the SLA appears imminent?
- Will punishment follow a failure or *repeated* failure to meet the SLA?
- What rewards, if any, will follow a consistent achievement of this SLA?
- Do dependencies flow from or to this SLA? (for example, failure to manage a SLA on power supply maintenance may have a catastrophic effect on the business, and effect all other SLAs, or the failure of a disk system SLA may effect all applications and services dependent on that system.
- Who owns this SLA in both the host company and the service provider's organisations?

This last point is critical. The IT department frequently selects what it believes are critical indicators of success for key business processes, and far too often it is wrong. If no one in the business wishes to take ownership of a SLA, it may be because it is unimportant or because it is absolutely critical. Find out which.

The last item to consider is how satisfaction with the SLA will be measured. There is a clear distinction between "meeting the measures" and "satisfaction". There are widely differing views of what constitutes a satisfactory experience. For example, a great chef may have produced a masterpiece in his kitchen, with perfect ingredients, exact cooking time, and splendid presentation. He will be upset and confused if diners leave the restaurant clearly dissatisfied, the dinner perhaps spoiled by one small thing such as an off-hand waiter or lukewarm coffee. So it is with SLAs. Meeting performance targets is not enough. The customer must feel they were "satisfied". The team must obtain agreement from the users that they not only agree on the output, but also that they accept the measures will provide satisfaction.

Finally, it is important to gain commitment from the user to take ownership for monitoring the performance of this measure. The host company cannot abrogate all responsibility for measuring to the service provider.

User involvement and ownership is critical to success. Karpathiou and Tanner note, "End user involvement in IT outsourcing decision making is only about 15% although the study does indicate that the involvement of end users does have a positive influence on the achievement of desirable outcomes."[62]

Setting measures

The difficulties with measures lie in agreeing the baseline, targets and future measures. That leaves nothing that is not difficult! This section considers some of the dimensions of setting measures:

- types of measures of performance
- current measures of performance
- future measures of performance

Before exploring these issues, the host company needs to be take heed of PA Consulting Group's advice: "In general terms, the service provider's interests lie in specifying low-level parameters, whereas the service user's interests lie in specifying and managing high-level outcomes." This is because the service provider can readily measure, manage and control these technical activities, and point to success, even in case of serious failure. For example, disk usage, transaction response and bandwidth usage may be entirely satisfactory, even if an important business output has failed abjectly.

Business outputs are more difficult to define, and are frequently affected by external variables. This makes them more difficult to measure, and service providers are inclined to fight shy of them. Success, however, comes from doing hard and difficult work, and for this and other reasons, the host company should seek to use an objective, expert third-party organisation to establish current measures and reasonable future goals.

The Commonwealth Bank of Australia did just that when entering into their multibillion contract with EDS: CBA appointed a project manager to oversee the baselining; Gartner Consulting provided financial and resource consumption templates; and Gartner Measurement provided benchmarking studies to compare CBA with representative peer groups.

Let us now explore some of the issues and opportunities with measures.

The balanced scorecard

The measures that are applied should cross all dimensions of the business. For this reason, consideration should be given to the framework advanced by Kaplan and Norton in their book *The Balanced Scorecard*.[63] They take a holistic approach to measuring performance, and encourage businesses to measure across four balanced perspectives, rather than focusing on financial measures.

The authors say:

> The balanced scorecard translates an organisation's mission and strategy into a comprehensive set of performance measures that provides the framework for a strategic measurement and management system . . . the scorecard measures across four balanced perspectives: financial, customers, internal business processes and learning and growth.

This seems a sensible way to measure an outsourcing agreement. The traditional approach of a single measure is rarely sufficient. The balanced scorecard approach may also help address the pernicious and persistent issue of "satisfaction" in performance measurement.

Measures of success that do not encompass customer satisfaction must be regarded as deficient. This is a persistent problem in SLA management, and conflict continually arises when the service provider points to 100% achievement of the SLAs but is still faced with a seriously dissatisfied customer. It is the old "chef and diner" issue: everything is perfect in the kitchen but a combination of factors at the customer interface leads to dissatisfaction with the outcome. The balanced scorecard can go some way to ameliorating the issue.

Operations measures

These are, in the main, well known to the IT professional. They are:

- back-up and recovery
- periodic processes, such as month-end and year-end
- disk farm management
- maintenance management
- batch management
- security management
- change management

Disputes arise in this area over:

- almost inevitable growth in file sizes that extend the back-up and recovery time. The host company needs to accept that the speed (and therefore duration) of these processes are limited by hardware and utility throughput. Shortening the duration may only be possible with the purchase of additional hardware or upgraded software;
- failure to consider that periodic processes need to be managed over weekends or public holidays. The service provider may overlook the need to pay penalty rates to staff for these periods;
- the host company baulking at the cost of purchasing systems management tools that are required to deliver improvements in operations management. These include network management, systems management, change control and security management products.

The host company and service provider should take cognisance of these factors from the outset. Some improvement in operations quality and efficiency can take place without substantial investment. However, both parties need to understand the investment necessary to move beyond that point.

Infrastructure measures

Infrastructure measures are, in the main, also well known to IT professionals. They will include:

- response times
- network error rates
- mean time between Failures (MTBF) on critical hardware.

Infrastructure measures often lie outside the service provider's direct sphere of management. Staff growth or changes to applications may affect response rates. Poor-quality cable or faulty equipment may cause network downtime. The service provider cannot directly influence MTBF: it is a manufacturing quality decision.

Service providers tell horror stories about irate clients who blame power failures, flood damage and hardware failure on the service provider's staff. Sadly, this is more common than it should be. Both parties should be clear about what is to be regarded as a "performance failure" and what is not, e.g. what is an "Act of God" or outside agency failure?

The parties also need to agree in advance on the limitations of the current infrastructure. For example, the user ceiling for the current network or the base on which application response time will be measured.

Project measures

Most companies would see "to time and budget" as an adequate expression of project measures. These will usually be set for individual projects, as it is virtually impossible to set a suitable standard framework in advance. Project measures are not without their difficulties. The aspects that cause difficulties are:

- the failure of host company staff to meet deadlines for sign-off and tasks such as user testing;
- inadequate user testing, which allows specification faults to carry into production;
- host company staff "approving" expenditure or change that has not been properly authorised.

The keys to introducing satisfactory project measures include:

- defining clearly the responsibilities and accountabilities of each party;
- defining the standard method or steps that will be followed for each project;
- sound change management process to ensure project deviation is properly approved.

Give sufficient thought to these issues in advance. Ensure all who are involved in IT projects are aware of them. Do not permit deviation from the rules, or the exception will become the rule and chaos will ensue.

Help desk measures

The help desk merits a section of its own. In many outsourcing agreements, it has become the focal point of criticism, and success or failure here seems to overwhelm all other measures. Yet it is often the one thing over which the service provider can exert little control, for the following reasons:

- Many of the problems relate to the use of packaged desktop software. IT staff may often have less reason to use word-processing, presentation software or spreadsheets than business people. They therefore lack familiarity with the software. Often, the request for support will require them to study manuals or call the vendors for help.
- The host company may be reluctant to implement a standard desktop operating environment (SOE). This leaves users free to alter configurations and settings and so trigger unpredictable and untraceable failures.
- The root cause of the problem may lie in user training. Analysis suggests that a significant proportion of calls to help desks is to ask how to carry out a simple task.

Companies seeking to control this area have followed a number of steps, including:

- implementing a standard desktop environment;
- removing diskette and CD drives to inhibit loading of unauthorised software;
- constraints on downloading software from Internet or bulletin boards;
- formal training as a prerequisite for software access;
- user self-help units, including "expert user" support in the business units.

Whatever steps are taken, both parties need to understand the limitations that apply to help desk management, and agree in advance what steps can and cannot be taken to control the user environment.

One warning: beware the risks of success where help desk calls increase because it does such a good job, and where business units that previously suffered in silence or learned to solve their own problems now call the help desk.

The parties must also agree and sign off the state of the current environment in all the above situations.

Current measures

The second aspect that must be managed carefully is the measurement of current levels of performance. The host company and the service provider need to agree on both the measures and the context in which these measures are achieved.

When measuring current levels of performance, consider measuring ranges, modes and medians to gain a complete picture of the pattern of current achievement. This is generally superior to a single number, which can be very misleading. For example, in a set of five closely spaced measures with one outlier, the average can be a very misleading number. Consider the pattern of numbers in Table 12.1.

Table 12.1—Achieved percentages for six months

Measure	Achieved percentage
January	98.0
February	98.5
March	72.7
April	98.0
May	98.5
June	98.0
Average	94.0

The risk here is that a performance level of 96% may be set which is 2% better than "average". However, this would allow delivery of a much poorer level of performance than has been achieved in five of the six previous months. In this example, the mode, or most frequent measure of 98% is a far sounder choice.

The second issue in taking current measures is to document properly the context or environment in which these measures were taken. The environment should define, where appropriate:

- the current numbers of users, preferably broken down into categories of light, medium and power users;
- the current hardware platforms, both servers and desktops;
- the current application scope, preferably listing all modules;

- the version of the operating systems (server and desktop), and network operating system in use;
- other infrastructure details, such as cable and hub router configuration.

These must be recorded, as a change in any of these environmental factors may affect the performance positively or negatively. The most pernicious change usually occurs in application software where incremental modifications add up to significant change over time.

One final word on current measures: As Michael Wilkins, Managing Director of Royal and Sun Alliance Ltd, puts it, they are very important in "guarding against the danger that people will develop a rosy view of past performance and past allegiances later in the contract."

Future measures

The single most awkward issue in defining future measures is that substantial and unpredictable change may take place, or need to take place, in the environment in which the future measures are to be delivered:

- Substantial changes may occur in the environment that might militate against the achievement of desired levels of performance. Business growth, changed applications, hardware, and infrastructure or business operations may drive these. These changes may take place quite separately to the changes foreseen to bring the measures up to a higher level.
- Future measures may require substantial change in the environment or business processes if they are to be achieved. At one end of the scale, the changes may demand business users conform to new disciplines. At the other end, it may require considerable expenditure on new equipment or tools. Make some allowance for the implications of such changes on processes, while never forgetting that the host company should focus measures on business outputs, not the inputs and processes.
- As mentioned, there will be inherent limitations in infrastructure capacity. Service providers have many tales to tell of customers who demanded transaction speed improvements with the same hardware, for operating windows to be extended without providing tools to reduce back-up time, or fewer breakdowns on obsolete equipment.
- Do not, under any circumstances, accept loose words such as "best efforts" or "best practice" in framing the agreement. Your legal advisers may tell you that "best endeavours" and "act within a reasonable time" have tested meanings in the courtroom. However, they are too vague for the cut and thrust of day-to-day management that keeps both parties out of the courtroom.

There is at least one other facet of the current environment that can lead to considerable angst if not trapped at this stage. This is the existence of shadow IT staff that currently participate in delivering those service goals. These may be subcontractors, business experts or suppliers who may not be available or accessible under the outsourcing agreement. Business staff who previously took ownership for quasi-IT processes will often distance themselves from the outsource management of the process. Subcontractors may not have been included in the cost model and suppliers who previously provided a high level of service to the host company may be far less willing to do so for a service provider, especially if the provider is also a competitor.

Future measures of performance need to be set with a clear understanding of the environmental changes required to reach the new performance levels.

In closing this section, there are three useful questions that should be asked about future performance criteria:

* Why has this been chosen as a measure?
* What benefit will the improved measure bring to the company?
* What changes are needed to realise the benefit?

In summary, when defining performance improvements, define the current state of the environment and capacity and capability of all resources involved in the process. Define, in outline at least, what hardware, software, skill improvements or staffing changes are required to bring about the change and maintain it.

Do not use the performance-setting process to win undeliverable commitments from the service provider. If it is physically impossible to deliver the improvements on the current infrastructure or with the current staff composition, then it stands to reason that improvement cannot be delivered unless these are changed.

Time and time again, the host company, aware that the service provider is under considerable pressure to win the account, pushes the service provider into unwinnable situations. To make matters worse, the service provider's sales team will often agree to host company requirements without the involvement of their line-of-service staff, who will be horrified at the commitments made. If unreasonable goals are demanded and agreed, then both parties will face future conflict and disagreement.

Motivation

Motivation for success should be considered from both the host company's and service provider's viewpoints. Both have much to lose if the agreement turns sour or fails. Motivations for success should be applied in at least two dimensions:

- The corporate dimension where the service provider's business pays penalties and host company pays rewards.
- The individual dimensions where both the service provider's staff and the host company's staff have some component of their remuneration at risk.

Neither form of compensation is easy to structure or is free of subjective judgements. However, I also urge that both penalties and rewards be subdivided further:

- The first category is purely performance-related, and is based on the achievement of essential business outputs or progressive milestones.
- The second category is satisfaction-related, and is based on customer satisfaction surveys, preferably conducted by a third party.

Both the host company and the service provider have complementary obligations and responsibilities. Both are responsible for success or failure of the agreement. Graeme Stevens of DMR Consulting Group explained that his then current assignment supported this view: "The project has two relationship directors, their man and myself . . . whose whole progression is based on benefits realisation."

The literature on individual motivation is wide and varied. Both parties should seek the help of human resources experts in structuring the at-risk compensation for both parties. Indeed, both parties should ensure that their incentive packages are complementary and consistent. Significant differences between the triggers and quantum of rewards for achievement between the parties may lead to unnecessary friction. The factors that govern the at-risk remuneration need to be complementary on both sides. It is critically important that the host company's staff is rewarded for the service provider's success, not for their ability to punish and extract payment for failures. Failure should benefit no one.

Corporate motivation is trickier. A word of warning: if the host company fails to stipulate rewards and punishments, then they should not be surprised if the service provider's other customers who do so receive more attention and get better service.

The final considerations for reward and punishment are documented below.

- Do not use a sledgehammer to crack a nut. Overly severe penalties can work against the host company for a number of reasons: they may lead the service provider to walk away rather than remediate; they can be so savage that the host company does not apply them, embedding acceptance of poor service; or they may create a climate of commercial fear in which the risk of progressive improvement is seen as too great.

- Address any service shortfall immediately. Kym Norley of Booz·Allen & Hamilton observed: "Companies need to make hard decisions, to draw the line when things go wrong, otherwise you abrogate your responsibility for performance." PA Consulting Group went further, drawing attention to the legal issues of accepting substandard service delivery: "If the penalty is too severe, the supplier can become confident that it will not be applied . . . and the likely outcome is ad hoc waivers to the contract terms . . . can be represented later by the service provider as a precedent, diminishing enforceability, at worst the service provider may claim estoppel[e], thereby preventing the penalty being applied thereafter."[64]
- Include customer satisfaction in the criteria that put part of the remuneration to the service provider at risk. This idea also came from PA Consulting Group, who observed: "One useful ploy is to have part of the service charge classified as 'discretionary' and subject to 'user satisfaction' rather than a specific service item. This can be paid proportionately to the measure of user satisfaction. This measure can be taken and judged by an external consultant to avoid any question of bias."[65] Andy Zaple of PA Consulting Group went on to tell of a customer and a service provider who agreed to a system of "credits". When the user satisfaction level was below a certain point, the service provider had to credit an "improvement fund". When the level was above the critical line, the host company credited the "improvement fund". The credits in the improvement fund were then used for improvements in the IT environment.
- The service provider should seek to extend the SLA performance model down the hierarchy to suppliers. The host company should encourage the service provider to enter into back-to-back SLA measures, with appropriate punishment and reward mechanisms. These SLAs should ensure that the service provider has adequate attention and influence with the companies supplying the business. There are few more frustrating experiences than to hear a service provider whining that they cannot provide a service because a subcontractor or supplier has let them down.

Performance measurement

A frequent problem experienced in outsourcing agreements is a failure to measure that which has been agreed. The responsibility for measuring lies on both sides of the fence. The host company must maintain measures over the outsourcer's

---

[e] A legal term defined in the *Concise Oxford Dictionary* as "being precluded from a course of action by one's own previous behaviour".

performance. The service provider must measure their own performance to ensure they are achieving the goals set for them.

The host company's measurement schedule can be smaller and less frequent than the service provider's. The goal of the host company is to establish whether major performance targets are being met. Indeed, it may be prudent for the host company to "outsource" this task to an independent third party that specialises in such measures, the benefits being:

- it will be done, as the third party's income is likely to depend on it being done;
- the measures are likely to be more objective.

Alternatively, an audit team or other individual removed from the day-to-day issues of the contract can carry out the measurement.

The service provider's measurement schedule should be much more frequent as they are measuring progress towards goals and lower-level improvement criteria. While the host company will be interested in business outputs, the service provider needs to know the quality and performance of all related business inputs.

Host companies are frequently surprised at the expense involved in taking regular performance measures. Domberger and Hall offer an explanation: "Provided performance evaluation can be implemented in a systematic way, the costs of monitoring need not be higher than monitoring in-house operations . . . the reason why it often appears monitoring costs are so high after contracting is that either little or no monitoring was previously undertaken or that its costs were not fully assessed."[66]

Finally, remember that if the host company does not measure, then it creates the perception that it does not care. After all the dust has settled and the SLAs have been agreed, both parties may be surprised how quickly attention drifts away from obtaining and verifying the measures. It is imperative that a regular scheduled meeting involving key players be set up to review SLA performance, understand why it is so, and recommend necessary steps to improve any areas where performance is substandard. Here are some recommendations:

- Select the half dozen key SLAs that matter to the business and monitor their performance.
- Review performance against these SLAs at least monthly.
- Review all SLAs for continued relevance, and cull those past their useful life.
- Add new SLAs where appropriate, bearing in mind the guidelines provided earlier.

If performance is constantly above or below target, then understand why. In some cases, it may be necessary to revise the goal.

Remedial actions

This is a very tricky area. An unnecessarily critical and aggressive approach may drive the service provider into an overly low-risk and obstructive stance. A generous approach may encourage inappropriate risk taking or imbed acceptance of poor service.

To make SLA achievement less of a contentious issue, ensure that:

- performance measures are based on statistical methods that provide sound "targets", ranging from bulls-eye accuracy to an acceptable, if not entirely satisfactory, achievement in a given period;
- performance measures are cumulative or based on an "average" result. For example, a company may set a monthly goal of 93–97% achievement, but punish if the average over any six-month period drops below 95%.
- penalties are small and frequent. Anecdotal evidence suggests that overly severe penalties are contrary to good performance. It appears that a large number of small penalties are more likely to bring about desired improvements than a savage penalty that is seldom or never applied.

Consideration should also be given to the way the penalties are "paid". Extracting cash payments in return for poor performance is probably best avoided, except as a last resort. Instead, the host company may find that requiring the service provider to fix the problem by providing extra specialist staff at no cost is a great deal more palatable. This is often easier for the service provider to do, as they may have spare consulting staff on the bench or can second a staff member from elsewhere to fix the problem.

Reward is equally difficult to manage effectively. Typical encouragement offers include bonuses for achievement of targets at an earlier date than envisaged in the contract, or early delivery of major system development projects. However, if these bonuses are known in advance, there is a danger that the service provider will ensure that the projected delivery dates are well within their comfort zone.

Changing

Businesses and service requirements change. Things that were important yesterday are often no longer important today. Accept that SLAs can change or become redundant, and review the SLAs periodically for continued relevance. Allow both parties to recommend additions, changes and deletions to the portfolio of SLAs. In each case, the new SLA should be defined in the manner set out earlier in this chapter. If a SLA is removed from the portfolio, the rationale for its removal should be documented.

Issues

The issues with SLAs are spread throughout this chapter. The list below provides a summary:

- Failure to link the SLAs to business outputs that usually results in other issues below.
- Low-level technical performance SLAs that are linked indirectly to outputs. John McNally of VicRoads spoke of "service providers being risk averse. They rate risk heavily and this acts as a disincentive to innovation, which is risky."
- Too many SLAs that try to manage every aspect of IT performance. For example, network packet collision, bandwidth usage, number of users logged on, etc.
- Inflexibility on the service providers part. According to John McNally, "Among the things that makes outsourcing hard is the fact outsourcers are often locked into their organisation's global system of doing things and can't adapt to your needs. You want customised service but they struggle to provide local customised solutions."
- Measures are often set without regard to implications and dependencies. Upgrading or maintaining performance may be impossible without upgrades to CPUs, memory, disk farms, network bandwidth and even desktop PCs.
- Lack of visibility is another issue that plagues SLAs. The service provider's sales staff may not have shared them with the staff responsible for delivering them. This issue also arises on the host company side.
- Relevance is another issue. The "Why?" question posed in the SLA checklist is designed to weed out irrelevant SLAs. These typically attempt to measure nice-to-have aspects that are of no relevance to the business. Typical examples are demands from a business unit for 24 hours a day, seven days a week coverage, when they only operate nine to five, Monday to Friday, or demands for reports "first thing Monday", which will incur weekend operations cost, but they are not utilised till late in the week.
- Distraction is another issue. The driver behind the limitation on the number of SLAs is to avoid distracting staff from key work by imposing valueless measuring and monitoring tasks
- Ignoring poor performance and laying the foundation for continued poor performance.

Tips

Some things that experienced outsourcing organisations have done to improve the SLA development, measurement and management process are:

- jointly developing the SLAs with the service provider in a workshop where the parties were forced to change sides and develop the SLA from the opposing perspective;
- using external parties, such as Gartner Measurement, to define performance measures;
- contracting an external "honest broker" to take monthly measurements on SLA performance and ensure both parties are adhering to the agreed obligations and responsibilities;
- including such items as vendor management within the SLA framework where the company sees continued good relationships with suppliers as critical;
- avoiding SLAs for the first year, until both parties have established a more thorough understanding of the issues surrounding the agreement.

Some or none of these may work for you. However, it is worth exploring all avenues in the struggle to define those few things that must be done well if you are to achieve success.

Checklist

1. Are you using an independent expert to develop SLAs?
2. Have you scoped the area to be covered by SLAs?
3. Have the outputs for those areas been defined?
4. Do they tie back to the objectives for outsourcing?
5. What is being measured?
6. Why is it being measured?
7. How will measurement be done?
8. Has the current performance level been agreed?
9. Has the current performance environment been documented?
10. What are the new measures?
11. Are the costs of achieving the new measures commensurate with the benefits?
12. What changes to the environment are required to achieve these measures?
13. What changes may take place that will alter these proposed measures?

14. What changes may take place in the environment between now and the achievement date?
15. Have you defined the accountabilities and responsibilities of both parties?
16. Has satisfaction been considered as a SLA component?
17. Are the measures statistically sound?
18. Have you considered the balanced scorecard?
19. What rewards and punishments attach to this measure?
20. What dependencies does this SLA have on other people or things?
21. Has change control process been defined?
22. Has a dispute resolution mechanism been agreed?
23. Has an at-risk remuneration package been agreed for both service delivery teams?
24. Have the SLAs been circulated to appropriate staff in the host company and the service provider organisations?

13 Managing transition

Transition is the process of moving from the insourced environment to the out-sourced environment. It will typically cover:

- managing the transition of IT staff from one company to another;
- familiarising the business staff with changed processes and rules;
- establishing some foundation tools and disciplines within the IT and business units.

Transition may well require that:

- site preparation activities have been completed by the contract activation date;
- plans and resources are established to move personnel, equipment and communication infrastructure;
- staff are orientated to their new company, and training given in new methods and procedures.

Commence transition well before the contract is signed. It is critical that continuity is maintained over this difficult period. It is also a period when all eyes will be on the project success, and circumstances and complexities of transition will militate against a smooth, successful handover.

Ideally, start planning for transition the day the concept of outsourcing is first given formal approval. Acknowledge that it will probably continue until at least six months after the contract is signed. The reason for this is that transition is the process of managing change—and the process of managing change should commence with the change, not half way through it as a reaction to issues arising.

Transition is often difficult. The advice of Michael Wilkins, Managing Director of Royal and Sun Alliance, is to "make sure everyone, including the outsourcer, knows the first six months are going to be rough. Also, don't make the assumption that changing staff over to the outsourcer will change the staff. They remain the same people they were before the deal was signed."

Many of the problems that arise in outsourcing agreements are people-centred. It is important that these issues are managed from the outset. The task of transition will be so much more difficult if morale is allowed to deteriorate and if negative attitudes are allowed to develop in isolation.

Transition has largely to do with culture change. The culture change and process change is required in at least four areas:

- Among the staff who are to be transferred to the outsourcer's payroll.
- Among the business staff who will now deal with the outsourcer.
- Within the service provider's business, which must accommodate new staff.
- In vendors and suppliers, who will often lose direct access to the host company's staff.

Cultural change is not easy. Sprague and McNurlin observed: "It is no easy matter to make radical change in the internal structure of a company, because it constitutes the 'corporate culture' that forms the basis of all employees work processes and habits."[67] Outsourcing is radical change, and it needs to be carefully managed and orchestrated.

There are other considerations in transition, such as licence and asset transfers, as well as familiarisation issues. These are comparatively pedestrian and are comfortably within the skill set of most managers. For this reason, they have not been given much attention in this chapter.

Transitioning staff

Those companies whose outsourcing plans include a transfer of their staff to the service provider report a wide number of disheartening issues. Typically, the problems start at the outset of the outsourcing project and persist until some 12 months after the contract is signed.

The problems experienced include:

- decline in productivity as morale is sapped and staff become uncertain about their individual futures;
- departure of the best staff, who are usually the most mobile;
- antipathy from business staff, who feel their colleagues are being "sold into slavery";
- significant workload on HR practitioners in coping with staff enquiries on options and industrial relations law;
- union demands on compensation for the staff or aggravation over continued terms and conditions;
- financial strains that arise from "packaging out" significant numbers of host IT staff.

Involve the company's HR unit from the outset. Do not rely on intuition, encouraging words or corporate hospitality as a means of handling a sensitive and potentially explosive situation. The issues are not peculiar to the host company. The service provider will face other, but similar issues. Involve the service provider's HR unit as soon as possible. This may be well before the contract is signed and should commence at the latest with due diligence.

Nick Kovari, formerly of CSC, observed: "In simple terms, outsourcing can be pretty awful for IT staff. They are squeezed by their new employer [service provider] for whom they may feel little attachment and then the customer, their old employer, squeezes them. Both organisations have different agendas. The outsourced staff may get the worst of both worlds and so they may get fed up and leave."

Both parties should work hard at ensuring open communication between the host company and its IT staff. This is often easier said than done. Staff often want cut and dried answers to uncertain issues. Some aspects of the outsourcing plans may, of necessity, be shrouded in commercial secrecy.

Staff often believe that the outsourcing project people know more than they are telling, even when this is not the case. Some staff cannot believe their individual fate has not been the subject of considerable discussion and complete career planning prior to even the RFI stage. However, open communication is part of the solution and it is best executed to a plan rather than as a reaction to issues. A suitable communication plan could include:

- staff briefing by the CEO at the outset of the project and at preplanned milestones;
- more frequent briefings by the CIO or chief IT executive, say every two weeks;
- weekly newsletter by the project team on progress;
- preplanned individual counselling sessions (if possible, do this for all staff; if sheer numbers makes this impossible, then seek to do it at least to team leader level);
- information packs on the project, including background information on preferred candidates that has been acquired through the RFI process;
- full briefing by CEOs of both the host company and the service provider when the selection is made;
- full information packs—preferably individualised—to all affected staff members;
- individual interviews and meetings for all staff with their new colleagues;
- farewell celebration for transitioning staff that recognises their contribution. *Caution*: do not try and gloss over the situation—cynicism will probably be running high and plain truth is likely to be more respected;
- welcome function by the service provider, followed by a well-structured induction and training plan;
- continuation of the CIO, project team and newsletter briefings for the first six months of the contract.

Both parties' human resources and change management teams will be better able to advise on the communication plan. Wayne Saunders, CIO of Southcorp Ltd, pointed out that "the outsourcer also faces the problem of absorbing people who were not hand-picked. People who have been in-house for a long time will be worried whether they can live up to the expectations of the service provider. Show them the brave new world is not threatening and support them and genuinely help them understand they aren't expected to become superstars." Some useful reference texts on the subject include:

- Kubler-Ross E, *On Death and Dying: What the Dying have to teach doctors, nurses, clergy and their own families,* Touchstone Press, UK, 1997.
- Cartright S and Cooper C, *Managing Mergers,* Manchester School of Management, Manchester, 1997.

Varying international industrial relations laws may prescribe process and conditions that govern transfers of staff and this may complicate the situation.

Thomas R Mylott III advises: "Don't transfer your troublemakers"[68]—he is correct. Troublemakers are troublemakers. Stonewall Jackson, a famous US Civil War general made a crude, if delightful, observation that you were better off with troublemakers inside the tent pissing out, than on the outside pissing in. Once they join the service provider, they are outside the tent.

Other HR-related issues that need to be considered in the transition include:

- asset ownership and transfer, e.g. laptops and mobile phones
- transfer of sick leave and vacation entitlements
- recognition for service where this effects remuneration or benefits
- payment of bonuses for the current year, especially if the transfer takes place mid-term
- commitments on educational or training and similar employee benefits
- pension and health insurance commitments and transfers.

Complications do arise when the service provider offers quite different conditions or corporate benefits. If the benefits enjoyed by the transferring staff are better than those enjoyed at the host company, this is not likely to be an issue. However, if the reverse is true, then there will have to be some compensatory arrangements made for the transiting staff.

As well as these commercial issues, there well may be other softer issues that need to be addressed, including:

- working conditions, e.g. moves from an office to a workbench or "hot seat" at the service provider's facility;
- apparent loss of seniority and changed reporting lines;
- perception that the service provider may not recognise their contribution in work at the host company and that they have to prove themselves all over again.

Nick Kovari described the situation: "The service provider gets lumps of people with quite different terms and conditions. Joining causes huge internal strains. Clashing cultural mixes and widely varying skill sets and quite different work ethics. These strains can be damaging to the service provider who is at the same time trying to do the customer's IT better."

Financial strains can also appear, and in several outsource projects the budget for packaging out staff and paying compensatory benefits has been grossly underestimated. This has usually been matched by a serious underestimation of the scale of effort required in both the host company and the service provider's HR units. I strongly recommend that every outsourcing project team includes a HR specialist, who is given the support and resources to do the job.

The transfer is traumatic for staff. Most of us like to choose who we work for, rather than having the decision made for us. People resent being "sold" as part of a business deal. The skills and capabilities expected by the service provider might well be higher than those possessed by the in-house staff at transition. They will also be unfamiliar with the methods and business processes in the service provider's company. These are all unsettling things that need to be managed properly.

Finally, there is the issue of changing the roles and mindset of the IT staff held by the host company to manage the outsourcing relationship. Graham Bull, Executive General Manager of IT Services at Telstra, says: "We believed once the outsourcing deal went through our IT shop would work like a commercial organisation. But both IT and ourselves lacked the experience for this to happen immediately."

However, as John McNally of VicRoads explained, the host company needs to be aware of the difficulties in changing retained staff from being "doers" to being "managers of doers".

Familiarising the business with changed processes

The major part of the change process needs to focus on the business and business processes. There is a natural tendency to focus on the IT unit, IT staff and processes, and overlook the significant change required in the business. The business will experience change in:

- personal relationships with colleagues, leading to a more distant relationship with the service provider's staff;
- processes for project and procurement approval, implementation and measurement;
- tighter delineation of roles with more push-back on accepting user accountability and responsibility on projects;

- discomfort at the visibility and extent of IT costs that may have been hidden previously;
- a demand for rigorous and accurate annual business unit IT plans and budgets;
- limitations on their overall flexibility in sourcing and managing their IT needs.

Graham Bull observed that one of the immediate impacts of entering into the contract was that people suddenly "became very careful, overcautious . . . they were second-guessing and double-checking everything." This reaction is understandable, given the level of visibility and the expectation of more rigorous scrutiny into how the IT cash is being spent.

Personal relationships are among the first things to suffer in an outsourcing relationship. Outsourcing forces a change in the relationship between the business users and IT staff. Business users find they can no longer rely, as they did in the past, on special favours. Instead, they find that the old friends in IT are often especially sensitive to their new employer's rules of conduct, and are demanding that due process is followed in all requests.

Many in the business find it hard to accept that they cannot just call on an old colleague on the help desk or a willing programmer to make "just one minor modification". This will surface in early customer satisfaction surveys, as the "favoured" clients of the old IT find themselves under a more democratic process that is not personality-driven.

Business staff are inclined to view these changes as obstructionist, unhelpful, less flexible and slower than they have been used to. They will not be inclined to see the big picture and overall benefit arising from a more structured balanced process that assigns priority on criteria other than relationships.

Processes for project approval or procurement are likely to be more thorough and disciplined under the outsourcing arrangement. The service provider is acutely aware that they must have approval for every staff-hour charged for on the monthly invoice. They will be equally conscious that they must show approval for all additions to software and hardware inventories.

There is little room for special favours or ad hoc requests for changes that are accommodated in in-house IT departments. Business units' direct IT investment in contractors, hardware or software will often be curtailed. Business units are likely to find that the service provider will wish to adhere to a method in project development, demanding formal business cases, project statements, project reports and budget allocation. The business will now face a formal process for requesting change and modification.

These disciplines are to be lauded. In the longer term, the commercialisation of the relationship between IT and other business units may be one of the greatest benefits of outsourcing. Indeed, one interviewee expressed the view that "outsourcing can provide an effective transition path to well-managed insourcing." However, in the short term, the disciplines are likely to be resented.

Role definitions will change. Internal IT shops grumble constantly about business units' lack of involvement and ownership, and the lack of consistency in their demands. Despite the grumbling, they are rarely in a position to insist that the business take accountability and responsibility for proper user requirements, budget management or testing, training or change management processes. The service provider will demand that accountabilities and responsibilities are defined clearly in role descriptions and service level agreements. These definitions will generally throw more accountability and responsibility back on business staff than they are used to.

The delineation is likely to be right and proper and based on sound systems development methods. However, this will also form a new and resented pressure on business unit staff.

Hidden IT costs may surface, which will add to the discomforts already mentioned. The formality surrounding outsourcing tends to force a true count of all IT costs incurred by business units. The literature suggests that the hidden costs of IT in businesses will sit between 20% and 30% of current IT budgets. The sudden appearance of another million dollars of costs in what was previously believed to be a three-million-dollar IT budget will not be welcome.

A sensible case should be made that this is merely the transfer of these costs out of a business budget into an IT budget, and does not represent an "increased cost". However, the business units involved may find the unveiling of these costs embarrassing.

Plans and budgets may also be a source of aggravation. Outsourcing agreements tend to be built around rigid control over annual plans and budgets for benefit delivery. Business units may be expected to consider, plan and budget for their IT needs in detail. They may find these subject to rationalisation processes as the corporate arm and the outsourcer work together to consolidate these plans into a coherent delivery portfolio for the coming year.

The change from submitting an unsubstantiated wish list to IT to providing a timeline of outputs required with supporting justification and business resource commitment may place unwelcome demands on business unit effort and skills.

These issues will be seen by many as limiting their overall flexibility in sourcing and reacting to their IT needs. Fundamentally, the change is analogous to the evolution from a soccer team of six-year-olds, where all the youngsters follow the ball like a swarm of bees, to the discipline of a world-standard team, where each player takes his appointed role and plays within an overall strategy. The international team will beat the six-year-olds, but the six-year-olds will complain that it is not as much fun as it used to be.

In short, outsourcing forces a commercial relationship between IT and other business units. One manager observed in an interview that it "forces upon an organisation a definition of the outputs required, service levels, and formal processes for the definition and management of change. All these are tools and processes that internal IT shops often wish they could implement in their own organisations to improve their contribution to the business."

The steps that should be taken to minimise these irritations are much the same as those that need to be directed to the IT department; the most critical aspects are communication and change management. The *business communication* plan should include:

- staff briefing by the CEO at the outset of the project and at preplanned milestones;
- management briefings by the CIO or chief IT executive, say every two weeks, focusing on the business impacts expected;
- business information packs outlining expected changes in planning, budgeting, project approval, procurement and change management;
- full briefing by CEOs of both the host company and the service provider when the selection is made;
- final information packs containing templates and forms for project initiation, procurement, help desk services, etc.;
- team briefings for key managers on handling the resultant changes;
- structured training plan to induct important business people into understanding their roles in any new methodology;
- information newsletter briefings for the first six months of the contract.

The HR and change management resources in the outsourcing team must be charged with managing this larger role in transitioning the business into the outsourcing arrangement. This side of the change management process is frequently overlooked or undervalued. It is the cornerstone of a sound outsourcing partnership. Michael Wilkins, of Royal and Sun Alliance, has had much experience in mergers and acquisitions; he gave these words of advice: "Don't expect immediate improvements. Tell the people in the business it is like integrating a takeover." This statement resonates in Greaver's observation that one of the risks facing organisations that outsource is that the "organisation fails to let go"[69].

The service provider must also adapt to change. One frequent complaint is that major service providers can be inflexible. Graham Bull of Telstra said, "Conflict can arise when mega-companies enter into outsourcing deals. They are both used to 'being in charge' . . . and large service providers find it difficult to change their processes because of their sheer size and bureaucracy."

Fail to manage the business change and there is a good possibility that the outsourcing agreement will disintegrate in an atmosphere of frustration, criticism and resentment.

Vendors and suppliers

Transition should also sweep in the remaining issues of dealing with vendors and suppliers. The discovery and due diligence process will have alerted many of them to the host company's intentions. However, there will be some fuzziness about the vendor and supplier positions until the preferred service provider is selected and the contract imminent.

It is at this time that the host company and selected service provider need to engage in sound vendor management practices. Some vendors may have tendered for the outsourcing contract. Others may perceive the selected service provider as a competitor. They may well raise issues concerning:

- confidentiality of their intellectual property and methods
- reluctance to grant the selected service provider maintenance rights on their software
- licence transfer surcharges.

I have been surprised at the extent of peevishness exhibited by bidders, particularly those who failed to win the outsourcing contract. I have been equally surprised at the readiness of vendors to sour long-term relationships by imposing licence transfer fees and other ridiculous charges on the host company.

The host company must also embark on the process of vendor management. It has many of the same attributes as are found in managing staff transition:

- Inform all vendors well in advance that the host company intends to outsource. This should be incorporated into the discovery process.
- Prepare an information pack for distribution to vendors outlining the changed processes and accountabilities in the agreement. Personalise this for large or important vendors.
- Introduce the service provider's key management to the vendor relationship managers at the earliest possible time.
- Provide a means for managing issues and disagreements over the service provider's management of the vendors.
- Drop vendors where a lack of cooperation may endanger your project.

It is disheartening to provide this advice, but unfortunately, it is a fact that even commercial relationships can be tinged with jealousy and bitterness.

Validating due diligence benchmarks

The transition process may well provide additional information to inform the contract definition. In practice, the following three activities inform the contract:

- discovery
- transition
- due diligence

It is desirable to keep the contract itself flexible and open to amendment, especially during the first six months of transition. It is during this time that the service provider will first take the wheel, and issues arise that have a major bearing on the long-term health of the partnership.

I again remind you of the view expressed by PA Consulting Group:

> To be successful, an outsourcing contract must be sufficiently "tight" to protect both parties from operational and commercial risks that may result, yet at the same time be flexible enough to enable changes to be made to the scope of services to be provided, the service levels to be achieved, or the basis upon which charges are to be applied (including payment of performance related bonuses or penalties).[70]

Checklist

1. Have you developed a communication plan for IT staff affected by the change?
2. Has a similar plan been developed to manage business communication?
3. Have vendors and suppliers been included in a communication strategy?
4. Does your HR team have experience in managing mergers and acquisitions?
5. Does the service provider's team have previous experience in absorbing host company resources?
6. Have all the elements of remuneration and benefits been considered?
7. Have issues of privacy been considered if transferring HR files?
8. Have appropriate and government agencies and unions been informed?
9. Have the second-order effects of employer change been examined, including taxation, continuing service provisions, etc.?
10. Have other interested parties, such as medical and salary continuance insurers, been notified?
11. Has counselling been made available to support the disenchanted or confused?
12. Have you put a safety net in place to protect essential employees?
13. Has the service provider's staff been counselled on welcoming the new staff to the company?
14. Has the service provider allocated work space or storage space in their offices for new staff?
15. Have security passes been updated?

16. Does the transitional staff have security passes to enter their new employer's premises? (Few things make a staff member feel less wanted than being treated as a security risk.)
17. Has an appropriate budget been allocated to "package out" employees who decide not to transfer?
18. Have arrangements been made to back-fill any vacant roles?
19. Have basic things, such as name plates, telephone directories and invitation lists, been updated?
20. Have you secured the services of a good industrial relations lawyer?

Five thoughts on effective outsourcing

If you are accountable for outsourcing your business information systems, think about these five things . . .

Plan for the end

Any sound contract expects that one day it will all end. If you commit your business systems to a third party—an outsourcer—ask yourself:

- What happens when the contract term is up?
- What happens if the outsourcer consistently underperforms?
- Can I relet the contract?
- What happens if your business decides that outsourcing is not its future?

One of these things *must* happen. If you are not able to resume control of your assets (hardware, applications and intellectual capital), then your business may have lost a major competitive advantage, and at the very least will suffer real disruption.

One successful mechanism has been to require the outsourcer to establish a subsidiary company with one client (you) with a predetermined ability for takeover by the client in certain circumstances defined by triggering events. Consider models that seek:

- to keep intellectual property rights with you;
- to allow you to purchase (for a nominal amount) the hardware, licences and contracts to keep running under any circumstance;
- to ensure that reasonable guarantees are in place to guarantee outsourcer viability;
- commitment of the outsourcer's staff to you.

Align the cultures

Once a contract is written, a good alliance will not require it to be consulted, other than, say, to check the deliverables and rates. Achieving a genuine alliance may, however, be more difficult than it may seem at first.

People in established businesses think and behave differently to IT professionals in many ways. Established businesses are just that—they may not be the rapidly expansive changing by the day industry that is IT. So, there may well be a culture clash between you and your outsourcer. Odds are that you will not have unlimited funds, time to pursue new technologies at the rate they emerge, or have the level of computer literacy in your firm that understands fully what the technical staff are saying.

You will need to educate your outsourcer to at least understand the mindset of your business and its ethos. Bring the outsourcer to your training sessions and work together in business planning. At the same time, teach your staff to regard the outsourcer's people as colleagues, not contractors. Break down the barriers and seek team accountability, not blame.

Let the outsourcer manage

The job of the outsourcer is to deliver IT. Your job is to ensure the outsourcer's deliverables align with the business needs (no more, no less), and that this is done to time and budget.

If they don't align, it may be because the needs are not developed or articulated (your problem), or because the outsourcer is not managing. You must have sufficient IT knowledge (including professional IT technical ability) to lift the covers on any problems before they become unmanageable. But you cannot afford to micromanage, since this will allow the outsourcer to abrogate their responsibility (or worse still, push the accountability back to you).

More often than not, the performance of the outsourcer depends on two things:

- the performance and attitude of the general manager of the outsourcing unit serving you;
- the preparedness of the outsourcer's parent to support the unit through times of difficulty.

A good outsourcing unit will be accountable for its people and especially for its subcontractors. In the event that the subcontractor is letting the side down, the outsourcer must have the wherewithall to step in and remove the subcontractor, and moreover guarantee the delivery of the work within the contract. This is a risk that you are rewarding the outsourcer to take.

Represent your business, understand the technology

When it comes down to it, your business people are your clients, and they will be under pressure from their (your firm's) customers and operators. This puts the outsourcer and their army of IT professionals more than a few steps removed from your customer base and the needs of the business. Accept that as an IT department, you are not regarded as part of the business—you'll be lucky if you are accepted as a corporate service rather than just an overhead.

The irony is that you and the business analysts sitting around the systems project table probably are in a position to know more about the business processes and other detail of the way things are done than the business people are. You have the process engineering and technology capability at hand, both key value adders. Use and share your knowledge without telling business people how to do their jobs and you will see value emerge.

Deal with expectations

Your people will probably see outsourced IT with a cargo cult mentality that says deliver it now, deliver it perfect, and deliver it with all of the add-ons that someone has just thought about or read about.

It will be a constant battle to manage "scope creep", which can pull down a system build or implementation. Both IT and business people will be guilty. The outsourcer will be motivated with all good intentions to deliver the best system possible, even when you can't afford it—and your people will want it anyway.

Business people genuinely believe that IT will always have a magic solution. If your one focus is to ensure that your outsourcer is delivering sound basic systems meeting the real needs of your business, then you are doing your job well.

Your biggest battle will be to manage IT with your board of directors, and some of your fellow executives. Most of your board may not comprehend IT; some may profess ignorance to distance themselves from it. There will be some directors with no IT experience—they will require (and respond to) education and assistance. Worse are those that think all good things come in a PC package—they will require careful persuasion. Take the time and effort to develop understanding, acceptance and support. Watch for those reluctant to share reality and stand accountable— they will compromise your success and that of your outsourcer.

Kym Norley
Senior Associate, Booz·Allen & Hamilton

Before joining Booz·Allen, Norley was General Manager Strategy & Systems at National Rail Corporation, where he managed National Rail's corporate strategy, management information and, through a single-purpose outsourcing company (Railtek Australia) under the DMR Group, development of National Rail's leading-edge Australia-wide IT throughout the company establishment and the first five years of its operations.

14 Managing the relationship

Management of the contract is a major ongoing task for the host company. Forget any idea that the business of management is now in the hands of the service provider. The host company will need to put significant effort into this area, directed at four levels:

- contract administration
- strategic management at the executive level
- portfolio management at the middle-management level
- help desk management at the operative level.

The host company will also need to ensure that it has included these costs in its ongoing budget—and that the service provider has likewise factored in the cost of managing the relationship as well as performing the service.

Most host companies retain a senior IT executive role within their business. Typically this would be a role similar to the chief information officer (CIO) in content and seniority. The role would hold overall responsibility for the success of the outsourcing project. Indeed, it may be the individual who managed the outsourcing process in the first instance. The incumbent is likely to be a senior, well-respected member of the executive management team and therefore in a position to influence and impose the structure where appropriate. Klepper and Jones stated: "Put the best, most capable managers in charge of the outsourcing evaluation and management of the outsourcing arrangement."[71]

The IMPACT Outsourcing Working Group reiterate the view: "Have an appropriate person manage the contract . . . a [contract] manager with the wrong attributes could quickly destroy the relationship with the supplier. The supplier could undermine a manager who does not have the support of business managers and end users."[72]

I cannot agree with Mylott, who believes that IT outsourcing can "minimise IS management responsibilities"[73]. It may reduce the volume of second-order work, but it does not diminish the responsibility.

The CIO should be held accountable and responsible for:

- the creation, maintenance and ownership of the strategic IT blueprint or architecture. The scope of the architecture should include applications, information

and technology. In some instances, the responsibility may extend to business
process or work architecture;
- corporate IT standards for hardware, software, security, operations, change
  control and human resources;
- ownership of the annual budget, and for all expenditure within that budget.
  This may be delegated in part to the service provider but never abrogated;
- the overall success of the outsourcing contract.

The CIO may require operational support in managing the contract. If so, set up a
contracts administration office, which should report to the CIO. The role of this
office is described below. Michael Wilkins, of Royal and Sun Alliance, added,
"Make sure your IT executive understands he is responsible for managing the
business delivery, not managing the contract."

Contract administration office

The purpose of this office is to monitor and report on the service provider's
adherence to:

- performance standards, including adherence to periodic reporting timetables
- budget management and financial reporting
- monitoring and approval of service provider site staff quality and quantity
- corporate principles and standards
- ensuring there is no deviation from key contractual clauses
- maintaining the issue register and participating in dispute resolution
- management of all variations to the contract, in conjunction with the CIO.

This office may also take on responsibility for managing regular contractual and
service audits of the service provider, and oversight of the implementation of
recommendations arising from audits.
  One or many people, depending on the contract scale and complexity, may staff
the office. If the contract is complex or broad in scope, then the contract administration office must include a senior contract manager. The senior contract manager should:

- have appropriate tertiary qualifications and some project management
  experience;
- have more than five year's experience managing contracts for provision of
  goods or services at a significant scale;
- demonstrate the ability to deal firmly and ethically with all issues;

- have sound negotiation skills training and experience;
- have a good understanding of the law of contracts.

If the outsource agreement is large, then additional support staff may be required, with good spreadsheet and financial analysis skills and sound report writing skills.

This office needs to be aware of the most intimate details of the contractual agreement, and have first-hand knowledge of the background negotiations that led to the outsourcing agreement. Ideally, the office should be formed at the outset, and play a key role in the development of the RFP and contract. At the very least, the office should be in place at the commencement of the contract proper.

The service provider likewise needs to staff and support a mirror image of this unit.

Executive management of the contract

It is often difficult to develop an appropriate level of involvement by the executive. The CIO's peers will regard managing the contract as the CIO's role, and to a large extent they are correct. Although it is one of the few business functions that directly and immediately affects the day-to-day operation of other business units, it is common for business units to ignore IT unless a crisis in technology affects them directly.

Outsourcing IT may worsen this level of apathy. However, the CIO cannot set IT strategy in isolation from the business. The IT strategy must be built on the business strategy, and reflect and support the direction in which the business is heading.

The senior executives must be informed of key performance issues with the service provider, and must inform the service provider about future changes, e.g. in product, distribution, reporting, location or structure.

Some methods that have been used to bring about executive-level involvement with the outsourcing agreement include steering committees, investment committees and workshops. Each is discussed below.

Many who have had the experience of sitting on IT steering committees will be familiar with the types of issues inherent in this approach, for example:

- An unbalanced focus, with the bulk of the time wasted complaining about minor performance issues or help desk gripes.
- Overly much detail in the form of reports, which focus attention on history, not the future.
- Domination of the agenda by a single department.
- Apathy and disinterest on a grand scale.

Traditional steering committees tend to be backward focused and political. They are a hangover from a time when IT was new and there was an understandable concern that a critical part of the business would be managed by a peculiar new breed of employee.

No similar structure exists for managing finance, marketing, operations or other business units, so the logic of overlaying the CIO's executive management with a steering committee in the present day and age may be superfluous.

Investment committees tend to be a more useful creation altogether. Typical roles filled by such committees include:

- approval for cross-functional projects that affect more than one department;
- court of appeal for deviation from corporate standards and architectures;
- approval for significant capital expenditures;
- monitoring progress and expenditure on significant cross-functional projects;
- audit committee that reviews and approves outsourcing audit reports, and implementation;
- reviewing and approving corporate IT strategy or blueprint;
- reviewing the serious issues register (see later).

These items are largely future-focused. The investment committee does not involve itself directly with projects that are completely within one business unit, help desk performance, hardware failures or any of the minutiae of daily IT management. The composition of such a group should include:

- senior financial officer
- senior strategic planner or marketing manager
- one other senior executive, perhaps the CEO
- the CIO
- service provider's senior site manager
- service provider's relationship manager.

Workshops provide a sound approach for involving a wider range of executives in the oversight of the outsourcing agreement on a sporadic basis. The workshops are formed to inform, review and discuss broad-ranging issues with a significant IT component. The workshops address new technology implications, or meet to develop a broader understanding and seek broader approval for large cross-functional projects. Some issues that the senior executive might workshop include:

- electronic commerce
- radio frequency mobile computing
- computer–telephony integration
- cross-system changes, such as the recent Y2K issue or broad changes to systems resulting from legislative changes, e.g. a goods and services tax.

The workshops need to be well-organised and facilitated. The ideal agenda should include at least the following items:

- Objective of the workshop, which should include the expected outcome.
- Questions and answers on the briefing papers, which should have been circulated at least 72 hours before.
- Review and restatement of the objective based on the discussion above.
- Key discussion points.
- Preferred option.
- Implications of the preferred option.
- Assignment of responsibility and accountability for tasks arising out of the workshop.

These can be arranged as required. Set a minimum cycle of four times each year (every quarter) to maintain executive involvement in IT direction. The workshops could also include invitations to other IT product and service providers to make presentations on new technology and its implications.

Middle-management or portfolio management

The portfolio refers to the group of applications and/or projects that are contained within one business unit, e.g. the group of financial systems and projects owned by a finance or accounting manager. The service provider should assign ownership for each business unit's portfolio to an individual within the service provider's framework. This has the following benefits:

- Staff have a single point of contact for all their business issues.
- The service provider builds deeper insight into the business area.
- Project coordination within the business unit may improve.
- Budget and expense management can be focused at the business unit level.
- The reporting and management of the unit's requirements can be done on a portfolio basis.

Managing business unit interaction with the service provider should take place under the watchful eye of the CIO and contract administration office, who retain accountability and responsibility for the management of the overall contract. One possible arrangement is:

- Establish a business unit portfolio management group (PMG). This should consist of two or three key managers from the business unit. If the business unit is multifaceted, then it may be appropriate to include a manager from each facet.
- Define the role of the PMG, including its accountabilities and responsibilities. Typically these might include:

- project approval within a limited budget and timeframe that comply with the corporate application, information and technical architectures;
- project review and monitoring on a regular basis—at least every two weeks and more frequently if the portfolio is large and active;
- the first level of issue resolution within the contract framework;
- preparing recommendations to the CIO on changes to performance standards or contract obligations.

Portfolio reporting should be skewed towards current project progress and performance criteria that directly impact that business unit. Help desk or desktop issues do not sit comfortably in the PMG's scope. These issues are often cross-functional and should be addressed by a separate body, described below.

Help desk management group

This is usually the most active, vocal, critical and contentious area in outsourcing. The rapid proliferation of desktop computing, built on rapidly outdated cable-plant and infrastructure, with very active software upgrade strategies and limited standardisation, has led this area to its position as the premier trouble spot for IT. Because of its potential to overshadow other aspects of the agreement during the initial stages, VicRoads retained the desktop support initially as it was closest to the people and therefore the most sensitive to change.

The IT unit's day-to-day experience with desktop software is often limited. Few programmers or operations staff are heavy users of word-processing, spreadsheet or presentation tools. Little pre-release training is available on new network operating systems. Parameters are many in number, powerful and user-controlled. The combination of hardware, desktop operating systems, switch and hub infrastructure and firmware, servers, server operating systems and applications that conflict or alter parameters on loading have created a Pandora's box for help desk support.

GartnerGroup estimated the yearly total cost of ownership (TCO) of a networked desktop PC lies between US$7000 and US$10 000 per year, and estimated that one help desk operative was required for every 50 users.

Few companies are prepared to staff and support PCs at these levels. Users are many, frustration is high, and no silver bullet has yet been cast, although there are significant improvements coming in desktop management software, standardisation and knowledge.

It is important to establish *one* cross-functional help desk user group with many of the characteristics of the PMGs. Do not use more than one help desk user group as multiple groups are likely to waste much time covering the same ground, introduce conflicting goals and products, and generally add to the mayhem.

The help desk user group should have as its prime focus the joint resolution of help desk issues with the service provider. This group must see itself as part of a self-help model, as the user is a significant contributor to the problem in help desk issues. Often, the underlying causes are poor training, poor password management, users fiddling with software and parameters, loading inappropriate software such as games, and poor appreciation of the need to consider the overall infrastructure in change management.

These user problems are often exacerbated by the tendency of service providers to spread their quality resources very thinly around their customer base. High-quality support staff in desktop and help desk services are few and far between. Service providers have to invest heavily in these keenly sought resources. It is here, on the help desk, that many outsourcing agreements founder, rather than in the expensive high-level consulting services that form the backbone of professional service organisations.

The help desk PMG should include:

- an executive who appreciates the issues and is determined to foster solutions;
- a senior representative from each of the key business units, preferably limited to four in total;
- a representative from the CIO's office or the contract administration office to oversee strategy and architecture compliance;
- the service provider's senior help desk manager, senior site manager and relationship manager.

This group should meet at least every two weeks, but may need to meet weekly if the situation is unstable. A possible agenda for these meetings could include:

- purpose of the help desk user group—its mission statement;
- training issues and their resolution;
- desktop standardisation issues and their resolution;
- review significant outstanding help desk calls, with a view to helping in resolution.

Each business differs in its emphasis on these issues, but the help desk user group must see itself as part of the solution, otherwise it will deteriorate rapidly into a focal point for complaints and exert a negative influence on the whole contract.

Issue management and dispute resolution

Issues and disputes will arise during the agreement. Even the happiest marriages have the odd spat. This section is not concerned with issues that can be dealt with readily between managers and resolved within 24 hours. Any well-managed business will deal with these as part of day-to-day management. Our focus is on sticky issues and those of a serious nature. These issues need to be recorded in an issue register, and the contract should include a process for resolution, and if appropriate, escalation. The issues register should record at least:

- a description of the issue
- why it is an issue
- who raised the issue, and to whom they reported it (two names)
- who has ownership of the issue
- steps that have been taken to resolve the issue
- the expected resolution date
- how we will know the issue has been resolved
- escalation steps to be followed if the issue is not resolved.

If the issue is escalated, then adequate records must be kept of all aspects of the escalation process. These would normally include names of people involved in the escalation, meeting minutes, arbitrator or mediator details and, if serious, the legal or mediation judgements.

One piece of advice: most serious issues can be resolved without the need for expensive litigation or arbitration. Here are some tips that can help avoid serious issues deteriorating into a financial opportunity for lawyers:

- Escalate the issue rapidly. If the initial group cannot resolve the issue within 48 hours, then bring in the next level of escalation.
- Brainstorm solutions to the issue. A group of people working to find a solution will achieve more than a group of people indulging in pointless verbal abuse.
- Adhere to the proper procedures set out in the contract. A failure to do so may weaken your case if the dispute does go to court.
- Before the issue becomes too heated, involve skilled negotiators, preferably from the law firm or advisers who helped form the contract.

Reporting

Reporting on the outsourcing contract will often be driven by insecurity, and demand an excessive level of detail. The content of reports should be pyramidal: the lower down the pyramid, the more detail, and vice versa. The scope should be inverse, i.e. the lower down the pyramid, the narrower the scope. The following are suggested reports for each level:

Investment management group

- High-level report on progress of any investment management group (IMG) approved projects or expenditure.
- Serious unresolved issue report—including architecture, standards and noncompliance.
- Performance against 7 ± 2 key targets.
- Proposals for new cross-functional projects or significant capital expenditure.

Portfolio management group

- Progress reports on projects within the business area.
- Monthly budget variance report for business unit.
- Business unit issues outstanding.

Help desk user group

- Progress report for cross-functional desktop projects.
- Performance against relevant 7 ± 2 key targets.
- Help desk issues outstanding.

The ideal report fits on one page and summarises the position on all aspects. A useful technique is to divide a normal A4 page into four squares, one for each of the subjects above, and limit the report to what will fit that area. An example is shown in Figure 14.1.

Insist on adherence to good meeting practice. Best practice guidelines for meetings include:

- Define the objective of the meeting.
- Decide who has to attend to allow the objective to be met.
- Prepare an agenda, including objective.
- Circulate the agenda and working papers at least 48 hours before the meeting.
- Set time limits for the meeting and, if appropriate, for individual agenda items.
- Stick to the agenda.
- Start and finish on time.
- Limit the detail; minute those things requiring action.

There are several relatively cheap and useful books on meeting management. It might be a sound idea to purchase copies of such books for all participants.

PROJECT PROGRESS	Actual to date	Budget to date	Budget remaining	Estimate to complete	NEW BUSINESS CASES
1. Network OS	A$23k	B$57k	R$49k	E$50	1. Improved upgrade invoicing system (budgeted)
2. Billing Module	A$37k	B$40k	R$40k	E$80k	2. New procurement system (unbudgeted)
KEY TARGETS	Actual		Target		**ISSUES OUTSTANDING**
1. Critical calls 20 min	90% (45/50)		100% (50/50)		1. Ex-budget approval for new tax calculations (all systems)
2. Network Up time	99%		98%		2. Removal of halogen gas system in computer room (new law)
3. TCO (running average)	$6700		$7000		

Figure 14.1—One-page report

Meetings

"Meetings, meetings, more meetings" is a complaint heard time and time again around business today. Meetings are a fact of life, and they can convey information quickly to a large number of people. They provide for a level of interaction impossible to achieve with mere reporting, and they facilitate progress—*if they are run well.*

Consider taking the following steps:

- Think carefully about the objectives, roles and composition of each group.
- Review these at least once a year.
- Get the contract administration office to draw up a calendar of meetings a year in advance.
- Adhere to good principles in running meetings.

Conclusion

The business of ongoing management of the service provider does not differ greatly from normal sound management practice. If the principles are sound, the standards agreed and the budget and annual plan well-defined, then management should be fairly straightforward. Appropriate incentive schemes and regular consultation can strengthen these things.

Michael Wilkins of Royal and Sun Alliance pointed out during an interview that the host company must also "make sure the outsourcer provides management and staff who understand they are there to fix business problems, not to just to deliver SLAs."

The inclusion of change management and dispute resolution processes may well lead to a more refined level of management than is normally achieved within the confines of a single company.

This chapter does not stand in isolation in the text. Other chapters, in particular Chapters 12 and 13, also contain some key insights into managing an outsourced relationship.

Checklist

1. Have you considered your management structure for running the contract?
2. Has the service provider established an appropriate management structure?
3. Have you both costed this management infrastructure into budgets and contract fees?
4. Are there incentives for both sides to deliver win–win outcomes?
5. Has an independent third party been selected for audit and performance measurement?
6. Can the service provider's structure and process meet reporting requirements?
7. Has the company developed and promulgated sound management principles?
8. Has the company established a change control programme that fits into the ongoing management process?
9. Have both parties agreed on an escalation and resolution process for disputes?
10. Have you established a meeting programme, preferably a year in advance?
11. Have you adopted sound meeting management code?
12. Have you set a review date for your reporting and management structures?

13. Is the contract administration office staffed appropriately?
14. Have the necessary interbusiness processes been agreed, e.g. with finance, strategic planning and audit?
15. Do all management roles on each side set out responsibilities and accountabilities?
16. Has an annual (or more frequent) planning and budgeting process been arranged?

Outsourcing mission-critical services: British Airways

British Airways (BA) is the world's largest international airline, and has an IT department that, as a separate entity, would rank as one of the UK's largest software and systems suppliers. Known as Information Management (Im), it supports 70 000 desktop devices and over 600 applications worldwide.

The Desktop Services group, a subset of Im, holds specific responsibility for safeguarding and maintaining the desktop functionality of the operation-critical IT infrastructure, such as the global network of ticketing and check-in computers. Systems failure could create an embarrassing and expensive problem.

PA Consulting Group worked with BA's Desktop Services group on a change programme to radically improve performance and achieve substantial cost reductions. Part of this project was a large desktop outsourcing arrangement.

Implementing change with no room to manoeuvre

Desktop Services set the ambitious goal of improving the cost and quality of its service by 20%. BA recognised the need for strong programme and project management skills to meet their challenging goal. The change programme had to adhere to tight budgetary and resource constraints alongside strict deadlines.

Working in partnership on multiple fronts

The initial shaping of the programme focused heavily on benefits and achieving the performance transformation. The transformation group concentrated on implementing a business-facing organisational structure, based on fewer, more focused staff. The group was restructured completely to support the principles and objectives of Desktop Services, introducing improved processes throughout. The consulting group provided the technical expertise to support the knowledge transfer and managed the transition to the new organisation. Best practice process and service levels were implemented and—paired with the outsourcing project— reduced significantly the time it takes to implement new equipment.

The joint client and PA team managed the outsourcing of desktop procurement, installation, maintenance and repairs designed to achieve dramatic service improvements and cost savings. This complex project comprising the selection of the preferred supplier through to full implementation of the outsourced service, is one of the largest of its kind in Europe.

Achieving over £1 million savings per annum

The outsourcing of several of the group's functions to an external service provider resulted in clear cost savings. The consulting group implemented SLAs, so that performance could be quantified. Improvements include reducing the delivery and set-up of new equipment from weeks to just five days, achieving extensive desktop standardisation, and a £1 million saving on the expected budgets for 1999–2000.

The results speak for themselves—there is a clear feeling that Desktop Services has achieved its targets, and one of the most significant barometers is the reduction in complaints from other cost centre managers. I'm glad to say that thanks to this change programme and our work with PA, Desktop Services is no longer the problem child of BA's IT department.

Linda Bartlett
Desktop Futures Manager, British Airways

Case Study reprinted by kind permission of PA Consulting Group.

15 Terminating or renewing the contract

Termination, restructure and renewal are covered separately in this chapter. The section on termination is common to all. Restructure is the process of remaking the agreement so that some of the environment is taken back in-house or turned over to another party.

Renewal infers that the contract will be renewed with little change. However, the process that is used to minimise the drawbacks of termination or restructure can play a useful role in ensuring a sound renewal.

Termination

Kym Norley of Booz·Allen & Hamilton pointed out: "One unshakeable fact is that at some time the contract will end. It must. It cannot go on in perpetuity. Therefore you must structure the agreement and contract so you can take your IT back in house." The triggers for termination, restructure or renewal might consist of:

- serious performance failure
- taxation changes that seriously undermine the cost–benefit model
- merger and acquisition of either host company or provider
- change of management philosophy
- wish to refine the model to gain additional benefits
- the contract has reached its expiry date.

The following circumstances may apply, regardless of the trigger for changing the status quo:

- The relationship between the host company and the service provider may be more hostile than it was at the outset of the outsourcing agreement.
- The host company is likely to be more vulnerable than it was when the contract was let.

Terminating, restructuring or renewing the contract is unlikely to be simple. According to Leonard Bergstrom, CEO of Real Decisions Corporation, "Once control of technology has been relinquished, it may not easily be won back . . . when you give away your data centre, it is very difficult to get it back because you lose the infrastructure and the people."[74]

The negatives facing the host company include:

- intimate knowledge of software construction and maintenance is now in the heads of the service provider's personnel;
- knowledge of complex operations and batch control procedures is now in the heads of the service provider's personnel;
- infrastructure, in the form of hardware and network, may have been sold to the service provider;
- software licences may have been transferred to the service provider and the transfer back may not be simple or cost-free;
- services may have been subcontracted to third parties and the implications of retrieving ownership and control over these arms-length agreements may be difficult;
- software and services may be operating on shared infrastructure that can not be disaggregated readily;
- office space and computer room environments may no longer be available;
- third-party (other vendor) contracts and relationships may be with the service provider rather than the host company;
- shared infrastructure and licences may have lowered costs to a point well below what any in-house operation can achieve;
- new technology may have been introduced such that the service provider has proprietary ownership and knowledge;
- it is probable that the termination, remodel or restructure will take place in an acrimonious atmosphere.

There are, no doubt, many negatives that face the company seeking to reverse or remodel its outsourcing agreement. There may, however, also be some positive points:

- The outsourcing project may have introduced greatly improved IT management skills amongst the host company's staff.
- The relationship between the parties will have reached a depth of maturity and intimacy that is positive. This is more likely if the change is driven by triggers other than failure to perform.
- The outsourced IT infrastructure may be in much better shape than when it was originally handed over.
- Documentation and procedures should have been greatly improved.
- The host company may have a better appreciation of the tools, skills and qualities needed to operate a quality environment.

However, Suh pointed to an undeniable truth that "companies that abandon control of their systems . . . can find that their knowledge of the business and their systems are permanently disconnected."[75]

For this reason, it is critical that the host company and service provider work hard to ensure that every aspect of a possible future divorce is well considered and agreed before they enter the contract.

Contract termination plans should form part of every host company and service provider's corporate business or disaster recovery plan. The difficulties and financial trauma are likely to strike both sides. Again, bear in mind that the termination may well occur in circumstances where the relationship is poisoned, which may exacerbate an already difficult task.

Forecasting the environment

One of the most powerful techniques that the parties can use is scenario planning. The basic steps that should be included are:

- understand the current environment
- project several probable future environments
- project the scenarios that may occur in those future environments that may lead to a change in the agreement.

Guidelines for understanding current and future environments can be found in Appendix A. More detailed coverage is given in Peter Schwartz's book, *The Art of The Long View*[76]. Schwartz observed, "Begin by looking at the present and the past . . . Before you can look ahead through scenarios, you need to understand your organisation as it has acted in the past, and your environment as it exists in the present." The bulk of strategic planning literature deals with the business of readying a company to face its future, and can provide a good source of professional advice.

The aim of scenario planning is to develop a mind and process readiness to deal with outcomes most likely to unseat the current agreement. Schwartz used an analogy of actors who are given the task of learning three plays, which are very different in style, time, place and character:

- Shakespeare's *The Tempest*
- O'Neill's *Long Day's Journey into the Night*
- Ionesco's *Rhinoceros*

Each night, the actors walk on to the stage and act the appropriate play. Until they arrive on stage, they do not know which play is on. The only clue will be the set. A shipwreck signals *The Tempest*, a New England living room *Long Day's Journey*, and a café table with a beer bottle *Rhinoceros*. The service provider and the host company are the actors; the future is the set.

The *Art of the Long View* sets out a number of steps to scenario building:

1. Identify the focal issue or decision. Here it is contract end for whatever cause.
2. Determine the key forces in the local environment. This is similar to the material in Appendix A.
3. Identify the driving forces. Schwartz refers to a set of social, economic, political, environmental and technological forces, which again is not dissimilar to Appendix A.
4. Rank scenarios by order of importance and uncertainty.
5. Select scenario logic, which are the axes on which scenarios will differ.
6. Flesh out the scenarios.
7. Develop the implications. The use of implications is referred to in Chapter 5.
8. Select leading indicators and signposts.

Schwartz is one of the world's leading futurists. His book is a useful addition to any manager's library.

The host company and the service provider should follow these five steps:

1. Define the current context.
2. Forecast the future context.
3. Project the type of scenario that could lead to contract end or contract restructure.
4. Model the costs, manpower and processes required to cope with the high-risk and high-consequence scenario.
5. Write the arrangements required for executing the scenarios into the contract.

Halvey and Melby said, "Although it is true that lawyers often plan the divorce before consummating the marriage, it is equally true that too many business people take the wedding vows before reading the prenuptial agreement."[77] The outsourcing contract must include the plan for the "divorce".

Some of the things that will need to be considered in the "prenuptial agreement" are the same as those in the contract, and will cover the whole sweep of what is the contract document. Challenging areas will be:

- continuing quality service through the disengagement process;
- disengagement and transfer of assets in the form of hardware and infrastructure;
- licence transfers including transfer fee responsibility;

- transfer of the library or repository of documented information on the whole system, as it may now contain information potentially damaging to the provider;
- transfer of staff back to the host company.

Andy Zaple of PA Consulting Group said, "The factor most often cited as preventing organisations from reversing their outsourcing arrangements is that the skills no longer exist in-house." There can be little doubt this is a serious concern. I know of one company that sought to have two clauses inserted in the contract to cover this. The first was a clause requiring the service provider transfer "nominated" staff back to the host company. The second clause was that the service provider should give the host company rights to nominate essential staff who were to manage the disengagement process.

The first clause was unenforceable, as the staff might prefer not to be transferred into the host company and could not be forced to do so. The second, while sounder on the surface, is only workable if the nominated staff are keen and interested in helping the host company part from their current employer, the service provider . . . an unlikely scenario.

However, I still endorse the view expressed by Peter Thornton of PA Consulting Group:

> One measure that can be effective . . . Is to include "enabling actions" in the contract provisions for non-performance. Where a service provider has been under-performing materially, the penalties should not include just a financial rebate, but also measures that would ease the transfer to an alternative service provider (or where it is more appropriate, a return to in-house provision).[78]

Restructuring

The term "restructuring" is used in this book to describe the process of remaking the agreement so that some or all of the environment is taken back in house or turned over to another party. This is, in fact, a partial termination, for restructuring need not be a negative process. John McNally of VicRoads said, "There is still plenty of room for some radical thinking on both sides on how the relationship should be structured and managed."

What distinguishes restructure from termination is that the service provider and host companies maintain an ongoing relationship. This offsets a number of otherwise troublesome issues:

- The host company still has access to the skills and knowledge of the service provider.
- The host company may be able to continue using infrastructure and equipment sold to the service provider.

- The service provider may be encouraged to provide support for the restructuring or hand over to the in-house or third-party organisation.

Restructuring should form part of the scenario-building exercises described in the section on termination. Restructure scenarios should consider the following emerging trends:

- business process outsourcing
- entry into the market of new service providers
- new pricing models
- best-of-breed provision

Business process outsourcing (BPO) is the handing over of a complete business function, say finance, to a third party. The third party may well run its own software and hardware with no need for the host company's, or alternatively it may require that the IT component, now in the hands of the outsourcer, is passed to them.

New service providers may offer opportunities that were not available at the time the original deal was struck. These new service providers may be able to offer substantial improvements in service or cost over the existing service provider.

New pricing models may emerge, for example "alliance pricing". This or other models may drive the host company (or the service provider) to seek a large-scale restructure of the deal that passes some work on to third parties, either at the service provider's or host company's behest.

The process is the same—understand the context, forecast the future, develop scenarios, and plan and define what will be done if any of the high probability scenarios eventuate.

If you have to restructure the contract or replace the service provider, follow *all* the steps outlined in this book that are set out for a first-time selection of an outsourcing partner. Just because the host company has done it before does not mean they can happily ignore critical processes in subsequent selection cycles.

If the restructuring is to bring some section of the outsourced environment back in house, then the host company should:

- define how the objectives that led to outsourcing in the first place have changed;
- define the CSF and criteria for successful in-house operation;
- follow due process to measure the in-house option against the current or alternative positions;
- enter a "contract" with the in-house provider, including setting SLAs;
- manage the transition in reverse;
- manage the reversed option as they would manage the service provider.

A failure to follow due process may lead to see-sawing of services from outsourced to in house.

Renewal

Renewal usually infers that the contract will be renewed with little change. The processes that are used to minimise the drawbacks of termination or restructure can also play a useful role in ensuring a sound renewal. It is now that the host company and service provider should take the opportunity to remove any remaining irritations in the outsourcing agreement and build on any ideas that have arisen over the course of the agreement.

However, the starting point is forward planning. All contracts have an "expire by" date. It is important that the contract also include a formal countdown to renewal. For example, six months before contract end, the parties should be required to indicate their intentions with regard to contract renewal, including:

- whether the intention is to renew the contract;
- the scope and model for renewal;
- expected duration of the renewal.

Three months before renewal, the parties should be required to commence formal negotiations on contract renewal:

- Finalise all contract alterations and additions.
- Sign "heads of agreement" on the renewal.

Finally, one month before contract end:

- confirm all aspects are covered (review this book, including this chapter);
- sign the renewed contract.

Ideally, you should publish a contract management schedule that sets out key tasks and dates over the whole life of the contract. A failure to develop a countdown process may lead to a panic renewal of the contract, which will benefit no one, or a termination by default, much to the chagrin of at least one of the parties.

Renewal alterations and additions

One danger facing contract renewal is that only issues that are currently front of mind will be addressed in the renewal phase. The host company or service provider may overlook innovative or constructive ideas that arose over the history of the contract. Deep-seated problems may be overlooked in favour of the most sensational but essentially trivial current issue.

I recommend you start planning for the renewal of the contract from the day the initial contract is signed, by creating two folders named "Yellow Book" and "Black Book" after Edward de Bono's Thinking Hats concept.[79] These are explained below.

Black Book[f]

Black Book contains the negative memories of the existing contract. The file is a repository of all the negatives experienced during the outsource agreement. A few simple tips for populating the file are:

- cut negative items out of minute papers, date them and drop them into the file;
- write standard file notes on issues and observations and slip them into the file;
- place press cuttings on other companies' negative outcomes in the file;
- photocopy articles from books and magazines that deal with outsourcing issues that may affect you.

In the months leading up to contract renewal, cull the file. Experience indicates that about 80% of what was collected will now prove of no value and can go straight in the bin. The other 20% should prove invaluable, and provide cues for:

- methods by which problems can be avoided in the future;
- pitfalls to be protected against in this renewal cycle;
- new impositions that you will demand the other parties meet;
- strong negotiation ammunition, which may help you obtain a better deal next time around.

It is unlikely that both parties entered a perfect contract or obtained ideal service in the first instance. The service provider also probably experienced a significant number of internal stresses and strains in servicing the business. The key to an improved contract is to reach two goals:

- Protect both parties against past issues—the things that caused problems during the current contract's life
- Protect against future issues—those things that could occur in the future, including things that have affected others, or could have been forecast.

Yellow Book

The other file holds the other side of the renewal process: the collection of good ideas and opportunities that could not be exploited under the old arrangement.

---

[f] De Bono stresses Black Hat is the hat of judgement and caution, not negative or inferior. After the cull the Black Book should more closely approximate de Bono's view.

"Yellow Book" in de Bono talk is the realm of good ideas. Many of the world's great thinkers, such as Michelangelo, Newton and Einstein, were great note-makers and diarists. These men wrote down good ideas when they thought of them. Often they revisited them later and saw the solution to a problem.

Become a Yellow Book person at least concerning the outsourcing contract. Into this file go:

- press cuttings on other companies' innovative solutions in outsourcing, not just in IT;
- ideas on pricing, and reward and punishment models;
- ideas taken from books and seminars on outsourcing or contract management;
- some outrageous ideas that may not seem so outrageous five years from now.

This file should contain a rich source of material that can be used to frame a better contract on renewal.

Clearly, neither party has to wait until contract renewal to introduce new ideas. Most should be introduced through contract variation during the contract's life. However, there will nearly always be a small number, which, for tactical or strategic purposes, need to be kept until their time has come. Most, like the Black Book contents, will be ideas whose time has past. Nevertheless, the Yellow Book should contain the seeds of significant improvement in the renewal phase.

The naming of these files is to stimulate a different mode of thinking about the renewal process and the material being collected. De Bono chose his "silly hats" idea because it provides a powerful metaphor for thinking about issues, breaking the discussion into the emotive, logical, creative, negative, positive and analytical facets.

De Bono's model is more conducive to stimulating the right thinking than a boring file labelled "Contract Renewal" that will probably be devoid of any useful material over its five year life.

Conclusion

Every termination, restructure or renewal will be unique. It would be impossible to develop a set of procedures and recommendations that cover all eventualities. However, the key to all these forms of contract termination is preplanning—before the parties enter the contract, not when the issue is surfacing. Service providers should also consider this, and must recognise the temporal nature of all contracts.

Finally, a word of warning to the host company. With your staff and expertise gone, and your hardware in the service provider's hands, you may be very vulnerable, with fewer and more limiting options, when it comes to restructuring or disengaging from the existing contract.

Checklist

1. Have current and future contexts been defined (see Appendix A)?
2. Have you developed scenarios for termination, restructure and review?
3. Have the scenarios been rated according to risk and probability?
4. Have the models for managing the high-risk scenarios been developed?
5. Does the contract define responsibility and cost for managing the scenarios?
6. Has the same attention gone into modelling restructure and renewal?
7. Does the contract include a timetable that leads towards an orderly renewal or contract end?
8. Have you considered a Black Book for recording issues over the contract life?
9. Have you considered a Yellow Book for recording opportunities at renewal?
10. Have you protected yourself against vulnerability?

Outside in—a personal view from outside the arena

If you had to go to Woodstock to be part of the 1960s, I suspect you have to have been retrenched to be part of the 1990s. For much of the past decade, the catch cry has been more with less. Unfortunately, this has led to a tendency for organisations to view staff as a cost to be diminished rather than as assets to be harnessed.

A changed world

Running an IT executive forum for the last five years, I am acutely aware of the pressure under which people now work. It is clear that the old notions of job security no longer exist. In their preoccupation with the bottom line, many organisations have outsourced noncore skills. It seems apparent that many businesses are viewing IT as a noncore competency.

False expectations

However, it is also clear that many organisations may be setting false expectations from outsourcing. In Australia, no industry sector has pursued outsourcing for cost savings as vigorously as the federal government. Unfortunately, the evidence to date has been that outsourcing has a poor record as a means of reducing government IT costs. For example, the Department of Health and Family Services believed saving assumptions were overstated by more than 30%. Furthermore, many had overlooked hidden costs in outsourcing such as the redundancy costs associated with dispensing with a large proportion of internal IT staff.

There are benefits

Nevertheless, the Australian Information Technology Experience Program (InTEP) sessions did stress that there could be significant gains generated from outsourcing. The point was made that outsourcing has the potential to instill a commercial relationship between IT and the business. In business, time is money. As such, no longer need the IT staff be held captive to requests for favours or for poorly articulated requirements. Furthermore, a contract ensures that these IT services are now defined so people know to what they are entitled and what is extra.

An interim step?

My own view is that the current focus on complete outsourcing will come to be seen as an interim but necessary step in the evolution of the IT department. In an increasingly online trading world, how can organisations describe information services as a noncore competency? Outsourcing may act as the catalyst for placing a commercial edge on the delivery of IT services. Eventually, though, many companies will appreciate that having IT personnel as direct employees will mean they have a deeper empathy with the aspirations and challenges of the business.

Peter Hind
IDG Communications

16   Why outsource?

One of my favourite reference books is *Taking Sides: Clashing views on controversial psychological issues* edited by Rubinstein and Slife.[80] *Taking Sides* reminds us that there are no monopolies on the truth, that "truth" itself is often a selection of preferred facts, and that science is littered with ambiguities and half-truths, statistics and lies.

Thomas Kuhn, in his text on scientific theory, reminded us that "philosophers of science have repeatedly demonstrated more than one theoretical construction can always be placed upon a given collection of data."[81]

The debate on outsourcing raises serious questions. Should we outsource a core function? Why should someone else be able to manage part of our business better? Does outsourcing save money? What risks does outsourcing raise? What benefits does it bring?

Sometimes the dialogue is emotional and overlaid by self-interest. Outsourcing poses a threat to the staff in IT, but poses a major earning opportunity to the service provider. Consultants are poised to make money either way.

In this chapter, I offer my views on these issues. Managers intending to outsource should become deeply involved in deciding how these "facts" apply to their decisions and beliefs.

Is outsourcing effective?—the case for

Here are some distinct arguments for outsourcing IT:

- Outsourcing is a well-proven process with a long history of success.
- Outsourcing achieves improvements that cannot be reached by the average IT unit.
- Outsourcing improves business and IT processes.
- Outsourcing offers cost-management controls not available with internal IT units.
- Outsourcing brings increased certainty over cost.
- Outsourcing improves the quality of service.

- Outsourcing enables a company to keep pace with its competitors.
- Outsourcing allows focus on core competency and revenue generation.
- Outsourcing is a valid way of achieving required cultural change.
- Outsourcing introduces qualities not found in internal IT departments.
- Outsourcing offers flexibility in the quantity of staff.
- Outsourcing provides access to specialist skills and knowledge.

A proven business process

Outsourcing is a proven business process. Over the past 50 years, companies have outsourced advertising, legal services, fleet management, building maintenance and production. Outsourcing is not new. Houghton asserted, "Outsourcing is a new name for an old practice. Services such as bureau services, contract programming and project management have long been outsourced."[82] So even IT outsourcing is not altogether a recent phenomenon.

Those that advance the argument that "IT is a core process, and therefore should never be outsourced" assume outsiders cannot improve a core process. However, automobile manufacturers have long outsourced the making of most vehicle components because it is more efficient and economic to do so. Many companies outsource processes like advertising, printing and legal services because others do it better or cheaper.

The argument that one should not outsource a core competence is a different thing. A core competence is one in which the company is more effective and efficient than the competition. The core competence is always related directly to the core product or customer-facing service of the company—which does not include running an IT department.

The argument that IT is complex and should not be outsourced overstates the case for IT. Motor vehicle manufacturers outsourcing arrangements make IT outsourcing complexity pale into insignificance, e.g. General Motors is said to have about 80 000 suppliers.

Cars are made up of hundreds of components sourced from as many suppliers. Every component must fit exactly into the overall schema of the car. Consider the complexity and interaction of the engine components, electronics, instrumentation, steering, gear systems, hydraulics, tyres, pressed metal and plastics that all need to combine in a harmonious whole in a wide range of models.

Another argument is that IT requires intimate business knowledge and therefore cannot be outsourced. This argument is dismissed by reference to the many other outsourced functions that are critical to business. For example, advertising requires an intimate knowledge of culture, image, business goals and markets if it is to be effective.

Outsourcing is old hat. It has been around forever.

Improvements that cannot be reached by average IT units

Andy Zaple of PA Consulting Group noted:

> One thing that outsourcing all or part of an IT shop forces upon an organisation is the definition of the outputs required, service levels and formal processes for the definition of requirements and change . . . Processes that internal IT shops often wish they could implement in their own organisations in order to improve their contribution to the business.[83]

This begs the question why the internal IT shops cannot achieve these goals. The answer, sadly, must be that they are unable to convince the business to accept these things because they lack credibility, competence or both.

It may be unfair, as Peter Hind, a consultant with International Data Corporation, said, that "the outsiders are treated like gods", but the reason they are so highly respected is because they have the competence and capability to bring about this substantial and needed cultural change in the business. The argument that outsourcing will achieve improvements rests on the simple premise that, right or wrong, the outsource service provider has more credibility than the in-house unit. In fact, any reputable outsourcer will not take on an agreement if the business is not willing to accept the imposition of these improved processes.

Improving business processes

It should not come as a surprise that outsourcing can improve business processes. The introduction of method and rigour in IT processes tends to flow on to the business. Professional service companies demand proper project approval and ownership, including business user management. They will herd business people through the door labelled "Manage your IT Right".

They also make it easier for the business project owner to manage IT effectively. They provide appropriate information and reports that ensure expenditure, progress and issues are visible and controllable. They encourage business-managed budget development and business-controlled expenditure. They encourage and demand proper business specifications and provide the skills to support the business in developing those requirements and managing change.

An added benefit is that smart companies adopt these processes and apply them to other business projects. The idea of project managing product releases or new product development will often stem from exposure to these processes in IT.

John McNally of VicRoads observed: "One thing outsourcing has done is turn the business into enlightened purchasers of IT. Business has come towards IT and made the effort to understand IT issues. The outsourcer has supported this enlightenment by introducing sound methods and processes."

Better cost-management controls

I am not advancing an argument that outsourcing cuts costs. This may well be true, but it is so poorly researched and justified that I will not debate it. Suffice it to say that a weak aspect of that argument is that it fails to project what IT costs would have been without outsourcing, or the burdens that ineffective IT has placed on the business.

GartnerGroup showed that spending in the USA on IT as a percentage of revenue has increased 93% in the last six years.[84] This factor does not seem to have been considered in many recent cost comparisons on the current costs of outsourcing versus costs at the outset of the contract.

It is evident that in general outsourcing brings with it a tougher cost-management regime. At the macro level, the agreement may set a fixed price for the outsourcing agreement and so limit cost within that framework, whatever the expense incurred by the service provider. However, the more common improvements stem from four other areas:

- More rigorous controls over expenditure in general. The service provider will normally face a tougher expense-control regime than an internal unit.
- Greater visibility over the true cost of IT. Outsourcing tends to bring to the surface and control the costs of shadow IT units. These typically represent a hidden burden of up to 20% of current IT budget.
- The service provider's staff are used only when needed. Anand Barry of Fujitsu put it well: "Flexible resourcing from the outsourcer can provide services that are available when needed, available when expanding or relocating, and not costing when not needed."
- Economies of scale from shared infrastructure, tools, utilities and specialist skills.

These aspects tend to tighten up cost management over the IT unit. Requests for additional IT staff are argued more closely, and approval (and therefore cost of ownership) is limited to the project or task in question. The service provider has to justify every one of their IT staff: basically they face a zero-based budgeting exercise every month.

Projects are tightly managed, as the service provider tends to provide better and more consistent information to the business. Service providers tend to demand the host company management participate and take ownership of the IT costs in their department. The old cosy relationship between IT and some departments disappears and a new and rigorous model rises in its place.

Outsourcing makes IT costs visible in a way that does not happen in traditional management reporting. All costs for manpower, supplies, maintenance and the like are identified and reported. This uncovering of previously concealed cost tends to bring about a demand for tighter controls.

Quality of service

The dynamics of the outsourced environment are quite different from those of the internal environment. The outsourcer is a different economic entity with profit at risk. Competition is fierce, and failure may have an unpleasant knock-on effect in the market place.

The service provider will strive to deliver quality at three levels, firstly in relationship management. They will communicate across the whole spectrum of the company: they have to. They need to be close to the CEO, business unit managers and operatives. In general, the service provider will seek to lift communication quality and frequency well above that achieved by internal IT units, which frequently have poor or nonexistent relationship management and communication processes.

The service provider will also provide quality in output, partly from implementing the improved definitions of outputs, requirements and change control, and partly from having staff with a higher level of skill and education than is found in many IT departments.

Finally, the service provider will often drive improved quality in planning and budgeting. Poor planning and budgeting can damage their revenues and profits. Because they have an arm's length commercial relationship, the service provider will address these matters and exercise quality control over them at a level beyond that of most internal IT units.

Keeping pace with the competition

This benefit is not applicable to all. However, many companies are hamstrung by lack of flexibility when faced with issues of capacity and capability in their internal

IT units. An outsourcer can generally provide resources reasonably quickly. This may allow the host company to acquire or construct new systems to support business activities, in a way that is not possible with a limited internal unit.

The improved process and output quality will also add to competitive strength. The rigours and controls that the agreement brings with it tend to ensure that systems are built better. The service provider will invest in state-of-the-art equipment and processes to provide the service because that is their core business. It is unlikely that the host company will have the same focus on IT, or be able to achieve economies of scale and management focus to justify the quality improvements.

Focusing on core competency and revenue generation

Put simply, IT is a distraction for many managers. Business units often find themselves micromanaging IT inputs. This issue is then often compounded by the need to test IT outputs at a microlevel because of poor quality.

Core competency is that which the business does well and ensures its success. Core competency relates totally and directly to the product the company sells, whether the product is manufactured, a service or a material such as petrol or coal.

IT is not a core competency for most businesses. Indeed, the rise of outsourcing is an endorsement of this fact. Businesses are not very good at running their IT. If they were, then there would be no need to consider outsourcing. IT may be a core process, but as we saw earlier, others may run our core processes better.

Vince Graham of National Rail, a CEO with a wealth of experience in outsourcing both within and outside IT, expressed the view that "even if outsourcing is more expensive it can be worthwhile to allow management to concentrate on revenue side changes . . . Success does not come from managing inputs, it lies in delivering outputs."

Outsourcing changes the dynamics. If the agreement is structured properly to focus on meeting business objectives through delivering outputs, then business managers are freed from micromanaging IT and can focus on revenue generation instead.

Nick Thornton of PA Consulting Group observed:

> improved focus on the core business. A major strategic benefit of outsourcing non-core activities is that management can concentrate on what it needs to do best. The valuable time of senior managers will not be taken up dealing with peripheral activities but, rather, they will be able to focus on the two or three core processes which provide competitive advantage.[85]

I take a view that the term should be "core competencies" rather than "core processes", but the argument is nevertheless valid.

A valid way of achieving cultural change

The literature on change management is large and varied. Two elements appear consistently. The first observation is that change is difficult to bring about. The second is that change requires a significant catalyst or trigger.

Ulrich, writing on earlier studies on culture change, noted:

> When these authorities tried to identify companies that had transformed their cultures, the resulting list was very short. While executives talked and academics wrote about culture change, neither group had yet experienced it.[86]

Culture change is often the unrecognised issue at the root of many outsourcing deals. Ulrich noted that "two assumptions frame the rationale for culture change: first, that culture effects the performance of the business [and IT] and second, that old ways are not new ways." These two issues are often central to the decision. Rarely, however, do they see the light of day in the rationale for outsourcing. However, it is often frustration with the cultural issues that lies at the heart of IT issues of quality, deliverables and business responsibility. Vince Graham, Managing Director of Australia's National Rail Corporation, said, "Outsourcing can be a valid way of breaking a culture so that you can later bring an improved unit back in house."

There can be little doubt that outsourcing can act as a broader catalyst for change throughout the organisation. It introduces the concept of considering the cost and quality of internal services, and challenges thinking about alternative forms of delivery of these services.

This argument will not explore all the tasks and environmental factors required to bring about change in organisations. Suffice it to say, however, that outsourcing is a powerful bulldozer of change. And this should be regarded as a benefit.

Management qualities

Anand Barry, Manager of Alliance Development at Fujitsu Services, stated in a conference presentation:

Outsourcing introduces discipline in defining and measuring service levels:

- services to be delivered are defined;
- measurement of these services is defined;
- data are collected and reported;

- trends are available for planning;
- efficiency [comes] from common management platforms.

In contrast, few IT departments measure themselves against benchmarks. An audit of most internal IT shops will reveal they lack any method for defining the services to be delivered. Rarely can one find an IT shop that measures its success in delivering these services. Data collection is poor or nonexistent, with limited capacity planning and projection.

Internal IT shops are also often lacking in their methods for delivering the services that are expected by the business, and formal methodologies will be few. The usual case for rejection is that the methods lack flexibility, are overly detailed and are onerous to follow. Translated, that actually means "They would force us to do our work properly, demand we understand the underlying complexities, and introduce rigour where we enjoy anarchy."

Environment control or change control processes will be equally weak or non-existent. This is how bad code gets into production. It is why month-end and year-end processes run into difficulty . . . why scripts and job control processes fail . . . why so many IT platforms are unstable and fragile. IT units counter with the argument that they don't have the time, resources or money. Rarely will they admit the truth: that they do not have the credibility, inclination or discipline to introduce proper management processes.

IT budgets are notorious for blowing out. Frequently, this is due to poor internal budget management processes. Outsourcing typically brings method, rigour and discipline to IT. And no, the staff will not like it. Even some users will hate it, as it brings their unfettered and often wasteful projects under tight control.

Flexibility in staff numbers

Most managers are poor at getting rid of poor-performing or excessive staff. The laws on unfair dismissal rightly demand we first attempt rehabilitation or redeployment. The problem with this is it takes a lot of time, effort, discipline, argument and legal advice to implement. Some people perform so slightly below a threshold of satisfaction that "counselling them out" is virtually impossible. Companies wind up with excess staff when major projects finish. Work swarms in to fill the gap, and they carry a hidden cost for a project well beyond its actual finish date.

Most service providers work on the consulting model. They own the pool of labour. You rent it when you want it, and then when you do not want it, you send it back. That is one of the great benefits of an outsourcing project. Projects finish, and resources depart. No counselling or due process required.

Quality in staff

Today, approximately 20% of staff in the "average" IT department are externally sourced workers (ESW).[87] They usually belong to one of two categories:

- The independent IT specialist, who seeks the challenges and change of contracting and does not want to be an employee of an insurance company, supermarket chain or bank.
- The consultant from a professional service company. These are increasing in number as IT professionals seek to work in IT companies, rather than as an adjunct to another business that limits IT careers and opportunities.

Some, but certainly not all, of the staff in an IT unit will lack the skills and characteristics necessary to be independent, or will lack the desire to be associated with professional IT firms. This clearly is an inflammatory statement, so it is important to state also that many good and capable people have chosen to remain in industry and are recognised for their contributions, intellect and skills.

Outsourcing can raise the quality of staff significantly. In one company surveyed, the quality of IT staff, measured in tertiary qualifications and experience, showed a dramatic change after outsourcing (Table 16.1).

Table 16.1—Quality of staff in a company before and after outsourcing

Criteria	Pre-outsourcing	Post-outsourcing
Tertiary qualified	20%	90%
IT experience	3 years	8 years
Business experience	2 companies	5+ companies

An argument could be made that these changes were as a result of hiring practices, and no doubt that is true in part. However, the changes are also due in part to the drift of quality staff to attractive, high-paying jobs with consultancy firms. Further, the service provider's staff will normally be trained in a consistent method, and will bring a coordinated and cohesive approach to the task. Everyone knows their task and how they are to accomplish it. An analogy with an army platoon is appropriate: the soldiers on point know what to do and how to interact with the others, as do the men on the "gun", the signalmen and the riflemen, who each cover their sectors so the unit behaves as a well-coordinated whole. In contrast, many internal IT departments' lack of consistent method provides a level of coordination analogous to a football team of seven-year-olds.

Access to specialist skills and knowledge

A distinction is made here between provision of higher quality and the access to specialist skills and knowledge. Like medicine, IT also has specialists. These may be data architects, strategic planners, network designers, or change control specialists, to name just a few. Only the largest IT shops, numbering in the thousands of staff, are likely to employ these people. Frequently they are not interested in maintenance work and therefore soon drift into consulting.

A professional services company will have a pool of these people available to their customers. These companies approach IT with rigour and professionalism. They have these skills in-house and will deploy them as needed.

A counter argument may be advanced that these people can be hired directly. This can prove difficult in practice. Importantly, when they come as part of the outsourcing package they will tend to be addressing your site as part of a coordinated whole, rather than attacking a spot fire in isolation from the bigger picture.

You can fire your outsourcer

But you cannot fire your IT department. If you think that does not make a difference to the way people work and behave, then think again. I do not encourage fear as a management tool, but I recognise that a little goes a long way.

Conclusion

Mylott drew the analogy that companies would not "build a dam to provide electricity to your offices, or render lard to soap for the washrooms."[88] The internal provision of IT services has some striking similarities.

The list at the beginning of this chapter of the benefits that can accrue through outsourcing may be large, but it is still incomplete. There is only one benefit I do not argue for: that is that outsourcing reduces cost. Indeed, I think that the increased premium, if any, paid for outsourced IT may be a good investment. Any company that is not realising the benefits listed in this chapter should look again to their contract.

Outsourcing is not always the best solution—a global investment bank

The situation—validating an outsourcing proposition

A global investment bank required an independent assessment of an IT outsourcing proposition that had been submitted by a major service provider. Within an environment of escalating IT costs and a poor track record of IT change, the bank was keen to bring in an external party to take on the global management of IT. However, before entering into the arrangement, the bank wanted to ensure that the supplier's proposed solution supported its overall business goals, and asked PA Consulting Group to carry out a review of the proposal.

The problem

The IT-related issues at the bank were significant, and the board had no confidence that the internal IT function could deliver. The board perceived in the IT function a lack of basic controls required for effective operation of a bank, and associated this with escalating costs and variable quality.

The solution—outsourcing?

The bank decided to engage a single supplier to perform a review of its IT situation. As a result, the supplier proposed a 10-year £1.4 billion global outsource arrangement as the solution, with itself as the outsource provider. However, the board remained unconvinced with the overall proposition and so took the decision to appoint an independent third party to validate it.

Prudence—an objective review

The major consulting group acted as an independent expert advisor. Working with the bank directors and the supplier, they validated the proposition against the bank's objectives of improving the delivery of IT, reducing costs and deploying IT globally to meet the business needs.

This highlighted the major weaknesses in the proposition and recommended significant improvements to the deal and its implementation. As a result, management decided *not* to proceed with the outsourcing proposition because of the mismatch between the proposition and the business ambition. It was decided instead to globalise the IT function and to implement an improved IT strategy to increase the value and performance of services provided to the business.

Enabling the bank to meet its IT objectives

As a result of this review, the bank moved away from the concept of outsourcing, and was consequently able to avoid entering into a disadvantageous arrangement that would have had a serious impact on its bottom line. The revised arrangement improved the prospective five-year impact on the bottom line by a potential £100 million.

Case Study reprinted with kind permission of PA Consulting Group.

Epilogue

Some, on reading the draft manuscript, offered well-made arguments against outsourcing. There are probably no "right" answers for outsourcing. Each issue remains open-ended and may be attacked from an opposing viewpoint.

Perhaps the truth about whether outsourcing is good or bad will always evade us. We will never know what would have happened had we not outsourced, or if we had approached outsourcing from a different perspective.

The information we have to deal with in the meanwhile will be a mix of opinion, factual data, interpretations and evidence all jumbled together and flavoured by personal values and experiences.

The outsourcing argument may be regarded as open-ended. We are all members of a jury that will one day judge to what extent this phenomenon as applied to IT was valuable (or not).

Appendix A
Future proofing the contract

Peter Schwartz writes in his book, *The Art of the Long View*,[89] "Begin by looking at the present and the past." This sage bit of advice should be followed by all whose work entails long-term commitments. Schwartz continues: "Before you can look ahead through scenarios, you need to understand your organisation as it has acted in the past, and your environment as it exists in the present." A company is both a product and a foil of its environment, and in order to understand the way the company is likely to behave in the future, it is necessary to study how it has reacted to stimuli in the past.

I recommend future proofing, as the outsourcing agreement will require changes to existing business practice, power structures and behaviour. It may also trigger external reactions, which the company may need to accommodate. The professional manager also understands that a company will face many challenges in the five to ten years of an outsourcing agreement. The business will improve the survivability of the agreement if these challenges are considered and planned in advance. The future proofing process consists of four steps:

1. Develop the internal context model, covering past, present and future.
2. Develop the external context model, covering the same three periods.
3. Analyse how the company coped with changes from past to present.
4. Forecast how the company will cope with changes going from present to future.

Developing context models

The first step is to develop three context models (past, present and future). Context models should be defined in two dimensions: internal and external. To develop the internal context model, I suggest a table similar to that shown in Table A.1. This is best done on a whiteboard or at least a sheet of A3 paper.

Products and services are those offerings the company made to the market at the time. For example, Honda initially manufactured only motorbikes. Now, they manufacture motorbikes and cars, as well as lawn-mowers, agricultural vehicles and four-wheel drives. In the future, they may manufacture light aircraft, trucks, hovercraft or something vastly different, such as computers.

Table A.1—Internal context model

Facet	Past	Present	Future
1. Products and services			
2. Markets served			
3. Distribution methods			
4. Financial position			
5. Organisation structure			
6. Company culture			
7. Change agents			
8. Point differentiation			

Markets served may be grouped by socioeconomic status, geography or other points of discrimination. For example, Honda's early customers for their small motorcycles were the emerging societies in Asia. Today, it is the global middle-class family. Tomorrow?

Distribution methods are the means of getting the product from the factory to the customer's point of purchase. Honda's original distribution was through small, lowly-capitalised motorcycle shops in Asia. Today, Honda products are sold in agricultural stores and car marts, and on the Internet. Tomorrow?

Financial position refers to the state of the balance sheet and the profit and loss (income) statement of the organisation.

Organisation structure is the business structure. In Honda, this changed over the years from the small autocratic management of a far-sighted and quality-driven individual, to a multinational enterprise.

Company culture describes the overall "style" of the company. For example, the contrast between the formal, blue-suited button-down-collar of IBM, and the jeans and T-shirt culture at Apple. Both companies would behave differently when faced with threats.

Change agents are the people, internal or external, who drive change in the organisation. These people need to be identified, as they will have a significant role in driving or impeding change.

Point of differentiation refers to the aspect of the business that makes it different from others. In Honda's case, it has probably been exceptional quality in design, engineering and style.

It is no small or easy job to identify these components in the past. Corporate myths and amnesia often smother harsh and unpleasant truths, and exaggerate virtues. Far better to rely on formal records to uncover the truth. Some suitable sources include:

- organisation charts
- company structure charts (showing holding and subsidiary companies)
- business plans
- financial statements
- marketing plans
- product portfolios or sales catalogues.

Clearly, it is important to pick a suitable point in the past. The point may be five years or more, depending on the organisation's industry and the rate of change. If the rate of change is high, then a more recent past may suit. For a mature company in an older industrial sector, it may be necessary to go back further. The key to picking a suitable past is that it should be a time when things were clearly different.

Developing the external context models

These models build on the framework suggested by Michael Porter in his work *Competitive Advantage*.[90] Porter, like Schwartz, provides a complete and more advanced treatment of the subject of the competitive environment than attempted in this chapter. The same table structure (Table A.2) is populated with data on the company's past, present and future environments. Again, a whiteboard or large sheet of paper may be needed.

Table A.2—External context model

Facet	Past	Present	Future
1. Competitors			
2. Regulators			
3. Suppliers			
4. New entrants			
5. Customers			
6. Substitutes			

The questions that must be answered to populate the cells in this table are:

- *Competitors*—who are they? What are they doing? How do they do it? Are they doing it better? How might it change our business?
- *Regulators*—which are the most important to us? Are they planning new legislation? How might that affect our business?
- *Customers*—who are they? Are there any indications of change in the way they deal with us? What does this mean for us? (e.g. banks and cash points.)
- *Suppliers*—who are they? Do we need to involve them in the decision? How will they react? (e.g. software suppliers who may insist you relicense software used by the outsourcer.)
- *New entrants*—are there any new businesses that now pose a threat to us? How will they do this? Who are they? (e.g. provision of financial services by new entrants, such as supermarket chains and telecommunications companies.)
- *Substitutes*—are there substitute products emerging that may alter our business, in the way that fax machines supplanted telex machines, or the TV altered the cinema?

Useful sources to determine the answers include:

- past and present business plans that may contain contextual information;
- industry research papers, often available from industry associations;
- lawyers, who can advise you on pending or planned legislation;
- business magazines and the business pages of newspapers;
- colleagues in marketing, finance, legal, distribution and administration;
- strategic planning or marketing departments—who should have done much of this work already.

Undoubtedly, it will be difficult to forecast changes over the next five years or so. However, it is the role of senior management to forecast and manage with a long-term outlook.

Once these tables (or their equivalent) are populated, then you can examine the way in which the company coped with past change, and make some forecast of the way in which it will cope with future change.

Analysing past change

The past is often shrouded in self-serving myths that may easily mislead the planner. The wise manager will examine documents and records to establish the facts. Useful reference documents include:

- annual shareholder reports and past business plans
- board or executive committee minutes
- public relations archives
- interviews with key staff.

The aim of this process is to identify:

- the type of changes that have occurred, and what triggered them;
- the company's reactions to these changes, and who led them;
- strengths and weaknesses in the company's style of coping with change.

It is said that the past is not a reliable indicator of the future. Nevertheless, it does inform the perceptive manager about the way a company may cope with coming change and the possible nature of such changes.

Coping with future change

In all circumstances, one would expect there to be some significant transformation in the external environment, and a shift in the internal context, over the life of the contract. The world does not stand still, and companies do not exist in isolation from the external environment.

The method proposed for this transformation is:

1. Write two or three short descriptive scenarios of the future environment. It is necessary to write two or three, as the future could unfold in many different ways.
2. Include a section that describes the things the company will have to do to survive in those scenarios. For example, shift to electronic distribution, close down plants, or outsource other essential functions. All of these examples would require changes in the contract. For instance, outsourcing finance may eliminate the management of a core application.
3. Review the contract to ensure that it accommodates the possible scenarios, or at least provides the flexibility to vary important aspects, should these things come to fruition.

It would be a sorry thing to be tied to a fixed-price contract that included support of applications that are no longer required, or to be tied to a service provider that could not deliver new-sprung services.

Elliott Jacques wrote in his book, *Requisite Organisation*,[91] "At Stratum 5 [the level of general manager, or senior project manager on large-scale projects] the person must judge the likely impact of changes or events—both from outside the business unit and from inside it—on any or all parts of the system, to pick out those parts where the impact is likely to be important, to trace the likely second and third order consequences of those impacts, and to sustain an active anticipation of what changes are likely to unfold."

Checklist

1. Will products or services change—and if so what else might that change?
2. How will markets change and what impact will that have on our business?
3. Will distribution change, e.g. will electronic distribution alter things?
4. How will product, market and distribution changes alter our differentiation?
5. Will these things alter our financial position for better or worse?
6. What sort of organisation structure will be required to support the changes?
7. Will these things change the company culture? How?
8. Have the people who will drive future change been identified? When do you need to enlist them in this project?
9. Who will the competitors be, and why? How might the future actions change our business?
10. What new areas of legislation are likely, and how might they affect our business?
11. Who will be our customers in ten years' time? How will they purchase? How will we behave as a customer? Will the outsourcing deal support or conflict with these changes in customer behaviour?
12. Will these changes alter our supply chain? Who will supply the company? What sort of products and services will they offer? Consider the evolution of IT service companies—what sort of businesses will offer outsourcing in the future and how will those services be delivered?
13. Are new entrants going to appear in the market? What will prompt them to enter our market? Do we need to consider this in our outsourcing contract?
14. Will substitute products emerge and alter the approach we are taking to outsourcing? (Consider how ATMs altered banking and banking technology.)

Appendix B
Indicative contract contents

1. Definitions
2. Objectives
3. Principles
4. Term
    4.1. Initial
    4.2. Renewal
5. Current environment
    5.1. Locations
    5.2. Budgets
    5.3. Business IT plans
    5.4. Hardware
    5.5. Software
    5.6. Network infrastructure
    5.7. Telecommunications
    5.8. Library/reference materials
    5.9. Furnishings and fittings
    5.10. Office equipment.
6. Ongoing management
    6.1. Budget preparation
    6.2. Planning preparation
    6.3. Accountabilities
7. Assets
    7.1. Inventory management
    7.2. Ownership
    7.3. Disposal
    7.4. Loss or theft
8. Human resources
    8.1. Core team
    8.2. Transition in
    8.3. Transition out
    8.4. Acceptability
    8.5. Turnover
    8.6. Training
    8.7. Benefits (pensions, bonuses, discounts, stock options)
    8.8. Equipment provision (phones, office equipment)
    8.9. Subcontractors

Appendix C
Position paper pro forma

---

1. Issue   *(Succinct description of the issue.)*
2. Issue rating   *(Describe the probability of the issue arising and its consequences, preferably quantified in monetary terms.)*
3. Options for dealing with the issue   *(Describe sensible options for dealing with the issue. Seek to include options that might be put by the opposing team.)*
4. Preferred outcome   *(Select the preferred option from those listed in section 3.)*
5. Reasoning   *(Describe why this is the preferred option.)*
6. Implications   *(Describe the implications of all the options, including the selected option.)*
7. Trade-offs   *(Describe any trade-offs that might be given away in order to obtain the preferred option. These should, of course, be items that are of significantly less importance from your point of view.)*
Issue owner   *(The name of the person who raised the issue. This is usually the person whose business unit is most affected by the issue.)*
Circulation   *(The names of the people who have received a copy of the issue paper.)*

Figure C.1—Position paper pro forma

Appendix D
Contract change control pro forma

Clause   *(Insert the number of the clause affected by the proposed change.)*
Owner   *(The name of the person requesting the change.)*
Circulation   *(The names of the people to whom the change request was given.)*
Issue   *(Give the reason for requesting the change.)*
Effect   *(Describe the effect of implementing the change.)*
Risk   *(Describe the probability of the issue arising and its consequences, preferably quantified in monetary terms.)*
Alternatives   *(Give any alternative to changing the contract, for example changing work practices or suppliers.)*
Legal opinion   *(The legal advice given on the change. If in summary, attach the full opinion.)*
Host position   *(The position of the host company on the change.)*
Service provider position   *(The position of the service provider on the change.)*

Figure D.1—Contract change control pro forma

Appendix E
Contract requirement statement

Clause   *(Insert the number of the clause or subject area if clause unknown.)*
Owner   *(The name of the person stating the requirement.)*
Circulation   *(The names of the people to whom the paper has been circulated.)*
Requirement   *(State the requirement in plain English.)*
Rationale   *(Describe the rationale behind the requirement.)*
Risk   *(Describe any risk associated with not obtaining the requirement. If possible, define in terms of probability and monetary risk.)*
Alternatives   *(Give any alternative to implementing this requirement.)*
Legal opinion   *(The legal advice given on the requirement statement. If in summary, attach the full opinion.)*
Other party's position   *(The position of the other party on the requirement. This may cross-reference to issue papers if they already exist.)*

Figure E.1—Contract requirement statement

Appendix F
Examples of principles

Below are examples of five principles (Figures F.1–F.5).

Principle 1
Issue *What guidelines will we issue on procurement of technical infrastructure?*

Options
    1. Procure on the basis of lowest price.
    2. Procure best of breed.
    3. Continue procurement from existing suppliers.

Preferred   (3) Continue procurement from our existing suppliers.
Rationale Outsourcing does not alter the objectives and rationale that led to the selection of the existing supplier.

Implications (positive)
    • We retain the benefits of a homogeneous infrastructure.
    • We retain the benefits of bulk purchasing from our preferred supplier.
    • This simplifies procurement processes and allows enhanced electronic purchasing.

Implications (negative)
    • Our infrastructure cost will not change as a consequence of outsourcing.
    • Our selected service provider will need to hold the appropriate skills to operate technology from our preferred supplier.

Approved: **Date:**

Figure F.1—Example principle

Principle 2

Issue
Will we allow the service provider to subcontract work?

Options
  1. No.
  2. Yes, unconditionally.
  3. Yes, provided the quality, cost, security and service standards are equal to or better than specified in service level agreements.

Preferred
  (3) Yes, provided the quality, cost, security and service standards are equal to or better than specified in service level agreements, and the service provider takes full responsibility for the subcontractor and all deliverables.

Rationale
The service provider cannot be expected to always have every possible skill and resource available at all times. On occasion, service demands may exceed the service provider's capacity and capability.

Implications (positive)
  - We enlarge our pool of labour without compromising quality, cost, security or service.
  - We are not constrained by the limits of the service provider's staff pool.
  - The service provider will be held accountable for delivery through contractual obligations.

Implications (negative)
  - The service provider will incur an overhead in controlling subcontractors, which they may try to pass on.
  - We will incur an overhead in auditing invoices and work that is subcontracted.

Approved: **Date:**

Figure F.2—Example principle

Principle 3
Issue *What formal methodologies will we use in our outsourced environment?*
Options 　　1. We will use our existing in-house methods and standards. 　　2. We will adhere to the service provider's methods and standards. 　　3. We will purchase an independent third-party method.
Preferred 　　(2) We will use the service provider's methods and standards.
Rationale The task of training all the service provider's staff in our method or a third-party method would be huge. This would also undermine one key benefit of outsourcing, which is the access to a pool of staff who share common methods.
Implications (positive) 　• We will now use a more broadly-based standard than our in-house standard. 　• No additional cost will be incurred to purchase a standard or train the service provider's staff. **Implications (negative)** 　• We may become more dependent on the service provider by relying on their standard. 　• Out staff will need to be trained and become familiar with the service provider's standard.
Approved:　　　　　　　　　　　　　　　　**Date:**

Figure F.3—Example principle

Principle 4
Issue *Will business units retain the right to fund, develop and manage small projects using their own resources?*

Options
    1. No, the service provider must undertake all systems development and operations.
    2. Yes, business units may retain their current authority.
    3. We will examine each project on a case-by-case basis.

Preferred   (1) No, the service provider must undertake all systems development and operations.
Rationale One of the drivers for outsourcing is rigorous controls over systems development and operation. These attributes are compromised by feral IT.

Implications (positive)
    • This should lead to a gradual improvement in the overall quality of systems development and operation in the company.
    • Better-quality IT should lead to lower long-term maintenance costs.
    • Previously hidden costs for IT will be visible and controlled.

Implications (negative)
    • Business units may express frustration and claim delays will occur because of this rigour.
    • Business units will need to plan and budget for all IT expenses in advance.

Approved: **Date:**

Figure F.4—Example principle

Principle 5
Issue *To what extent will we hold the provider responsible for adherence to the annual plan and budget?*
Options 1. Adherence to the plan and budget will be the responsibility of the host company. 2. Adherence to the plan and budget will be the responsibility of the service provider. 3. Both parties will share ownership of the plan and budget.
Preferred (2) Adherence to the plan and budget will be the responsibility of the service provider. Deviation to plan or budget must be authorised by the host company CIO.
Rationale The service provider is to manage procurement and staffing to the agreed plan. It is the service provider's responsibility to deliver commitments to the agreed plan and budget.
Implications (positive) • Cost containment is likely to be stronger than would be exercised by business units. • Only work within plan and budget will be undertaken by the service provider, as they know we will not pay for unauthorised work.
Implications (negative) • Business units may express frustration at the resultant cost and planning controls. • There may be some conflict when the service provider rejects business people's projects because there is no allocation of funds for them.
Approved: **Date:**

Figure F.5—Example principle

Appendix G
Outsourcing timetable

Table G.1 aims to give some indicative measures of the time (duration) that should be allowed for structuring an outsourcing agreement. The time taken to outsource the management of the local area network (LAN) of a 500-person company in one building will vary considerably from that required to outsource the complete IT management and operational infrastructure for a large government department with offices in every major town.

Table G.1—Timescale for structuring an outsourcing agreement

Task	Lower range	Higher range
Identifying goals and objectives	10 days	20 days
Developing CSF and criteria	15 days	30 days
Discovery	15 days	60 days
Setting principles	10 days	30 days
Preselection of service providers	15 days	40 days
Preparing RFP	15 days	60 days
Issuing RFP (time to respond)	30 days	60 days
Evaluating RFP responses	15 days	40 days
Due diligence	15 days	30 days
Forming contract	20 days	60 days
Defining SLAs	Within contract	Within contract
Managing transition	20 days	120 days
Totals	**180 days**	**430 days**

The "lower range" is based on a medium-sized company with an IT unit based in a single location, running a comparatively simple application suite on mid-range servers running some variant of UNIX, and a LAN serving the majority of employees. The higher range assumes a larger enterprise, similar to a regional bank, employing around 5000 staff in less than ten locations, two or three regional IT centres, and a large but relatively well-documented and defined IT infrastructure centred largely on mainframe computers with regional LAN/WANs (wide area networks).

Clearly, some of these tasks may be overlapped, and some may be discarded if the IT component to be outsourced is trivial or complete asset registers exist for hardware, software, people and other resources.

The times given in the table are provided with the aim of giving the novice some idea of the scale of these tasks, and an understanding that following a sound process to select your provider will not be a ten-day task.

Appendix H
Business case template

Organisations tend to have an existing template for business cases. They vary widely in content, emphasis and rules for completion. The template below is simple and may serve as a guide if you have no existing model.

- *Introduction*—describe what this business case is about, e.g. outsourcing LAN management.
- *Purpose*—describe the purpose of the business case, e.g. to obtain funding to carry out a feasibility study, up to and including issuing the RFP.
- *Rationale*—describe why the business case was developed. Include:
  - current situation
  - any identified goals or objectives that led to the initiation of the outsourcing project
  - options considered, including high-level costs, benefits, risks and implications of each option.
- *Preferred option*—describe the preferred option in detail. Acknowledge that the detailed process of outsourcing may lead to modification of the business case.
- *Indicative costs*—describe:
  - indicative costs of the outsourcing project
  - indicative cost of the outsourced function, including both one-off and recurring costs.
- *Indicative benefits*—describe:
  - indicative benefits of the outsourcing project
  - indicative benefits of the outsourced function, including both one-off and recurring costs.
- *Risks*—describe:
  - risks of the outsourcing project
  - risks associated with outsourcing the function.
- *Schedule*—include schedule showing timeline for:
  - the outsourcing Project
  - the transition process.
- *Resources*—identify the resources required to execute the project, including:
  - role descriptions for in-house and consulting/contracting staff;
  - contractors and consultants, including legal;
  - research materials;
  - equipment and office space, if required.
- *Process management*—describe how the process will be managed and approved, for example:
  - role of steering committee

- indicative approval milestones
- indicative meeting schedule for the committee or other participants
- reporting schedule, including report type and contents.
- *Appendices*—include any appendices, for example:
  - financial models
  - research extracts
  - current budget and expense levels
  - working papers

This temple is not comprehensive and is intended to serve only those companies who do not already have a standard approach to developing a business case.

It must be emphasised that the business case must be reviewed during the outsourcing process. Significant changes and their implications must be researched, and the team must obtain formal approval for these. It would be prudent to adopt a formal project management methodology, such as PRINCE-2,[g] or to use an experienced consulting group to manage the overall process.

---

[g] Project Results In Controlled Environments, UK Central Computer & Telecommunications Agency (CCTA) 1989—the UK government standard for IT project management.

Appendix I
PA Consulting Group's SMART model

PA helps organisations to obtain the best possible advantage from sourcing and partnerships arrangements. Our comprehensive and pragmatic approach to IT sourcing focuses on three key stages: establishing a sourcing strategy, procuring and implementing an outsourced service, and managing the service. We continually refine our approach to reflect the changing nature of both the outsourcing market and our clients' requirements.

PA Consulting Group's model of best practice for the development and implementation of strategic sourcing strategies is reproduced in summary below.

S   Strategy and services analysis

Establishing the business services required now and into the future to achieve the overall business strategy and identify candidates for outsourcing. Such candidates will be identified following an understanding of the costs and value added by business processes, their classification according to the organisation's competence at performing it, and the criticality of the process to achieving business objectives.

M   Market capabilities

Establishing the capability of the external market to provide suitable suppliers of outsourced services.

A   Assessment of in-house capability

A thorough review of existing in-house capability resulting in an analytical view of internal performance and identification of opportunities for process improvement, in addition to confirmation of outsourcing potential.

R   Risks and rewards evaluation

The evaluation of outsourcing candidates against an agreed set of identified risks and rewards, establishing which business services should be outsourced, and indicating the criteria against which outsourcing decisions should be made.

T   Transition planning

Producing high-level project plans covering the outsourcing of services, improvement to in-house services, and the organisational change required to operate effectively with the newly outsourced services.

Further reading

Collins R (ed), *Effective Management, CCH*, Auckland, 1993.

De Bono E, *Six Thinking Hats*, Penguin, Harmondsworth, 1985.

Domberger S and Hall C, *The Contracting Casebook*, AGPS, Sydney, 1995.

Festinger L, *A Theory of Cognitive Dissonance*, Stanford University Press, Stanford, 1957.

Gay CL and Essinger J, *Inside Outsourcing*, Brealy, London, 2000.

Greaver MF II, *Strategic Outsourcing*, ANACOM, New York, 1999.

Halvey JK and Melby BM, *Information Technology Outsourcing Transactions*, Wiley, Somerset NJ, 1996.

Hindle P, *Pocket Strategy*, Economist Newspaper Ltd in association with Profile Books, London, 1998.

Jacques E, *Requisite Organisation*, Harvard Business School Press, Arlington, 1985.

Kaplan S and Norton DP, *The Balanced Scorecard*, Harvard Business School Press, Boston, 1996.

Karpathiou V and Tanner K, *Information Technology Outsourcing in Australia*, RMIT, Melbourne, 1995.

Klepper R and Jones WO, *Outsourcing Information Technology Systems and Services*, Prentice Hall, Englewood Cliffs, 1998.

KPMG, *Best Practice Guidelines*, HMSO, London, 1995.

Kuhn, TS, *The Structure of Scientific Revolutions*, University of Chicago Press, Chicago, 1996.

Lacity MC and Hirschheim R, *Beyond the Information Systems Outsourcing Bandwagon*, Wiley, Somerset NJ, 1995.

Martin J with Leben J, *Strategic Information Planning Methodologies*, Prentice Hall, Englewood Cliffs, 1989.

Martin J, *Information Engineering II: Planning and analysis*, Prentice Hall, Englewood Cliffs, 1995.

Mintzberg H, *The Rise and Fall of Strategic Planning*, Prentice Hall, Harlow, 1994.

Mylott TR III, *Computer Outsourcing—Managing the Transfer of Information Systems*, Prentice Hall, Englewood Cliffs, 1995.

Niessen K and Oldenburg P, *Service Level Management*, CCTA, Norwich, 1997.

Ohmae K, *The Mind of the Strategist*, Penguin, New York, 1982.

Porter ME, *Competitive Advantage*, The Free Press, New York, 1985.

Robbins S and Mukerji D, *Managing Organisations*, Prentice Hall, Sydney, 1994.

Schwartz P, *The Art of the Long View*, Currency Doubleday, New York, 1996.

Sprague R, *Information Systems Management in Practice*, Prentice Hall, Englewood Cliffs, 1986.

Strassman P, *Politics of Information Management*, Information Economics Press, New Canaan, 1995.

Thornton N, *Developing Business Led Outsourcing Contracts* (discussion paper), PA Consulting Group, London, 1996.

Thorpe J, *The Information Paradox*, McGraw-Hill, Toronto, 1998.

Tozer J, *Leading Initiatives*, Butterworth Heinemann, Port Melbourne, 1997.

Trout J, *The Power of Simplicity*, McGraw-Hill, New York, 1999.

Ulrich D, *Human Resource Champions*, Harvard Business School Press, Boston, 1997.

Van der Heijden K, *Scenarios: The art of strategic conversation*, Wiley, Chichester, 1996.

Weill P and Broadbent, M, *Leveraging the New Infrastructure*, Harvard Business School Press, Boston, 1998.

Zaple A, *The Keys to Outsourcing Success* (discussion paper), PA Consulting Group, Sydney, 1998.

References

1   Lu Yun in Birrell AM (translator), *Chinese Love Poetry—New Songs From A Jade Terrace—A Medieval Anthology*, Penguin, London, 1995, pp. 262–303.
2   Lacity MC and Hirschheim R, *Beyond the Information Systems Outsourcing Bandwagon*, Wiley, Somerset NJ, 1995.
3   Collins R (ed.) *Effective Management*, CCH, Auckland, 1993, p. 214.
4   Karpathiou V and Tanner K, *Information Technology Outsourcing in Australia*, RMIT, Melbourne, 1995, p. 8.
5   Hindle T, *Pocket Strategy*, The Economist Newspaper Ltd in association with Profile Books, London, 1998, p. 127.
6   Karpathiou V and Tanner K, *Information Technology Outsourcing in Australia*, RMIT, Melbourne, 1995, p. 63.
7   Festinger L, *A Theory of Cognitive Dissonance*, Stanford University Press, Stanford, 1957.
8   Robbins S and Mukerji D, *Managing Organisations*, Prentice Hall, Sydney, 1994, p. 120.
9   Robbins S and Mukerji D, *Managing Organisations*, Prentice Hall, Sydney, 1994, p. 120.
10 Lacity MC and Hirschheim R, *Beyond the Information Systems Outsourcing Bandwagon*, Wiley, Somerset NJ, 1995, p. 20.
11 GartnerGroup, *Inside Gartner*, **XV**, 31, 4 August 1999.
12 *Office Magazine*, November 1989, p. 19.
13 Lacity MC and Hirschheim R, *Beyond the Information Systems Outsourcing Bandwagon*, Wiley, Somerset NJ, 1995, p. 24.
14 Robbins S and Mukerji D, *Managing Organisations*, Prentice Hall, Sydney, 1994, p. 119.
15 Strassman P, *Politics of Information Management*, Information Economics Press, New Canaan, 1995, p. 302.
16 Sprague R, *Information Systems Management in Practice*, Prentice Hall, Englewood Cliffs, 1986, p. 73.
17 Strassman P, *The Politics of Information Management*, Information Economics Press, New Canaan, 1995, p. 310.
18 Ohmae K, *The Mind of the Strategist*, Penguin, New York, 1982, p. 22.
19 Lacity MC and Hirschheim R, *Beyond the Information Systems Outsourcing Bandwagon*, Wiley, Somerset NJ, 1995.
20 Strassman P, *The Politics of Information Management*, Information Economics Press, New Canaan, 1995, p. 312.
21 Ohmae K, *The Mind of the Strategist*, Penguin, New York, 1982, p. 15.
22 Collins R, (ed.) *Effective Management*, CCH, Auckland, 1993, p. 207.

23 Strassman P, *The Politics of Information Management*, Information Economics Press, New Canaan, 1995, p. 71.

24 Ohmae K, *The Mind of the Strategist*, Penguin, New York, 1982, p. 77.

25 Kaplan S and Norton DP, *The Balanced Scorecard*, HBS Press, Boston, 1996.

26 Robbins S and Mukerji D, *Managing Organisations*, Prentice Hall, Sydney, 1994, p. 79.

27 Karpathiou V and Tanner K, *Information Technology Outsourcing in Australia*, RMIT, Melbourne, 1995, p. 30.

28 Suh, R, "Guaranteeing that outsourcing serves your business strategy", *Information Strategy: The Executive's Journal*, Spring, pp. 39–42.

29 Lacity MC and Hirschheim R, *Beyond the Information Systems Outsourcing Bandwagon*, Wiley, Somerset NJ, 1995.

30 Domberger S and Hall C, *The Contracting Casebook*, AGPS, Sydney, 1995.

31 Greaver MF II, *Strategic Outsourcing*, AMACOM, New York, 1999, p. 48.

32 GartnerGroup, *Inside Gartner* **XV**, 31, 4 August 1999.

33 Strassman P, *The Politics of Information Management*, Information Economics Press, New Canaan, 1995, p. 29.

34 Klepper R and Jones WO, *Outsourcing Information Technology, Systems and Services*, Prentice Hall, Englewood Cliffs, 1998, p. 105.

35 Karpathiou V and Tanner K, *Information Technology Outsourcing in Australia*, RMIT, Melbourne, 1995, p. xiv.

36 Strassman P, *The Politics of Information Management*, Information Economics Press, New Canaan, 1995, p. 46.

37 Strassman P, *The Politics of Information Management*, Information Economics Press, New Canaan, 1995, p. xxvii.

38 Strassman P, *The Politics of Information Management*, Information Economics Press, New Canaan, 1995, p. 79.

39 Strassman P, *The Politics of Information Management*, Information Economics Press, New Canaan, 1995, p. 78.

40 Strassman P, *The Politics of Information Management*, Information Economics Press, New Canaan, 1995, p. 7.

41 Strassman P, *The Politics of Information Management*, Information Economics Press, New Canaan, 1995, p. 84.

42 Strassman P, *The Politics of Information Management*, Information Economics Press, New Canaan, 1995, p. 84.

43 Domberger S and Hall C, *The Contracting Casebook*, AGPS, Sydney, 1995, p. 7.

44 Domberger S and Hall C, *The Contracting Casebook*, AGPS, Sydney, 1995.

45 Greaver MF II, *Strategic Outsourcing*, AMACOM, New York, 1999, p. 217.

46 Domberger S and Hall C, *The Contracting Casebook*, AGPS, Sydney, 1995, p. 6.

47 Domberger S and Hall C, *The Contracting Casebook*, AGPS, Sydney, 1995.

48 Domberger S and Hall C, *The Contracting Casebook*, AGPS, Sydney, 1995, p. 27.

49 Lacity MC and Hirschheim R, *Beyond the Information Systems Outsourcing Bandwagon*, Wiley, Somerset NJ, 1995, p. 11.

50 Karpathiou V and Tanner K, *Information Technology Outsourcing in Australia*, RMIT, Melbourne, 1995, p. 100.

51 Halvey JK and Melby BM, *Information Technology Outsourcing Transactions*, Wiley, Somerset NJ, 1996, p. 43.

52 Halvey JK and Melby BM, *Information Technology Outsourcing Transactions*, Wiley, Somerset NJ, 1996, p. 36.

53 Gay CL and Essinger J, *Inside Outsourcing*, Brealey, London, 2000.

54 Klepper R and Jones WO, *Outsourcing Information Technology Systems and Services*, Prentice Hall, Englewood Cliffs, 1998, p. 5.

55 Thornton, N, *Developing Business Led Outsourcing Contracts* (discussion paper), PA Consulting Group, London, 1996.

56 Halvey JK and Melby BM, *Information Technology Outsourcing Transactions*, Wiley, Somerset NJ, 1996, p. 35.
57 Halvey JK and Melby BM, *Information Technology Outsourcing Transactions*, Wiley, Somerset NJ, 1996, p. 18.
58 Halvey JK and Melby BM, Information Technology Outsourcing Transactions, Wiley, Somerset NJ, 1996, p. 50.
59 Klepper R and Jones WO, *Outsourcing Information Technology, Services and Systems*, Prentice Hall, Englewood Cliffs, p. 12.
60 Zaple A, *The Keys to Outsourcing Success* (discussion paper), PA Consulting Group, Sydney, 1999.
61 Gay CL and Essinger J, *Inside Outsourcing*, Brealey, London, 2000, p. 27.
62 Karpathiou V and Tanner K, *Information Technology Outsourcing in Australia*, RMIT, Melbourne, 1995, p. xiv.
63 Kaplan RS and Norton DP, *The Balanced Scorecard*, Harvard Business Press, Boston, 1996.
64 Thornton N, *Developing Business Led Outsourcing Contracts* (discussion paper), PA Consulting Group, 1996.
65 Thornton N, *Developing Business Led Outsourcing Contracts* (discussion paper), PA Consulting Group, 1996.
66 Domberger S and Hall C, *The Contracting Casebook*, AGPS, Sydney, 1995, p. 8.
67 Sprague R and McNurlin E, *Information Systems Management in Practice*, Prentice Hall, Englewood Cliffs, 1986, p. 60.
68 Mylott TR III, *Computer Outsourcing: Managing the transfer of information systems*, Prentice Hall, Englewood Cliffs, 1995.
69 Greaver MF II, *Strategic Outsourcing*, AMACOM, New York, 1999, p. 39.
70 Zaple A, *The Keys to Outsourcing Success* (discussion paper), PA Consulting Group, Sydney, 1998.
71 Klepper R and Jones WO, *Outsourcing Information Technology, Systems and Services*, Prentice Hall, Englewood Cliffs, 1998, p. 1.
72 KPMG, *Outsourcing Best Practice Guidelines*, HMSO, London, 1995, p. 20.
73 Mylott TR III, *Computer Outsourcing*, Prentice Hall, Englewood Cliffs, 1995, p. 2.
74 Karpathiou V and Tanner K, *Information Technology Outsourcing in Australia*, RMIT, Melbourne, 1995, p. 30.
75 Suh R, "Guaranteeing that outsourcing serves your business strategy", *Information Strategy: The Executive Journal*, Spring, pp. 39–42.
76 Schwartz P, *The Art of The Long View*, Currency Doubleday, New York, 1996, p. 232.
77 Halvey JK and Melby BM, *Information Technology Outsourcing Transactions*, Wiley, Somerset NJ, 1996, p. 35.
78 Thornton N, *Developing Business Led Outsourcing Contracts* (discussion paper), PA Consulting Group, London, 1996.
79 De Bono, E, *Six Thinking Hats*, Penguin, Harmondsworth, 1985.
80 Rubinstein J and Slife BD (eds), *Taking Sides: Clashing views on controversial psychological issues*, 3rd edn, Dushkin Publishing Group, New York, 1984. (Copyright © 1984 by Dushkin Publishing Group Inc. Reprinted by permission of Dushkin/McGraw-Hill, a division of The McGraw-Hill Companies.)
81 Kuhn TS, *The Structure of Scientific Revolutions*, University of Chicago Press, Chicago, 1996, p. 76.
82 Quoted in Karpathiou and Tanner, *Information Technology Outsourcing in Australia*, RMIT, Melbourne, 1995, p. 8.
83 Zaple A, *The Keys to Outsourcing Success* (discussion paper), PA Consulting Group, Sydney, 1998.
84 GartnerGroup, *Inside Gartner* **XV**, 31, 4th August 1999.

85   Thornton N, *Developing Business Led Outsourcing Contracts* (discussion paper), PA Consulting Group, London, 1996.

86   Ulrich D, *Human Resource Champions*, Harvard Business School Press, Boston, 1997, p. 169.

87   GartnerGroup, *Inside Gartner* **XV**, 17, 28 April 1999.

88   Mylott TR III, *Computer Outsourcing*, Prentice Hall, Englewood Cliffs, 1995, p. 21.

89   Schwartz P, *The Art of The Long View*, Currency Doubleday, New York, 1996, p. 232.

90   Porter ME, *Competitive Advantage*, The Free Press, New York, 1985.

91   Jacques E, *Requisite Organisation*, Cason Hall, Arlington, 1988, p. 69.

Index